MAMPHELA
RAMPHELE

LAYING
GHOSTS
TO REST

Dilemmas of
the transformation
in South Africa

TAFELBERG

Tafelberg
An imprint of NB Publishers
40 Heerengracht, Cape Town, 8000
www.tafelberg.com
© 2008 author

Set in Ehrhardt
Cover and book design by Nazli Jacobs
Cover photograph by Nick Aldrige
Index by Mary Lennox

Printed and bound by Paarl Print, Oosterland Street, Paarl, South Africa
First edition, third printing 2009

ISBN: 978-0-624-04579-3

CONTENTS

INTRODUCTION
A Ghost Story

MY CHILDHOOD WAS SHAPED IN THE IDYLLIC VILLAGE OF KRANS-poort at the foot of the Soutpansberg Mountains in what is now the Limpopo Province. Both my parents were teachers at the local school, the Stephanus Hofmeyr Primary School.

My early memories are dominated by my fear of darkness. This fear was crippling for a child in a rural setting where darkness was everywhere. There was no electricity, and water had to be fetched from the single tap at the centre of the village to meet the needs of individual households. We carried the water on our heads in twenty-litre containers – a chore largely reserved for women and girls.

In our family, my mother insisted that every child participate in household chores. My brothers helped by transporting two water containers at a time by wheelbarrow. We stored water under an orange tree in large earthen pots. Our long-drop toilet was outside, in a remote corner of our relatively large property. Every domestic task seemed to involve having to venture into the dark.

My siblings teased me mercilessly about my fears. My mother had little patience with my anxieties, and I was physically punished for breaking household utensils in my frantic flights from the dark into the safety of our house as I rushed to complete any errand outside. I always had the sense that something would come out of the dark-ness to get me. Often I fell as I ran in and out of the house, suffering countless bruises to my then skinny knees.

My fear of darkness came from the many ghost stories that circu-lated in our village. According to legend, there were two prime haunted sites. One was the thorn-bush forest just beyond the main gravel road that bordered our village on the southern side. For many decades there had been settlements in the forest of the Seakamela clan. Then, in the 1950s, the Seakamelas were forcibly removed by the apartheid government and resettled in a remote, dry area. Their forced removal was part of the clearance of 'black spots' in 'white areas' that was one of the hallmarks of 'separate development' under the apartheid regime.

Disgruntled ancestors of the Seakamela people, whose graves remained in the forest, were said to have become furious ghosts. Their fury was reputedly expressed through inexplicable occasional streaks of light that flashed across the night sky above the thorn trees. Only two other properties separated our home from the gravel road bordering on the forest. In my view, we were too close for comfort. Whenever I had to venture out into the dark, I steadfastly avoided looking south. I did not want to risk encountering the furious ghosts.

The second haunted site was the tallest tree in our village. This tree, known as *Mphata* in the local Sepedi language, stood almost in the centre of the village, just outside the school property on the mountain end of our street. It had a solid metre-and-a-half-wide trunk with a suspicious-looking hollow area near the bottom, big enough for a small person to hide in. I could imagine some ghost-like figure lying in wait there to scare unsuspecting passers-by. The tree barely had any branches and even fewer large, greyish leaves.

This haunted tree seemed unavoidable in our daily lives. We walked past it to and from school, to and from the central tap, and to and from our local Dutch Reformed Church (DRC). I made sure I never fell behind on our way home after evening services, keeping close to adults or my siblings as we passed this formidable tree. The ghosts of villagers who had passed on were said to visit it at night. It was rumoured that they had been unhappy people who could not find peace in the afterlife.

There was only one man in the village known to be able to lay ghosts to rest, Uncle Paulos Moshapo, a tall, soft-spoken man of slight build. He had soft, watery eyes and the constant suggestion of a smile playing on his serene face. He was also one of the church elders and worked as a gardener for the local conservative DRC missionary, Rev. Lukas van der Merwe.

Uncle Paulos managed his relationship with this tyrannical, racist man by keeping his head down. Whenever Van der Merwe called out loudly for Uncle Paulos, he would fling his frayed, sweaty hat into the nearby bushes and run as fast as his frail-looking legs could carry him in the direction of the summoning voice. He cut a pathetic figure standing near the missionary, silently awaiting instructions. But somehow he was able to regain his composure and dignity after each episode. He would slowly retrace his steps, pick up his hat and go about his daily chores in his quiet, unassuming way.

Uncle Paulos confronted each ghost by name. He would plead with the ghost to make peace with whatever unfinished business was troubling it, and find rest. Should the ghost persist, he would become quite aggressive and command it to go and join its fellow departed and stop frightening the children.

I was in awe of this man, and grateful that he had taken on the responsibility of keeping the ghosts at bay. Uncle Paulos also seemed to have been at peace within himself. Was it the power he wielded over ghosts that gave him the serenity that shone through strongly even to a child's eye? I shall never know. Village legend had it that he had been born with his placental sac intact – a sign of being special.

Whatever truth there was to the ghost stories that shaped my childhood, one thing stood out: ghosts could be laid to rest by calling them by name. The distinction between ghosts and ancestors appeared to stem from the nature of the relationship between the living and the dead. Troubled spirits roam as furious ghosts. Spirits at peace, on the other hand, are protective ancestors. In the Christian faith they are known as saints.

What Uncle Paulos did in each instance was to acknowledge the ghost by calling its name. This acknowledgement opened a channel of communication between the living and those in the afterlife. Unfinished business was acknowledged and peace was made. Uncle Paulos was an effective mediator between the living and the dead.

Rituals and ceremonies practised by many South Africans place ancestors at the centre of their lives. Moments of transition at milestones along one's life journey are marked by rituals. Transitions such as births, baptisms, initiations, graduations, changes in places of abode, acquisitions of important property, marriages and deaths are communicated to ancestors. Key ancestors in each household or clan are called by name, and asked to participate in the significant occasion and bless it. Such key ancestors are usually fathers, mothers and grandparents. Whenever appropriate, ancestors are visited at their graves and informed about matters for which thanks are due and blessings are requested.

In the event of personal or work-related problems, rituals are performed to appease the dead and restore good relationships. These rituals enable the living and those who have passed on to make peace and maintain it. It is this peace that is believed to open up opportunities for present and future prosperity.

Post-apartheid South Africa has done much to make peace with the past. The Truth and Reconciliation Commission (TRC) in particular played a major role in the ritual processes aimed at exorcising the ghosts of our past.

The process of transformation to normalise South Africa has at its core the laying to rest of these lingering ghosts lest they continue to haunt our future. The most stubborn ghosts are those whose names we are often too afraid to mention: racism, ethnic chauvinism, sexism, and authoritarianism. Yet effective transformation is predicated on acknowledgement of each ghost by calling it by name, engaging with it to transact unfinished business, and bidding it to make peace with bygones.

We have been fortunate to have in our midst transformative leaders with special qualities who have laid some ghosts to rest already. But the task is not yet complete, and much work remains to be done.

PART ONE

Dealing with
the past

CHAPTER 1

The challenges of transformation

Transformation of a society entails a complete change in both form and substance, a metamorphosis, as happens in the life cycles of insects such as butterflies. The transition from an invisible egg, to a larva, then a pupa, and finally a flying insect with all its beautiful colours takes the butterfly through significant changes in form and substance.

The scale and scope of the transformation South Africa embarked on after apartheid is without precedence. The country has had to wrestle simultaneously with political, economic and social transformation at all levels. The term 'transformation' is used here to denote fundamental changes in the structures, institutional arrangements, policies, modes of operation and relationships within society.

Transformation of our society calls for its reorientation from past values and practices defined by racism, sexism, inequality and lack of respect for human rights towards the values reflected in our national constitution.

A successfully transformed South Africa would be characterised by the antithesis of all that was bad about the apartheid system: non-racialism, non-sexism and social relationships consistent with the observance of human rights and greater equity.

Achieving this shift requires radical changes in values, attitudes and relationships at all levels. This would create the platform for embedding the roots of civic-mindedness that ought to characterise the public service as well as community and interpersonal relationships in our new democracy.[1]

Transformation of this magnitude is complex. The urgency imposed by the political-settlement process in the early 1990s added to the pressure of managing such a multifaceted change. South Africa did not have the luxury of sequencing stages of the change process so as to tackle one element at a time. Once agreement had been reached on 'talks about talks' towards a negotiated political settlement, attention had to turn to all the elements that needed to be changed to begin the process of closing the long painful chapter in the country's history. South Africa has no model to guide its transformation from the apartheid past to its envisaged future. It has had to find its own way.

Few countries have had the privilege to see their dreams take shape in real life over as short a period as South Africa has witnessed over the last decade. It is a good moment to reflect on where we are as a nation in the aftermath of the euphoria of the celebrations of the first decade of democracy.

Much has been achieved. There are signs of success everywhere. We have a national constitution that is widely acclaimed. We have a solid legal and judicial system. We have woven the fragments of our divided past into a nation that calls itself South Africa. We have accomplished some transformation feats in the public sector that were unthinkable. Welding together multiple government departments serving sectional interests into unified entities to serve all South Africans is a major accomplishment.

Learning to live and work together as black[2] and white South Africans is another achievement in which we can take pride. We have a strong and growing private sector that is also increasingly coming to terms with the challenges of broadening the base of participation by black people in growing the wealth of the nation.

But we have much more to do to turn our remaining challenges into opportunities for further success. A central challenge in the transformation process is the quality of the human-capital base we have inherited from apartheid. It is not simply a question of the legacy of poor education and health-services provision for the oppressed majority. Nor is the challenge only related to the low levels of skills across sectors that are struggling to meet the demands of running a modern socio-economic and political system. It is also about the reality that South Africans, black and white, have had no experience of themselves as citizens of a modern, non-racial democracy on their home ground. How does one make up for these gaps in skills and experience as we consolidate our democracy?

The future for which South Africans are yearning has to be built on the foundations of the past we have inherited. That past has its beauty. It also has many ugly parts. We have little choice but to embrace the reality of that past as a whole. But how does one embrace such a difficult past, and isn't there a risk of being tainted by such an embrace? Or can one choose to embrace only that aspect of the past one can call one's own? What about the 'other' that has now become part of one's 'self'? The leap of faith required to fully embrace our ugly past in order to transform it is often underestimated.

We continue to face many challenges in coming to terms with our past, although we have already taken bold steps towards confronting it. The many compromises reached in the negotiated settlement that ushered in democracy are the products of courageous, visionary leadership. Seeing through the Truth and Reconciliation Commission (TRC) process took inspirational leadership. Many South Africans have reached out across boundaries to touch their fellow citizens.

Yet we still struggle to find closure on many issues related to that past. This is in part because the wounds are still raw. It is also because we have difficulty acknowledging the depth of our trauma. Our wounds fester partly as a result of our denial of their extent and their impact on attempts to transform society. Past wounds have a long history. The road to healing will also be long.

We also should not underestimate the psychological legacy of three centuries of colonial rule followed by apartheid. Both black and white South Africans have work to do to lay the ghost of racist stereotyping to rest.

Frantz Fanon, writing about oppression under French rule in North

Africa in the 1950s and '60s, was one of the first to point out how one's historical and political context becomes a personal psychological experience. In *Black Skin, White Masks*[3] he showed how the colonial situation has debilitating consequences for oppressed people's personalities and identities. The structures of colonial society condition them to see the world, including themselves, through the eyes of the oppressor. Such societies are always hierarchical, with the oppressors and their culture valued as 'good', and the oppressed and their culture as 'bad'. The oppressed, adopting this view themselves, become alienated from themselves and their own cultures. Fanon called this the 'scarring of the black pysche'. Some of the symptoms of this condition include a socially induced inferiority complex, self-hatred, low self-esteem, jealousy of those seen to be progressing (both black and white), suppressed aggression, anxiety, and sometimes a defensive romanticisation of indigenous culture.

In South Africa in the 1970s, Stephen Bantu Biko, founder of the Black Consciousness Movement and leader of the South African Students' Organisation (Saso), took up a similar theme. His central message was that psychological and cultural liberation of the mind of black people was a precondition for a successful struggle for political freedom. As Biko put it,

> the most powerful weapon in the hands of the oppressor is the mind of the oppressed. Once the latter has been so effectively manipulated and controlled by the oppressor as to make the oppressed believe that he is a liability to the white man. Hence thinking along the lines of Black Consciousness makes the black man see himself as a being, entire in himself, and not as an extension of a broom or additional leverage to some machine.[4]

Finding the courage to acknowledge this scarring and to set about reclaiming 'the mind of the oppressed' remains a major challenge of South Africa's transformation.

At the same time, white South Africans also need to confront the impact of racism on their psyches. The assumption by many that the material benefits white people enjoy reflect their superior abilities hampers their own development as self-reflective beings in a non-racial society. It is often difficult for white people to accept that they now have to live, collaborate and compete with black people as equals and fellow citizens. This non-reflective tendency leads to resistance on their part to contribute to the normalisation of our society.

Laying ghosts to rest entails transcendence beyond normal human experience. Transcendence is usually associated with the spiritual realm. In a sense, South Africa's transformation has at its best moments delved deep into the collective consciousness and touched the spirit of the nation. It was at those moments that we rose above the ordinary and achieved extraordinary things. Transcendence requires openness to a radically different frame of reference; it takes one beyond the known into the unknown, demanding courage and a willingness to take risks.

Most analyses of our society tend to focus on material issues in the socio-economic and political domains. Yet human beings as the main actors in history are framed in significant ways by spiritual and psychological impulses that go beyond material needs. We are inclined to underestimate the importance of deep matters of the soul that distinguish humans from other members of the animal kingdom. We are at our best as humans beings when our souls and minds are in harmony with what we do and how we relate to others.

Think back to the first encounter between Nelson Mandela and P.W. Botha. Here were two men who reached deep into themselves to find a way out of the dead end of apartheid intransigence on the one hand, and a costly anti-apartheid struggle on the other. It was their mutual recognition of the need to go beyond the divisions between them that enabled them to respond to each other as elderly men with a shared responsibility to future generations. Here the jailer and the jailed were able to move beyond their then reality to contemplate a different and shared future. They transcended their respective realities in the interest of a better future for their country.

The same possibility of transcendence came to the fore at the TRC hearings where perpetrators of human-rights abuses and those they had wronged were able to go beyond their woundedness towards mutual recognition of the need for healing through acknowledgement of the wrongs committed. Forgiveness became possible when those who had been wronged moved beyond the common tendency to seek revenge. Their willingness to forgive contributed to a stronger foundation for a united nation.

For those who have had traumatic experiences, transcendence is essential to moving forward on life's journey. The experiences of being oppressed on the one hand, and being oppressors on the other, have left South Africans traumatised. There is a need for all of us to transcend that past in order to build a shared future, drawing on the collective strengths we bring to our democracy. Such transcendence would enhance our ability to take ownership of the new democracy with its rights and responsibilities.

It is inconceivable that we can become 'whole' as a people without focusing on the incalculable damage done to our ability to love ourselves as individuals, to love our families, our communities and our entire society with the passion that grounds our patriotism. Our ability to develop and sustain the same inner commitment that characterised the best amongst us during the struggle for freedom would benefit from such a spiritual journey. Material freedom disengaged from inner spiritual freedom puts us at risk of losing the focus on the larger purpose of freedom – freedom to be fully who we can be in our democracy.

Our reticence to tackle matters spiritual or psychological is understandable. Such issues are difficult to deal with, and airing them inappropriately outside a professional, supportive environment can do more harm than good. In addition, there is a stigma attached to psychological or mental problems, which are often seen as reflections of a 'weak' character. The very nature of the struggle for freedom that brought about this democracy demanded a resolute frame of mind. Weaknesses, whether real or apparent, could easily be exploited by the apartheid system to frustrate the march to freedom. By now we should acknowledge that those risks are behind us, and open up space for people with persistent wounds to find healing. We also need to create opportunities for nurturing our souls to keep our ideals alive in our everyday lives.

Another reason for the marginalisation of spiritual matters in our transformation process has been the influence of Marxist thinking on the struggle for freedom. Marx's critique of religion as the 'opium' of oppressed people found resonance in activist ranks, especially amongst members of the South African Communist Party (SACP). This created ambivalence within the anti-apartheid movement in a society that has very strong religious roots across many faiths. The misuse of religion by the apartheid system to justify racism did not help. Many activists did not make their religious stance known until well into the new democracy. Even now, few base their social actions on a spiritual foundation.

From the late 1960s, liberation theology added a spiritual dimension to the discourse and practice of resistance politics. Liberation theology was inspired by activist priests in Latin America and elsewhere who stood on the side of the oppressed. Martin Luther King's leadership of the Civil Rights Movement in the USA in support of equal rights for African Americans also added spiritual tones to the struggle for freedom. The Black Consciousness Movement embraced it and popularised it as Black Theology that influenced theological students who became part of the wider radical student movement. Trevor Huddleston's stance against apartheid embodied in his 1950s work as an Anglican priest amongst people of Sophiatown, Johannesburg, inspired the likes of Desmond Tutu and others to stand on the side of oppressed people in their ministry. The 'conversion' of people such as Beyers Naude, a member of the Afrikaner establishment Broederbond who became an anti-apartheid activist, reflects the impact of the spiritual on the freedom struggle. Those who lived in exile before this infusion of spiritual discourse missed out on an important dimension.

Jonathan Sacks, Chief Rabbi of the United Hebrew Congregation of Great Britain and the Commonwealth, presents an interesting perspective from Judaism: 'In Judaism, faith is not acceptance but protest, against a world that is, in the name of the world that is not yet but ought to be . . . It is impossible to be moved by the prophets and not have a social conscience . . . The world will not get better of its own accord. Nor will we make it a more humane place by leaving it to others – politicians, columnists, protesters, campaigners.'[5]

Sacks's critique resonates with the actions of many religious leaders and practitioners across the spectrum who act out their faith in socio-economic and political terms. What we appear to have lost as a nation is the voice of morality in our public discourse. In the new dispensation, only a handful of religious leaders are willing to speak out for poor and vulnerable people. We seem to have retreated into religion as private practice rather than infusing political action with spiritual understanding. Archbishops Desmond Tutu and Njongonkulu Ndungane are notable exceptions. This loss of voice by those who ought to care about vulnerable people prompted Nelson Mandela at the Steve Biko Memorial Lecture in 2005 to appeal for an RDP (Reconstruction and Development Programme) of the soul.

Analysts of our transition to democracy are inclined to either romanticise what has been accomplished thus far or be overly critical of the persistent gaps between the idealism of the envisaged transformation process and the socio-economic realities of citizens' everyday lives. Both sides are apt to underestimate the complex processes involved in managing the urgent multiple challenges that had to be addressed to secure a successful transition and lay the foundations for orderly transformation. The mood of the nation tends to swing between euphoria and pessimism as it confronts the challenges of closing the gaps between commitments to the founding principles framed in our national constitution and the weaknesses of execution at many levels in our society.

Even though there are no comparable models to guide our transformation, South Africa has had the opportunity of learning from transitions in other parts of Africa about what has worked or not worked, and why. For example, the approach of many anti-colonial activists that focused on 'seeking first the political kingdom, then all others would be added'[6], has largely been discredited by historical experience. This dictum of Kwame Nkrumah, the first president of post-colonial Ghana, proved a dead end for the pioneering country that in 1957 became the first black African state to win its independence.

Political freedom without economic power has proved meaningless to countless post-colonial countries. This becomes apparent when one compares the post-colonial development of African countries with that of the 'Asian tigers' (Hong Kong, Singapore, South Korea and Taiwan). These Asian countries first achieved economic power, which led to high levels of economic growth and industrialisation, resulting in their establishing themselves as developed countries by the end of the 20th century.

Many African countries, though politically free, continue to suffer from inadequate attention to appropriate economic reforms to underpin sustainable socio-economic development of their societies. Uhuru[7] remains an empty shell for many poor people of Africa. In this regard, South Africa's post-apartheid governments have done a remarkably good job in focusing on deep macro- and micro-economic reforms to minimise the trap of empty freedom.

It is, however, important to acknowledge that some of our policy choices as a new democracy could have benefited from lessons derived from elsewhere. Transformation of the education and training system is an area where we could have done better by learning from others' experiences. Countries as diverse as South Korea, Finland, Ireland and Zimbabwe were all able to increase mass access to education and training while improving the quality of outcomes. In our case, improved access to education has not necessarily translated into improved outcomes where it really matters – in the lives of poor people.

Equally important are lessons learnt from the Old Mutual/Nedcor transition scenarios exercise that was conducted between 1991 and 1992. Transitions from authoritarian rule to democracy forged on elite pacts between incumbent political leaders and heads of liberation movements pose special challenges and opportunities. Such pacts are characterised by the voluntary handover of power by sitting governments, as ably analysed by Guillermo O' Donnell and Philippe Schmitter.[8] These authors found no example of success in raising incomes of citizens after transition to democracy unless there had been a successfully performing economy beforehand. An analysis of successful political transitions in Colombia, Venezuela, Spain, Turkey and Chile indicated that they were preceded by rising incomes.

The strong relationship between economic performance and successful transitions is supported by other literature. For example, 20th century history suggests that democracy is more stable in high-income countries than in those with weak economies. Medieval Europe was a brutal and unstable place compared to the Europe of today. There was little room for democratic principles to emerge and be embedded in the survival-of-the-fittest cultures of the Middle Ages. An understanding of the relationship between economics and politics informed the support of the European Union (EU) for poorer fellow countries through social funds to facilitate economic reform.

Three waves of successful transitions to democracy in Europe attest to this. The first was the reconstruction and development after World War II inspired by the Marshall Plan. Then came the social reforms and accelerated economic growth of poor member countries such as Ireland, Portugal and Spain in the 1970s. The third wave was in the form of socio-economic reform of former Soviet Union client states as a prerequisite to their joining the EU after the end of the Cold War.

Countries of the former Soviet Union made their transition in the early 1990s in an environment in which their success was of interest to all their neighbours. The former German Democratic Republic was even more fortunate in having a natural brother that immediately embraced it. East Germany's transition was guided and largely financed by West Germany. It also automatically became part of the EU, a club that not only sets standards of performance but provides structural funds to help bridge transition costs. Other East European and Central Asian countries also benefited from being in a neighbourhood anxious to support their successful transition. Political imperatives linked to ensuring that the fallen Soviet Empire would never rise again kept the United States (US) focused on bringing in multilateral development institutions, notably the World Bank and the International Monetary Fund (IMF), to support the successful development of market economies in Eastern Europe.[9]

South Africa's economy was anything but successful at the time of its transition to democracy. Democratic change was a non-negotiable part of the settlement process. How was the country to achieve a successful transition to democracy against such odds? There would be no Marshall Plan, as many Western political analysts made clear to South Africans trying to make a case for material support. There was also no 'big brother' with a vested interest in South Africa's transition willing to bankroll it. South Africa had to make do with what it had inherited, and make a success of the transition despite the weaknesses in the economy. The Old Mutual/Nedcor scenario analysis indicated four key weaknesses of the South African economy at the time: declining incomes, declining investments, rising unemployment and huge inequalities.[10]

These weaknesses posed serious challenges to the transition process. There was widespread fear in the early to mid-1990s that populist demands on the post-apartheid government would lead to instability that could derail the transition to democracy. The perceived influence of the South African Communist Party (SACP) and the Congress of South African Trade Unions (Cosatu) on policy-making within the Tripartite Alliance with the ruling African National Congress (ANC) was regarded as a threat to sound economic policies. Pessimistic analysts contributed to a nearly self-fulfilling prophecy in the mid-1990s by creating an environment of low expectations of the outcome of the transition.

However, lessons with regard to economic-policy choices derived by the ANC leadership from the Mont Fleur Scenarios[11] protected South Africa against populism. The ANC leadership chose to focus on the Flamingo Scenario – slow to take off but ultimately soaring gracefully in perfect formation – in contrast to the Icarus Scenario of populism, which is characterised by early apparent success that fizzles out in the harshness of reality.

South Africa's transformation process also rests on a weak social-capital base that is often unacknowledged. 'Social capital' is used here to denote the complex web of networks of support, trust relationships and intergenerational transfer of values and wisdom that sustain a reasonable quality of life for human community. The burden of the struggle for freedom borne by young people in the post-1976 period left deep fissures in relationships between individuals, families and communities, and in the wider social system.

Intergenerational transfer of wisdom and guidance was fractured by the radical reversal of roles between parents and their children, and mistrust between and within generations undermined social relationships. The protracted civil war left deep wounds and scars in our society that are still crying out for attention. In addition, our progress is undermined by mistrust that still exists between and within sectors of the South African population.

The transformation of South Africa into the kind of society characterised by the principles and values envisaged in our national constitution confronts us with major dilemmas.

The first set of dilemmas stems from the elite pact that led to our transition. Inevitably compromises had to be struck. Attention to the socio-economic rights of the majority of the population was judged to pose risks to the delicate balance on which the political-settlement process rested. The TRC was confined to examining gross violations of human rights, leaving the violations of socio-economic rights unaddressed. The sorely needed closure on the socio-economic front was left to the Reconstruction and Development Programme (RDP) of the post-apartheid government.

More than ten years' experience with redressing socio-economic inequities suggests that this challenge has been grossly underestimated. Socio-economic transformation is a demanding task under any circumstance anywhere in the world. In South Africa, the challenge is compounded by the inadequate capacity of the post-apartheid state and ever-moving targets for performance as expectations rise amongst those at the bottom of the socio-economic pyramid.

Persistent inequalities are an inevitable outcome of the elite pact. The dilemma is how to acknowledge this reality without exacerbating tensions between the haves and the have-nots. As Raymond Aron has reminded us, 'the existence of too great a degree of inequality makes human community impossible'.[12]

The second set of dilemmas relates to the scale and scope of transformation that spans the political, economic and social systems of our society. How does one undertake such a major, complex task while keeping all these systems going? Political analyst and businessman Frederik Van Zyl Slabbert coined an apt metaphor for what we were trying to accomplish in the early stages of our transition: 'It is like changing the engines of a Boeing 747 in mid-air!'

Yet, this is precisely what our post-1994 governments have been trying to accomplish – changing the constitution, the laws, the policies and practices of our nation while keeping South Africa functional. It is a massive and courageous undertaking by any measure. Whatever mistakes were made should be understandable in such a context. Avoiding mistakes might not be possible, but the key question is whether or not we learn from our mistakes to improve performance as we go forward.

Third, we face dilemmas in transcending the divisions and values we inherited from apartheid. Forging an identity as a non-racial, non-sexist, egalitarian society, the kind of society to which we committed ourselves in our constitution, requires us to lay to rest the ghosts of racism, sexism, ethnic chauvinism and authoritarianism. These are stubborn ghosts that will not be easily exorcised, with an enduring global resonance that has proven tenacious even in mature democracies.

The fourth set of dilemmas revolves around the impact of the legacy of the past on the capacity of individuals, institutions and systems to contribute effectively to the transformation and prosperity of society. The deliberate underdevelopment of the human, intellectual and social capital of the majority of the population as part of the apartheid system has left our society with a weak base on which to mount this immense transformation agenda.

The major predicament both individuals and the government face is how to acknowledge and tackle capacity problems without undermining the credibility and effectiveness of those involved. How does one acknowledge state capacity problems without creating loss of confidence by the public in state institutions and those operating within them? Acknowledgement of weaknesses is further complicated by the fear of fulfilling racist or sexist stereotypes in a society still wrestling these ghosts.

The fifth arena of dilemmas relates to the extent to which we as a young democracy can or should be our neighbours' keepers. There is a body of opinion across the political spectrum that questions our ability to tackle our own considerable transformation challenges while paying the significant attention we do to the challenges of our neighbourhood. The dilemmas we face in this regard pertain to whether South Africa can afford to relegate its neighbourhood issues to a lower priority and still succeed in becoming a prosperous democracy.

Each one of the dilemmas facing South Africa points to the need for a shift in our frame of reference. Using known approaches to transitions to democracy and promotion of sustainable development is likely to limit our horizons. We need to take the risk of venturing into the unknown to explore new possibilities.

Tackling dilemmas successfully requires the willingness to abandon the tendency of dealing with issues on an either-or basis. Traditional economics tends to overemphasise the importance of trade-offs. For example, development-policy advice over many decades has been to first ensure macro-economic stability and then look at broadening the base of participation in the economy. Essentially, this means that poor people have to take the pain in the short term in the hope that benefits would trickle down to them as the economy grows. This view is thoroughly discredited by evidence of the benefits flowing from investing in both human capital and macro-economic stability at the same time.

A holistic approach that exploits links between clusters of problems and their solutions allows one to harness synergies by marrying apparently contradictory policy frames. For instance, the tendency to see the empowerment of black people and that of women as competitive domains is threatening to undermine the gains we are making in our transformation process. Tackling race, class, gender and other markers of discrimination simultaneously has the potential of turning competing claims for redress into a greater surge of energy from all the talents that are forced to confront fundamental problems of power relationships.

Instead of black men protecting their new-found turf by focusing only on fighting racism, solidarity with women in the continuing struggle for gender equality is likely to lead to a more concerted, fundamental anti-discrimination cultural change. Worldwide, the energies of liberated women have been shown to help build better partnerships, families, communities, companies and societies.

Freedom is indivisible. One cannot be free as a black person and yet still be bound by traditionalism as a woman. Nor can we fully enjoy our freedom if some sectors of our society are not free. Promoting greater equity within society also unleashes the energy and talents of those previously excluded so that they can become contributors to the common good instead of recipients of charity and welfare transfers.

Embracing a comprehensive framework for transformation that reflects the indivisibility of freedom requires a focus beyond the material domain of life on which major revolutions tend to concentrate. Shifting the frame of reference is about transcendence. It is a deeply spiritual matter that forces one to be true to deep convictions even if one may be going against conventional wisdom. It is about making oneself vulnerable by abandoning known ways of seeing the world and engaging with others to explore different approaches.

Leadership is vital for this shift to occur, whether at the personal, family, community, institutional or societal levels. Good leaders expand the boundaries of possibility to enable others to reach beyond what they thought were their limits.

In this book I would like to explore how we have fared so far in tackling the dilemmas stemming from the legacy of our past. Underlying all the themes is a plea for us to move beyond denial to acknowledgement of the burden of that legacy. We would then be in a better position to shift our frame of reference for our transformation process from the known past and present towards a bolder imagined future. Courageous, visionary leadership is essential to success.

CHAPTER 2

A miracle that never was
Living with ordinariness

SOUTH AFRICA'S POLITICAL SETTLEMENT AND TRANSITION TO democracy have often been characterised as a miracle. Both South Africans and international observers have repeated this so often that they have come to believe it to be true. The idea of a miracle – an act of divine intervention – is seductive. It makes South Africans feel very special. It makes our democracy special. That the Divine singled us out for intervention is at once humbling and flattering.

We are not alone in appropriating this special status of the chosen ones. The Afrikaners, winning their freedom from the dominance by British colonials following the 1948 election victory of the National Party, also felt special. They believed that they were the chosen people in a hostile land that they had had to tame to fulfil their covenant with the divine. Their theologians went on to justify apartheid as ordained by the same divine force that had given them South Africa as their heritage.

Die Stem, the Afrikaner national anthem, captured the spirit of this covenant:

> *Uit die blou van onse hemel*
> *Uit die diepte van ons see*
> *Oor ons ewige gebergtes*
> *Waar die kranse antwoord gee*
> *Oor ons ver verlate vlaktes*

Met die kreun van ossewa
Ruis die stem van ons geliefde,
Van ons land Suid-Afrika.
Ons sal antwoord op jou roepstem,
Ons sal offer wat jy vra.
Ons sal lewe
Ons sal sterwe
Ons vir jou, Suid Afrika.

This anthem was intended as a powerful call to arms for the Afrikaners to defend their God-given land. It translates as follows:

From the blue of our skies
From the depth of our sea
Over our eternal mountains
Where the crags echo in response
Over our remote, desolate plains
Where ox-wagons creaked
Calls the voice of our beloved,
Of our country, South Africa.
We shall answer your call
We shall sacrifice what you demand
We shall live
We shall die
We for you, South Africa.

It took the courage of people such as Beyers Naudé and Theo Kotze, both Afrikaner theologians, to challenge apartheid theology in the late 1960s. They were inspired to join the struggle against inequities of the society. It was the theological challenge that strengthened the resolve of many to fight apartheid at home and abroad. The demystification of apartheid, showing that it was a system of oppression that could not have been sanctioned by any divine power, enabled many South Africans to question the racist assumptions of our society.

The history of apartheid should caution us in the post-apartheid era against the temptation to regard ourselves as a special people singled out for divine intervention. The notion of Afrikaners as a chosen people was also based on their experience of having been delivered from suffering and humiliation. The suffering endured in the concentration camps of the Anglo–Boer war and especially the deaths of many women and children remained fresh in the minds of many Afrikaners. Their resilience throughout these traumas was seen as a sign of the hand of the Divine being upon them. Suffering was seen as strengthening the chosen people for service.

The temptation to regard suffering as ennobling needs to be resisted. History is full of examples of people who had been oppressed turning into oppressors of others weaker than themselves.

The miracle formulation, suggestive of being singled out for special treatment by the Divine, heightens the risk of entitlement to wield power over others. Our young democracy needs to manage this significant risk. Given the role of liberation theology and the participation of religious leaders in the struggle for freedom, the notion of a miraculous transition is emotionally and intellectually appealing. As a society, we have a high rate of participating in religious belief systems, including indigenous African, Muslim, Hindu, Christian and Judaic. In addition, former struggle activists often share strong ideological convictions similar to religious convictions, permitting little room for doubt. The emotional boost we derive from being special needs to be tempered by historical lessons that should inform our conduct and public accountability within the human rights constitution we have adopted.

The notion of a miraculous settlement and transition is a convenient formulation for some international observers as well. Those who had given up hope of a political settlement ever coming to South Africa in the 1990s can feel vindicated. They can rationalise their failure to raise their voices against the injustices of apartheid by pointing to the hopelessness of any attempt to challenge the apartheid system. Only divine intervention could succeed in changing such an entrenched system. Thus, those who remained silent in the face of human-rights abuses were absolved from guilt by association.

The miraculous transition notion also vindicates those who believed the propaganda that the struggle for freedom was a communist ploy to take over the only 'civilised' part of the African continent. They do not have to re-examine their earlier assumptions, because the Divine intervened to convert terrorists and communists into reasonable leaders willing to negotiate a political settlement. The metamorphosis of Mandela the terrorist into Mandela the international statesman could only have come from above.

The miracle characterisation of the transition leaves unexamined the past role of those who today define themselves as the defenders of freedom and democracy. How would they otherwise square their professed roles now with their defence of apartheid and sustenance of its hegemony in southern Africa over so many decades? The miracle idea serves as a good cover for the changed foreign-policy stances of the US and UK political establishments. Hostility to the ANC as a liberation movement in the 1960s through to the 1980s changed to support for its ideals and leaders in the period after 1990. They could partly justify this change in stance to their constituencies as reflecting the change of heart of an ANC that was inspired by some divine power. The fall of the Soviet Empire provided a bigger impetus to this change of sentiment towards and within the ANC. The ANC itself had to accept a negotiated settlement given the reality of the disappearance of a major ally.

The miracle idea also permits amnesia of the betrayal of black people by the UK as the former colonial power in South Africa. The granting of self-governance by the UK to the Union of South Africa in 1910 that excluded the majority of the population from full political participation set the scene for the formalisation of apartheid. The opportunity to include the majority was again lost in 1961 when South Africa left the Commonwealth and became a Republic.

Ironically, the same UK refused to grant independence to Rhodesia because of the then Prime Minister Ian Smith's insistence on excluding black people from full citizenship. Rhodesia made a unilateral declaration of independence (UDI) in 1965. A brutal civil war followed before a negotiated settlement was reached in 1979, paving the way for the birth of Zimbabwe in 1980. Inconsistencies in the unfolding of histories of nations often reflect the changing interests of key players. The UK is a prime example of a country that has evolved from an imperial power to a major advocate of democracy in international affairs. Nevertheless, the UK's national interests, as is the case with most countries, remain paramount in the conduct of its international relations.

There are risks attached to holding on to the myth of a miraculous political settlement and peaceful transition. One is the risk of losing lessons of history. It is difficult to learn from a miracle. After all, one cannot direct miracles at will. Understanding the underlying dynamics of our political settlement and transition is critical to learning history's lessons.

There is also a risk of promoting fatalism in political affairs through interpretations of historical events in the language of miracles. If radical political change comes from divine intervention, what motivation would there be for governments to negotiate settlements, or for citizens to take the risks of shaping their own destinies by challenging unjust authority and holding public officials accountable?

Let us look at some of the historical realities and lessons from transitions to democracy. Both internal and external forces propelled South Africa's political settlement. The fall of the Berlin Wall in 1989 was a decisive moment in shifting the geopolitical terrain in favour of democratisation. The Eastern and Central Europe region was not the only beneficiary of this momentous event. With the Soviet empire crumbling, the US no longer had strategic interests in continuing its support of the apartheid government. The same geopolitical considerations applied to the UK. The apartheid regime that had over the years positioned itself as a bastion against the communist threat lost its strategic importance, and constructive engagement with it no longer held any appeal. Both the US and UK governments became more responsive to pressure from their own constituencies to press the apartheid government into a negotiated settlement.

It was ultimately the struggle mounted by both internal and external anti-apartheid movements that forced open the space for political dialogue. Sports boycotts, academic and cultural isolation, disinvestment campaigns, boycotts of South African goods and produce and other symbolic acts all added to the pressure. South Africa's liberation is a product of collective effort by activists inside and outside the country that made the alternative to change 'too ghastly to contemplate' – to borrow the late President John Vorster's words.

Nelson Mandela's visionary strategic leadership was a key factor in the creation of a climate for dialogue, the success of the negotiations that produced the political settlement, and the transition to democracy. It would be a mistake, however, to credit Mandela with everything that led to the settlement. Those eager to sustain the miracle characterisation of the process also tend to imbue Mandela with magical powers. If the Divine did not intervene directly, then surely Mandela must have been the chosen one sent to implement the will of the Divine.

There can be no denying the extraordinary leadership that characterises Mandela's role in history and the gifts with which he has been blessed. But by attributing this merely to 'magic' we run the risk of losing lessons from his leadership style that can be of value to other leaders. His greatness comes from his willingness to take risks and to break new ground even if it means going against popular sentiment.

Negotiating with the enemy was not a popular concept in the late 1980s when Mandela first suggested it to his comrades in prison. The purists among them believed that only when they were released could proper negotiations be conducted, in full consultation with the liberation movement leadership. But Mandela was wise enough to know that little progress could be made unless risks were taken to break the impasse between the oppressed and the oppressors, and he met clandestinely with his captors to test the possibilities of 'talks about talks'.

As he wrote in his autobiography, 'My solitude would give me an opportunity to take the first steps in that direction, without the kind of scrutiny that might destroy such efforts.'[13] The change in the circumstances of his imprisonment in 1985 at Pollsmoor Prison allowed him to take advantage of an offer by prison officials to occupy a 'three-roomed facility: bedroom, study and exercise room'. The leadership of the Robben Island ANC had been transferred from Robben Island to Pollsmoor Prison in 1982.

Mandela's strategic leadership qualities enabled him to negotiate single-handedly with his captors for months on end. They had all the professional strategists on their side. They had the machinery of state. He had only his convictions and wits. In his encounters with tough negotiators he was greatly assisted by his knowledge of the Afrikaners' history of their struggle against British domination. He could draw on lessons from key historical moments to illustrate why his proposals made sense in the light of the Afrikaners' own history. It was a classic case of knowing your enemy well enough to charm them into respecting you.

A colloquial expression used in South Africa's townships describes someone with the knack to make the right decisions at appropriate moments: *u ne timing* (he has timing). Mandela is also a master of choosing the right time to raise issues. This 'sense of timing' was crucial to the success of his solo negotiations.

Much of the respect Mandela earned from his captors came from the manner in which he conducted himself throughout the long 27 years in prison. His approach was to respect the rules and the officers who enforced them without allowing them to violate his dignity. He cautioned his fellow prisoners against disrespect for those in authority as strongly as he insisted on prisoners being treated with respect. Prison life was as harsh for him as for everyone else, but his inner dignity was protected by an iron will.

It helped that Mandela is a highly disciplined man. He used his imprisonment to establish a regime of exercising regularly, eating a balanced diet, reading widely and studying subjects of interest. When I first visited him in Pollsmoor Prison in 1988, I was amazed at how well he looked for a man of 70 and how well informed he was about contemporary issues.

In 1976, as part of a group of Black Consciousness Movement activists in the Eastern Cape, I tasted some of the 'luxury' of leisure time during a stint as preventive detainee in King William's Town Prison under Section 10 of the Terrorism Act. Our group of detainees was part of the wider liberation movement, mobilising politically through practical community programmes under the aegis of the Black Community Program (BCP) headquartered in Durban.

I read a lot. I slept a lot. We exercised daily and held self-help yoga classes using a book sent to us by a fellow detainee, the late Gibson Kente. We came out of prison trimmer and healthier. Imprisonment can be turned into an opportunity for reflection and personal growth. We were able to focus on the future and to continue believing in our capacity to shape it.

Mandela's incisive mind and exceptional memory served him well in his negotiations with his captors. These endowments also made him the legendary president he became. His attention to details of the lives of people he meets is extraordinary. This matters if one is to win the confidence of the other party in the negotiation process.

He has an astounding grasp of national and international issues. Unlike many leaders in more sophisticated societies who have a range of trusted expertise at their disposal, Mandela did not have adequate technical backing as leader of his country. Apartheid robbed the ANC leadership of highly trained experts in the various fields essential to understanding alternative policy choices and complex contemporary politics. The low level of trust of expertise from outside the ANC led to reliance on limited intellectual resources within the movement. Mandela had to rely on his own wisdom and trust his own intuition. This has served him well over the years.

What stands out about Mandela's leadership style during the first years of our transition is his ability to make people feel that with him around, everything is possible. Benjamin Zander, conductor of the Boston Symphony Orchestra for many years, has likened great leadership to inspirational conducting. The members of an orchestra are the specialists in their fields, but they need a conductor to make their performance more than the sum of their individual endeavours. Zander refers to this type of leadership as

> '. . . an enlivening way of approaching people that promises to transform you as well as them. It is a shift in attitude that makes it possible for you to speak freely about your own thoughts and feelings while at the same time you support others to be all they dream of being . . . [It] transports your relationships from the world of measurement into the universe of possibility.'[14]

The 'Madiba magic' mania that spread like wildfire in the five years Mandela was president stemmed from this ability to inspire confidence and self-belief in others. He became associated with the country's many sporting achievements during his presidency, which were seen as 'miraculous' in the context of South Africa's years of isolation. Mandela's embrace of sporting codes which previously excluded black people from representing their country in national teams had a conciliatory and healing impact on society. One of the best examples of this was his televised appearance in a Springbok rugby jersey to wish the team well before their 1995 Rugby World Cup Final encounter with the All Blacks at the Ellis Park stadium in Johannesburg. His presence gave the players wings and opened up possibilities for them to see themselves as winners.

Andrew Feinstein, a former ANC MP who resigned in 2001 in protest at the failure of the ANC to openly investigate the multibillion rand arms deal that continues to reverberate in our body politic, had this to say about Mandela's leadership: 'Like most people I was in awe of the man-myth . . . Part of Madiba's extraordinary charm is his ability to humble himself through humour, so that while you know you are in the presence of greatness the knowledge doesn't overawe or paralyse.'[15] Mandela's greatest virtue, however, is also his most significant fault – loyalty to comrades in the struggle and those close to him.

Mandela's self-confidence inspired South Africans in all walks of life. He also set new dress codes by refusing to bow to the Western-style 'black tie' that he derided as 'penguin dress'. It reminded him too much of the Robben Island penguins that had been part of his environment for more than twenty years. Instead, he introduced loose, colourful shirts that have become known as Madiba shirts, thereby redefining casual- smart dress for men in South Africa.

While the miracle notion of South Africa's transition tends to encourage excessive focus on Mandela as an individual, Mandela himself always takes care to emphasise the importance of other leaders in the struggle. Once the ice had been broken between him and the apartheid government negotiators, he made sure that he consulted regularly and widely both inside and outside South Africa. It is this awareness and appreciation of the contribution of others that also marked him as a leader well suited to forge consensus not only within the liberation movement but with the apartheid government.

He specifically acknowledges the late Oliver Tambo, his partner in law and politics and leader of the ANC in exile, for his courage and wisdom in keeping the movement going during those long, cold years. His love and respect for Tambo and his wife Adelaide was deeply and publicly acknowledged. We now know that Tambo had also been instrumental in promoting dialogue between ANC leaders in exile and Afrikaner establishment figures that had a major impact on both sides of the political divide.

Mandela also had a special fondness for the late Walter Sisulu as his mentor, friend and leader. Sisulu, with a low-key and conciliatory leadership style, is credited with having kept the ANC alive through the tough times of the 1950s as its secretary-general.[16]

It is to Mandela's credit that the bloodbath in KwaZulu-Natal was halted just before the elections in 1994. He had been overruled by his own comrades in the ANC from charming the leader of the Inkatha Freedom Party (IFP), Chief Mangosuthu Buthelezi, early on in the negotiation process[17]. His self-confidence allowed him to acknowledge the role of Buthelezi as leader without fearing that it would diminish his own stature. But it took the loss of many lives before the cost of exclusionary competitive approaches to power by his comrades within the ANC gave way to reconciliation between the ANC and Inkatha. Mandela understands the historical lessons that it is often up to those in a stronger position to reach out to weaker adversaries. The reconciliation with Buthelezi paved the way for the Inkatha Freedom Party's participation in the seminal 1994 elections and the government of national unity.

The myth of our transition as having been 'peaceful' is belied by historical facts. Acknowledging the loss of life in the run-up to the final settlement would detract from the mystique of a miracle. But there could also be another, less generous interpretation. If the profile of those killed had been predominantly white and not young black people, would the same assertion have been made?

It is estimated that no fewer than 30 000 people died between 1976 and 1994 in the anti-apartheid struggle that had all the hallmarks of a civil war. According to the South African Institute of Race Relations (SAIRR), nearly 24 000 political fatalities occurred between 1985 and 1996.[18] Most politically related deaths took place in the four years leading up to the first democratic election on 27 April 1994 – in this period 14 000 deaths and 22 000 injuries were recorded.[19] Many more undocumented young people paid the ultimate sacrifice, their remains hidden in unmarked graves or worse. A white right-wing gunman, Janusz Walus, assassinated Chris Hani, a very prominent ANC leader, only a year before the first elections in 1994. The miracle idea plays down the sacrifices that were made by many.

The miracle idea also ignores the hard work that went into making peace with the past. As will be explored more fully in the next chapter, poor men and women participated in the rituals of reconciliation at the TRC, and were able to forgive those who had wronged them thus enabling our society to move on. There was no material or emotional compensation for their losses. Theirs has been a selfless gift to their society – a peace offering to allow it to move on. Many continue to live in poverty in the new democracy they have helped to stabilise through their generous acts of forgiveness.

There is a sense in which those South Africans who have the means to lead comfortable lives in the post-apartheid era can indeed afford to 'let bygones be bygones'. New elites can look forward to a rewarding professional life, a comfortable home, healthy and happy children, a sense of accomplishment of their ambitions, control over their lives.

The real heroes and heroines of our transition to democracy are those many men and women who remain marginal, disempowered and miserably poor, and yet are prepared to forgive and make peace with the past. They are the ones who had to make the extra effort to heal the nation. They are the wounded healers to whom society owes much. It is this extraordinary generosity that has not been sufficiently acknowledged. The notion of a miracle does an injustice to those who gave so much up in order to transcend the past.

It may be that the lacing of our transition with so much ritual and symbolism also gave an impetus to the idea of a miraculous process. Take the inauguration of Mandela as the first president of a free South Africa. The setting was apt. The Union Buildings with their magnificent plaza provided a fitting space for the ritual of transition towards a more inclusive society.

The Union Buildings, situated on a ridge on the edge of the city of Pretoria, bear the imprint of the celebrated British architect Sir Herbert Baker. They showcase superb architecture that pays attention to detail while making a statement of majestic proportions.

Mandela has a knack for the dramatic. Three moments in his inauguration ceremony stand out, capturing the complexities of ritual and symbolism in the transformation process. They enacted the movement of African people from the margins to the centre stage of politics, and also signaled a more inclusive politics. The first moment was praise singing by a traditional Xhosa artist in full regalia. His role was to present Mandela in the context of the cosmology of his people as well as in the political history of his country. Never before had African praise singing been accorded pride of place in modern South African politics, let alone on a world stage. On 10 May 1994, African praise singing burst into millions of living rooms worldwide.

The second moment ritualising the birth of a new nation was the singing of the two South African national anthems – each dear to each side of the divided society that was coming together to inaugurate their president. The one was a prayer, *Nkosi Sikelel' iAfrika* (God Bless Africa), sung in isiZulu, isiXhosa and Sesotho by generations of those yearning for freedom in South Africa. It had served those in the anti-apartheid struggle in times of mourning their fallen heroes. It also rang out proudly in times of celebration of small victories along the long road to freedom.

Die Stem (The Voice) is an Afrikaner nationalist call to patriotism, as explained earlier. It remains dear to those who saw themselves pitted against threats to their heritage – a South Africa led by white people. Both anthems were accorded the dignity they deserved as a mark of the coming together of the two main strands of our society in 1994.

In 1996 these two anthems were merged to become what is now
South Africa's official national anthem. In that act Mandela's visionary leadership again came to the fore. His leadership overcame objections from both the right and the left to combining the traditionally
revered *Nkosi Sikelel' iAfrika* with the highly emotive patriotic Afrikaner anthem. The result is a goose-bump-raising prayer for peace, a
pledge to patriotism and a commitment to unity:

Nkosi sikelel' iAfrika
Maluphakanyisw' umpondo lwayo
Yizwa imithandazo yethu
Nkosi sikelela, thina lusapho lwayo

Morena boloka sechaba sa heso
O fedise dintwa le matshwenyeho
O se boloke!
O se boloke Sechaba!
Sechaba sa Afrika
South Afrika

Uit die blou van onse hemel
Uit die diepte van ons see
Oor ons ewige gebergtes
Waar die kranse antwoord gee

Sounds the call to come together
And united we shall stand
Let us live and strive for freedom
In South Africa our land!

The third moment in President Mandela's inauguration rose physically to the highest ritual realm. The fly-past by the South African Air
Force had a strongly symbolic element to it. In saluting their new com-
mander-in-chief, they were at once displaying the best of South Africa's
military prowess and making a statement about the richness of the

technological heritage that was now owned by all citizens. South Africans left the Union Buildings plaza mesmerised. In one fell swoop
they became a united nation. They learnt to share the pride and joy of
their country's achievements and its potential to overcome its past.

Alan Paton, one of the founders and leader of the Liberal Party in
the 1950s and the author of the classic novel *Cry the Beloved Country*,
must have heaved a sigh of relief from his grave. On this mild winter's
day in May 1994, the cry of the beloved country had turned into song.
Each of the songs that rang out at the inauguration ceremony expressed
some part of the significance of the occasion that could not have been
conveyed through speeches alone.

African praise singing is about everything but singing. It is a performance. The praise singer is both the choreographer and actor. His outfit
of colourful African cloth, beads and animal skins is part of the
choreography and defines his personality. Every move is part of the
performance, with each step calculated to communicate both mystique
and authority. Certainty and mock uncertainty are played out to enter-
tain the audience. Mock uncertainty accentuates the boldness of the
sure steps the praise singer takes at appropriate moments to emphasise aspects of his song.

The power of opposites is exploited to the full in this genre: strengths
and weaknesses, the living and the dead, the ordinary and the extraordinary are all placed together to accentuate the points made to depict
the complexity of life. The praise song is performed in a measured
rhythm that harmonises physical movement with the rise and fall of
the voice. Pauses are interspersed for maximum effect to hold the audience in suspense.

The praise song itself brings biography, past and present into harmony. It exploits the rich store of idiom from African languages. It
straddles poetry and prose. The praise singer has poetic licence to use
language as a pliable medium. The subject of praise singing has to be
presented nestled within the embrace of his or her ancestors. The
ancestors have to be brought into the occasion to witness one of their
own attaining an important milestone. Their blessing is critical.

Praise singers also have their feet firmly rooted in the present. They are masters of the moment. They electrify and are electrified by the present. But they also have the licence and obligation to express hope of a better future. They implore the subject to take future responsibilities seriously. They remind the subject that the hopes and dreams of many are pinned on him. Failure is not an option for those whose praises are sung.

Mandela's royal blood added to the dignity of the occasion. The praise singer was burdened by this knowledge, but also energised by it. Who would not be honoured to sing the praises of one with such a pedigree? Mandela's isiThembu lineage was acknowledged and the bravery of his AbaThembu ancestors from the great place celebrated. Mandela's clan name, Madiba, was put into context and branded into the hearts of many around the world.

The significance of placing African praise song on the world map was not lost to Madiba's praise singer. He had to give it his all. He dug into the deepest of isiXhosa idiom to showcase the beauty of the language. He played on its many clicks. He flew high above the understanding of all but a few native speakers. African praise singing is like opera in the best Italian idiom. One does not have to understand the words. It is to be enjoyed as a melody and a performance.

The inauguration provided South Africa with an opportunity to finally acknowledge its Africanness. It stopped the pretence of being part of the 'Western world' that found itself by some accident of history at the southern end of the African continent. It redefined itself as being of the African soil. All its children are African by virtue of being citizens. They are all embraced by Mother Africa.

Nkosi Sikelel' iAfrika has pride of place in the hearts of Africans within and beyond South Africa's borders. Its creator did not live to see how widely his hymn would be used. Enoch Sontonga, a deeply spiritual composer, choirmaster, teacher and photographer who taught at a Methodist school in a Johannesburg township, composed this anthem in 1897 as a Xhosa hymn for his pupils.

Enoch Sontonga died in 1905 at the young age of 32 and was buried in an unmarked grave in a segregated cemetery in Braamfontein, near downtown Johannesburg. In 1996, on 24 September which is celebrated annually as Heritage Day in South Africa, his grave was transformed into a national monument. He had waited more than 90 years to be honoured with this recognition.

Sontonga too must be smiling in his grave each time the nation fills its lungs with his anthem. *Nkosi Sikelel' iAfrika* also rings out in the highlands of Kenya, Zambia and Zimbabwe. It is an African anthem.

That it had taken so long to sing this anthem heartily to usher in the new South Africa only added to the emotion of the moment. White people who had never bothered to pay attention to *Nkosi Sikelel' iAfrika* found themselves swept into the tide of overflowing emotions. Its genius lies in the anthem being translatable into many indigenous African language groups: isiXhosa, isiZulu, Sesotho and Kiswahili. As a solemn prayer, it implores the Creator to bless Africa, guide her leaders, guard her children and give her peace. As a song, it is captivating in both its melody and provision of space for harmonising the four major voices: soprano, alto, tenor and bass all share the moment. Men and women, young and old, find their place in this harmonious song.

The hardest part of the inauguration process for the majority of South Africans was to bring themselves to sing *Die Stem* (The Voice). For many it remained the personification of Afrikaner nationalism. In a cruel twist of irony, *Die Stem* was an instrument of the celebration of the denial of a voice to the majority of the population. In the silence, the voice of the minority was amplified and vested with the power to override the will of the majority.

But if one permitted oneself to listen to the words and the melody, one could not help being struck by the anthem's poetic beauty. It expresses passion and love for our beautiful country, and pledges the loyalty of citizens to live and die for this land.

Reflecting on *Die Stem* brings to mind Aubrey Mokoape, a friend and colleague at the University of Natal Medical School in the 1970s. Aubrey was a man with strongly held views on many issues. He refused to even acknowledge the poetic beauty of *Die Stem*, finding it difficult to see anything attractive in an anthem employed for such unjust ends. While sharing his abhorrence for the system this anthem was mobilising white people to defend, I could not help drawing attention to the power of its celebration of the beauty of our country's landscape.

Today, I find myself moved to tears each time I join in singing our national anthem. *Die Stem* has at last been liberated from its exclusionary prison and has become part of a shared heritage. We have all found our voice at last – black and white South Africans can raise their voices with pride.

I was not in my country to celebrate Nelson Mandela's inauguration on 10 May 1994. Like the rest of the world I watched it on television, from my sabbatical home in Cambridge, Massachusetts. Earlier that year, on 27 April, I had voted for the first time at the ripe age of 46. That too was an experience I shared with South Africans who lived or were travelling abroad at the time.

It was an emotional moment at the Boston City Hall on that April day. For that important first vote for the new democracy, Boston City Hall became a piece of South African soil. After voting, I went back to our apartment in Cambridge and watched the rest of South Africa snaking its way to voting booths countrywide. Freedom had come at last. I watched the televised voting process and the inauguration with tears of joy and pride. We had at last crossed the river Jordan into the 'Promised Land'. The inauguration of President Mandela was the finale.

Designating South Africa's transition as a miracle also justifies the unrealistic expectations that are placed on this young, fragile democracy. It is often forgotten how long it has taken today's mature democracies to get to where they are. The US has been consolidating its democracy for over two hundred years punctuated by a painful Civil War and conflict. Even now, they have unfinished business. The Civil Rights Act of 1965 notwithstanding, many African-American poor people have yet to experience the positive impact of living in the wealthiest nation of all. Making democracy work for every American remains a challenge in the 21st century. Europe has been through a prolonged period of revolutionary and evolutionary change. Yet the last century saw two world wars originating on European soil. Transitions to democracy take time and effort.

Conferring the status of a miracle on South Africa's democracy makes South Africa vulnerable to the overconfidence of triumphalism. The seduction of the miracle designation is very strong. It gives us prominence and a special place in international relations. It cushions us against the harsh realities of a competitive global socio-economic environment.

But challenging the miracle designation poses a dilemma for us. On the one hand, the miracle idea emboldens us as a special people and gives us the self-confidence to face the future with optimism. On the other hand, it makes us vulnerable to denial of anything that might be seen to undermine our special place in history. Such denial poses a serious risk to our capacity to be honest with ourselves about what we have done well and where we have fallen short during the more than a decade of freedom. That honesty requires self-confidence and being comfortable with both our strengths and weaknesses.

Facing our ordinariness as a young, fragile country is essential to the maturation process of the new democracy. We need to heed Neville Alexander's caution against underestimating the challenges we face in transforming our country. He suggests that 'in South Africa after the abolition of apartheid as a system of laws and social, political and economic institutions and practices based on the concept of "race", we are in fact dealing with a very ordinary country, one which has come very late to the table of the comity of nations.'[20] We have every right to celebrate our extraordinary achievements in getting to where we are over the last decade and a half. But we need to become much more open to reflecting on our strengths and weaknesses as we strive to become the society we aspire to be.

Our transition to democracy is anything but a miracle. The tree of freedom in South Africa was nourished by the blood of many martyrs over the years of struggle. It benefited from the fall of the Berlin Wall and the shift in geopolitics. It is the product of careful strategic leadership by Nelson Mandela and others. Its road was paved by the extraordinary sacrifices of all those who fought for freedom at home and abroad. It was made easier by rituals and symbols that helped victims and perpetrators of human-rights abuses to face up to the ghosts of the past and make peace with them.

CHAPTER 3

Laying ghosts to rest
The dilemmas of the Truth and Reconciliation Commission

We are charged to unearth the truth about our dark past; to lay the ghosts of that past so that they will not return to haunt us. And that we will thereby contribute to the healing of a traumatised and wounded people – for all of us in South Africa are wounded people – and in this manner promote national unity and reconciliation.[21]

THIS WAS SAID BY DESMOND TUTU ON 15 APRIL 1996 AT THE OPENing ceremony of the first hearing of the Truth and Reconciliation Commission (TRC), in East London. The enormity of the commission's task weighed heavily on each of these words. A nation struggling to be born faced the dilemma of laying the ghosts of a dark past to rest with neither retributive justice nor promotion of a culture of impunity. How much success could be expected? How would we manage the inevitable fall-out from those demanding more justice before reconciliation?

Rituals need appropriate masters if the full benefit of their healing effects is to be exploited. In President Mandela's mind there was only one person suited for the role of TRC chairperson: Archbishop Desmond Tutu.

Ritual is the stuff that Anglican archbishops are made of. But Tutu perfected it into an art. At critical moments during the struggle for freedom and in the transition period ritual had to be summoned to weld together what logic could not.

The TRC could not have succeeded to the extent it did without Tutu at the helm. Some objected to the imposition of Christian rituals on a society whose citizens include adherents of many different faiths as well as atheists. But in the end almost everyone acknowledged the importance of ritual in healing the wounds of the past. Christian rituals did not hurt. Everyone was held in a communal embrace that was at once a gesture of sharing pain and expressing gratitude to those prepared to forgive, so that society as a whole could be healed. The individual survivors became the weavers of a new and stronger social fabric from the fragments of the one torn asunder by years of the abuse of human rights.

Wounded healers are often better at accompanying others on a journey of healing. The mothers of seven young men from Guguletu Township in Cape Town, who had been lured by an informer into a trap set by security police and then shot dead in cold blood, exemplified wounded healers. The perpetrators' act of making a full disclosure enabled the mothers to transcend their anger and sadness. The Guguletu Seven mothers, as they have come to be known, were able to embrace the repentant informer who had asked for a private session with them in which he begged for forgiveness. This is a profound philosophical approach to the healing of the women's own wounds, those of the informer, and those of their society as a whole.

The involvement of religious leaders in the struggle for freedom as well as in facilitating the negotiation process had contributed to the insertion of the language of divine intervention in our political processes. Despite the diversity of their political persuasions – non-violent activists, holy-war protagonists and 'middle-of-the-roaders' – these leaders were united by their belief in the righteousness of the struggle.

Diverse views on what constitutes justice in post-apartheid South Africa do not detract from the important role of religion in our politics. Tutu has been consistent in reminding all South Africans that forgoing retributive justice is the price that had to be paid for peace following the negotiated political settlement. Settling old scores was not part of the package. How else could those in power have been will-ing to let go? This is an unpalatable political reality for many, but it is necessary medicine to swallow as part of the healing process.

As a leader, Tutu is very different from Mandela. They share the same pride in their heritage but their authority derives from different bases. Tutu is a traditionalist with a strong spiritual base who lives his beliefs. He is faithful to his daily office – the ritual of prayer and cele-bration of sacraments. The Divine is at the centre of his life. He is also a strong believer in the episcopacy of the Anglican Church lead-ership structure. In his view, bishops have to lead in both matters of doctrine and practical theology. It is not for nothing that Tutu is widely referred to as 'the Arch'. More than any of his predecessors, he put St George's Cathedral in Cape Town on the global map. That he was the first black archbishop of Cape Town was a major factor in the deep imprint he left on the cathedral.

Tutu's personality set the stage for his success as the Archbishop of Cape Town in the dying days of apartheid. He is fearless and yet not arrogant. He reaches out to touch all those he encounters. Through-out his life he has set the tone for a ministry that speaks truth to power. His small frame seems to be magnified in size whenever he takes on a major challenge. Arms outstretched, he launches forth into tough situ-ations and demands to be heard.

Tutu's activist ministry and mobilisation of anti-apartheid soli-darity preceded his enthronement in 1986. It was as the secretary-general of the South African Council of Churches (SACC) that he be-came a world figure. His defence of the SACC against the onslaught of the 'dirty tricks' of the apartheid government's security forces bent on discrediting it, demonstrated the courage of his convictions. The Nobel Peace Prize bestowed on him in 1984 was in recognition of the critical role he played to keep hope alive in a tough and violent anti-apartheid struggle.

He spoke out against violence on the part of both the oppressed and the oppressors. He was particularly vocal against the gruesome 'neck-lace' murders activists used in the 1980s to punish suspected apart-heid spies. A tyre filled with petrol was placed like a necklace around the victim's neck, with the victim often being forced to strike a match to set him- or herself on fire. The chanting crowds would then rejoice in hearing the screams and seeing the agony of a slow death ending with the explosion of the victim's cranium.

Tutu was undeterred by the criticisms of those in the struggle who accused him of blaming the victims of apartheid for the ruthless manner in which they responded to threats from collaborators of the system. He was concerned about the brutalisation of a society that tolerated such acts, and appalled by the prospect of a democracy built on the foundations of such violence. In this case, it was the worst form of violence against the self – black people were waging war against their own who were accused of 'selling out' to the apartheid enemy.

The impact on young people who had been involved in such horrific acts against fellow black people is yet to be acknowledged in the post-apartheid era. The increasing brutality of violent crime in South Africa could in part be traced back to tolerance of violence in the past.

In looking at the dilemmas of the TRC and some of its unfinished business that continues to pose challenges to our society, it is useful to remind ourselves of strategic choices that had to be made at the time. Inevitably, the choices as to where the focus of the commission's work would lie had implications for the new democracy.

The architects of the transition to democracy had an unenviable task. As retribution was not an option in a settlement where there were neither victors nor vanquished, a middle road was to agree on a process of seeking to tell and hear the truth about the past as a precondition for amnesty. Truth-telling and amnesty became the anchors of the ritual of finding closure.

The strategic choice to place the emphasis on gross violations of human rights reflected the wisdom of not allowing perfection to become the enemy of the good.[22] The first element of this choice was the focus on individuals and their actions in violating the rights of other individuals. But this shifted the burden of responsibility and the focus from the system that had created the climate that made violation of human rights part of the normal business of governance. Letting the system off the hook had implications for our future in that there was a risk of perpetuating a culture of impunity.

Focusing on gross violations of human rights meant that violations of the socio-economic rights of the disenfranchised majority were left unexamined. This, too, had consequences for the new democracy. How would citizens learn to assert their socio-economic rights in the new era if the worst intentional violations of those rights were not explored, and those rights were not seen to have been paramount within the context of the political-settlement process? Yet one has to concede that inclusion of socio-economic rights in the TRC process would have complicated what was already a complex undertaking.

The strategic focus on individuals as agents of history in the perpetration of violations of human rights was in many ways logical. It is doubtful whether the South African society could have found even a semblance of closure if the focus of the TRC had been on the very system that formed the pillars of the government with whom negotiations had been conducted. Would the then incumbent government have agreed to settle knowing that the system of which they had been the architects would have to stand 'public trial'? It is unlikely that a political settlement could have been reached under such conditions.

Nonetheless, the compromise of focusing on individuals had unintended consequences. Individual agents of the state such as policemen, army conscripts and civil servants who had enforced laws that violated fundamental human rights of fellow citizens were held responsible for acts they had committed 'in the service of their country'. Some had even been decorated by their political superiors for the same acts they now had to confess to the TRC without any acknowledgement of co-responsibility by their leaders. The foot soldiers ended up bearing the responsibility for crimes they had committed with the blessing of politicians who sought to distance themselves from all atrocities. Many feel deeply betrayed by their political masters.

Some white people remain baffled by the turn of events. Many were mere children at the close of the apartheid era and feel unfairly blamed for the errors of previous generations. Some feel labelled as perpetrators of human-rights violation purely by virtue of the colour of their skin. Dave Steward, a former senior civil servant during the apartheid era and now executive director of the F.W. de Klerk Foundation, probably spoke for many white people when he wrote in 2006:

> The TRC also stamped whites with an almost indelible mark of guilt and created the perception of moral inferiority. Even loyal white ANC supporters like Carl Niehaus have said that they accept that their grandchildren will have to go to the end of the queue in South Africa.
>
> The assumption of blanket white historical guilt and the unwillingness of most whites to acknowledge it is the wedge that continues to create the chasm between us. It explains why Archbishop Tutu still feels so strongly that whites have not given proper recognition to the generosity of blacks for 'not wanting to knock their blocks off'.
>
> Characterising racial groups with negative moral labels is a very dangerous business. When married to self-interest or the search for scapegoats, it can be a recipe for dehumanisation and catastrophe.
>
> In a *Sunday Times* article earlier this year, Nkosinathi Biko of the Steve Biko Foundation wrote that if white South Africans did not accept history for what it was, and if they tried to palm this responsibility off on their children, they would be reminded by the next generation, not 'through the power of the pen, but by any means necessary'.
>
> The moral worth of people cannot be judged according to their race but only according to their actions and their motives as individuals. To suggest otherwise opens the way to alienation and conflict — and to the potential negation of Archbishop Tutu's words at the end of the TRC process: 'Never again'.
>
> One of the weaknesses of the TRC was that its mandate dealt primarily with the conflict after 1960 and not with the real problems of colonial domination and apartheid.
>
> We still need a reconciliation process in which genuine

representatives of all our communities must hammer out a version of our history with which we can all agree. Not unsurprisingly, white South Africans and the political parties that they had supported emerged as the villains of the piece. In the perception of many whites, they were welcome in the new South Africa only as supplicants for forgiveness and as payers of reparations.

Given our traumatic history, this was perhaps understandable. But it did not constitute real reconciliation. Reconciliation requires that the narratives and perspectives of all sides should be reflected in a commonly accepted version of history. As it is, black and white South Africans emerged from the process with different maps of our past. And without a common map it remains difficult for us to move forward together into the future. [23]

Was it politically feasible in the mid-1990s to deal with the real problems of colonial domination and apartheid without upsetting the settlement applecart? It could also be asked whether it is actually possible to hammer out a shared version of history on which all South Africans can agree. History is in most cases a reflection of the views of victors and of those with the power to impose their version on those who have been conquered or are in less powerful positions. In the case of South Africa there are neither victors nor vanquished. We have a contested history.

Our contested history goes beyond black and white views of history. The 'narratives and perspectives of all sides' to which Steward refers point to the problem that even within broader 'white' or 'black' versions of the past, the histories of some sectors of society, black as well as white, have been and continues to be marginalised. Even within the black community there is a contest over how the history of the struggle for freedom is recounted, documented and utilised as a resource.

First, there is the question of leadership of the struggle for freedom and the role played by various movements and parties. Supporters of the ANC frame the history of the struggle with the ANC at its centre. While few would contest the major role played by the ANC since its inception in the early 20th century, many are concerned about the silence about the role of other parties at critical stages in our history.

Take the role of the Pan-Africanist Congress (PAC) in re-energising the struggle for freedom in 1960. In 1959, Robert Sobukwe and others had broken away from the ANC due to fundamental differences over strategy, the influence of white and Indian communists on the ANC, and the general direction and effectiveness of the struggle. Sobukwe became an advocate of an Africanist perspective.[24] The anti-pass campaign of 1960 reflected a focus on those issues that mattered most in the daily lives of poor Africans. On 21 March 1960, 69 anti-pass protesters among a group who had campaigned peacefully were shot dead by police at Sharpeville, setting off countrywide protests. The PAC regional secretary for the Western Cape, Philip Kgosana, led a march of 30 000 protestors from Cape Town's townships to Parliament.[25]

The Africanist perspective of the PAC emphasised the importance of African leadership and agenda-setting within the struggle, and challenged white leadership and domination within the 'multiracial' Congress Alliance the ANC had fostered. The PAC's stance in 1959 resonated with that advocated by the ANC Youth League of the 1940s. The success of the PAC's 1960 anti-pass campaign, and the brutal response to it, raised the visibility of the anti-apartheid struggle in the international community in an unprecedented way.

After serving a three-year prison sentence for incitement, Sobukwe was detained without trial for six years on Robben Island under a special clause in the General Law Amendment Act of 1963. After his release in 1969, he was banned and banished to Kimberley where he was under twelve-hour house arrest in his home in Galeshewe Township. He had been an ardent pipe smoker, and eventually died of lung cancer in 1978.

Yet in post-apartheid South Africa Sharpeville Day – 21 March – is commemorated annually as Human Rights Day without any acknowledgement of Sobukwe's leadership or the role of the PAC on that historic day. He has been written out of history. There is no significant public memorialisation of Sobukwe's name in our streets, parks or buildings outside his birth place, Graaff-Reinet.

The silencing of heroes of our struggle through the re-writing of history to suit those who are in power today robs young people of important lessons. Robert Sobukwe embodied visionary leadership that was willing to take risks to expand the boundaries of possibility at a difficult time in our history.

Many more heroes of the struggle, both men and women, have been buried in silence. Acknowledging the role of others need not detract from one's own laudable efforts. The struggle for freedom was a collective effort in which ordinary South Africans made huge contributions. Failure to recognise the efforts of ordinary people is disempowering and risks laying the ground for apathy and over-dependence on those in authority to provide all the solutions to the challenges of everyday life.

While white people may resent being unfairly blamed for past wrongs, many black people also feel unhappy about the outcomes of the TRC process. In their view, the TRC bent over too far backwards to find closure by giving amnesty to people who had committed atrocities in the name of a system from which they benefited. Many of those who defended the old regime are seen to be continuing to enjoy the ill-gotten gains, whilst the majority of black people remain poor and vulnerable.

In addition, young people such as Nkosinathi Biko have unspeakable personal wounds that refuse to heal. They perceive that there is lack of remorse from those who were in positions of authority when they suffered their losses. White people who may feel aggrieved about being labelled by an 'indelible mark of guilt', need to bear in mind the anguish of those young people who were denied the basic right of a child to be nurtured by a father. Nkosinathi's father was brutally murdered by the system that was bent on protecting white privilege. His anger is not directed at individual white people but at the system of white racism that remains unacknowledged by many who continue to benefit from its legacy.

Steward also confuses being blamed for past wrongs with the imperatives of putting right what those wrongs have bequeathed to us. Carl Niehaus's children may have to stand at the back of the queue not because they are personally guilty of any crime. But their status as beneficiaries of generations of white privilege puts them ahead of many of their black compatriots in the competition for scarce resources. They are likely to have been brought up in a stable family, gone to better schools, been supported by educated parents and grandparents. They also would enjoy a network of friends and relatives who can guide them to opportunities in ways that many young black people cannot even dream of. Affirmative action in the context of promoting greater equality of opportunity would rightly rate the achievements of young black people who have pulled themselves up by their own bootstraps higher than those of products of a privileged background.

These contested versions of history are unlikely to be put to rest by either letting time heal the wounds or by pretending that they have been resolved. The TRC's successes need to be built upon by dealing with the unfinished business of reconciliation. This has to be done delicately to minimise undermining the significant gains made with the help of the public rituals of the TRC.

In looking at some of the unfinished business of the TRC, it is important to acknowledge the successes of the commission in creating space for both survivors and perpetrators of crimes under apartheid to find healing.

Tutu managed tensions that inevitably arose within the TRC itself about how to approach the most controversial cases, such as that of Winnie Madikizela-Mandela. Here was a woman who used to be revered as the 'Mother of the Nation' as the wife of the most famous political prisoner. Winnie was also idolised for her courage and contribution as a leader in her own right. She had been an inspiration to many – young and old. Her beauty and elegance were, and remain, breathtaking. She carried herself like royalty. She still does.

Winnie had also been subjected to severe abuse by the apartheid regime. She emerged from long periods of solitary confinement, detention without trial, and banishment orders stronger than ever. Her defiance reached a point where she began to act as if she were above the law. The illegitimacy of the apartheid laws added to the boldness of her resistance. She came to symbolise the anti-authority ethos that permeated the activism of the time. Ordinary people saw her as untouchable and loved her for it. She was able to do what they lacked the courage to do. They lived their dreams of freedom through her defiance of the apartheid system.

It is difficult not to be seduced by power under such circumstances. Leaders who are treated as if they are superhuman often behave as such. Loss of contact with reality thrust this revered leader into situations that culminated in tragedy and scandal. Those around her were fans rather than advisers. They could not provide a reality check when she needed it. The death in 1989 of Stompie Seipei, a fourteen-year-old activist, marked the nadir of her free fall into leadership without accountability.

Stompie had been beaten at Winnie Mandela's Soweto home. Dr. Abubaker Asvat, called to attend to the boy, advised that he be taken to hospital, given the serious injuries he had sustained. His advice was not followed. According to Jerry Richardson, the man convicted of Stompie's murder, who was at the centre of the activities of the Mandela United Football Club, 'I . . . slaughtered him. I slaughtered him like a goat. We made him lay on his back and put garden shears through the back of his neck.'[26]

Stompie's body was found days later in a field in Soweto. Dr. Asvat was subsequently killed by gunmen in his Soweto surgery. In 1991, Winnie was charged with the assault and kidnapping of Stompie Seipei. She was convicted of kidnapping despite denying any responsibility and given a suspended sentence, converted to a fine on appeal. Stompie and other missing persons' relatives brought eighteen Human Rights violations by the Mandela United Football Club,[27] including eight murders, to the TRC to seek the truth about their loved one's deaths or disappearances.

At the TRC hearings Winnie Madikizela-Mandela continued to deny any involvement in the beatings that witnesses said had been instigated by her, and in which she had also participated. Tutu failed to coax her into acknowledging responsibility for having created conditions that culminated in this tragic death. He acknowledged the suffering she had to endure. He praised her for her heroic role in the struggle. In the end, he literally dictated words to her that went as close to acknowledgement as she was prepared to go. He appealed to her as a father, not just a spiritual one, but one who knew her intimately and loved her. He got her at long last to say the words: 'I will take this opportunity to say to the family of Dr. Asvat how deeply sorry I am: to Stompie's mother, how deeply sorry I am . . . I am saying it is true, things went horribly wrong . . .'[28]

Tutu embraced her. Stompie's mother immediately signaled her willingness to forgive Winnie. Tutu encouraged Winnie to extend a hand of friendship to Stompie's mother, which she did. Stompie's mother later offered to welcome Winnie to her home where a ritual goat was to be slaughtered to bring closure. Winnie is reported not to have taken up the offer in spite of promises to do so.

Critics both inside and outside of the TRC were concerned that Tutu had bent over too far backwards. Here was someone given amnesty for a crime she continued to deny to the end. Some felt that, as a privileged person, she had been treated leniently. The courts, in giving her a suspended sentence at the conclusion of the 1991 trial for kidnapping, had also treated her leniently as the wife of a future president.

Tutu's judgment call was based on his awareness of Winnie's own wounds. By the time she appeared at the TRC in 1996, she was a broken woman and a tragic figure. She was divorced from President Mandela and had fallen from grace. He saw her need for healing and responded to it even though she did not seem ready to ask for it. Not everyone in the commission agreed with this decision, but what were the options? Imperfect beings have to accept imperfect outcomes. The past needed to be made peace with, however imperfect the outcome. Stompie, too, needed to have his spirit laid to rest.

Another controversial case was that of former President P.W. Botha. He refused to co-operate with the TRC, rejecting it as a tool to discredit Afrikaner history and his ancestors' contributions to South Africa. Tutu courted him in many ways. He was allowed months to

respond to questions from the TRC. Tutu visited Botha at his residence in the Wilderness, Southern Cape, in an attempt to convince
him to own up to the consequences of policies pursued on his watch.
Botha was unrepentant to the end. The Afrikaners had done nothing wrong, he said. They had done what they had to do to fulfil their
God-given responsibility to protect Christian national values against
terrorists and communists. Tutu treated Botha with great respect
and generosity even though he disagreed with his stance.

The court arraigned Botha for refusing to obey a subpoena to
appear at the TRC hearings. Even in court Tutu did not give up on
Botha and the opportunity for healing the nation. He suggested a
way out for Botha to acknowledge that the policies of his government had led to wrongdoing by various government officials, for
which he was sorry. But Botha was stubborn to the end. Here Tutu's
charm completely failed to move a sick and stubborn old man.

Some members of the commission again thought that Tutu had
bent over backwards for an unrepentant perpetrator. This was not
just anyone, but one who had played a leadership role. Should he not
have been made to take responsibility for acts of human-rights violation under the system of government over which he had presided for
so long? Others pointed to the risks attached to humiliating President
Botha at that time. The threat of a right-wing revolt was significant
given the fragility of the new democracy. Imprisoning an old, sick
man was just not an option. An elegant way out had to be found.
Leaving it in the hands of the courts to enforce the subpoena was
the best option.

Tutu described the outcome of the court case as follows:

> He was convicted and sentenced to a suspended gaol sentence
> and a fine by the magistrate, but subsequently acquitted on
> a narrow technicality. (We had bent over so far backward to
> accommodate him that we left issuing our subpoena too late.
> On the day we issued it, our mandate had expired and Presi-
> dent Mandela had not yet signed the new mandate.) Morally
> and politically, he had been called to account, faced victims

and perpetrators of his policies, and politically he had been isolated. He looked such a pathetic figure in court that I felt deeply sorry for him.[29]

There were also remarkable moments of true healing at the TRC. Take Eugène de Kock, a man journalist Jacques Pauw depicted as 'Prime Evil' in a documentary on South African national television. De Kock had been recruited and trained to kill to sustain apartheid over more than two decades. He distinguished himself in the war against the South West African People's Organisation (Swapo), the liberation organisation that had finally won freedom for the people of Namibia in 1990. In recognition of his skills he was put in charge of a killing machine headquartered at Vlakplaas, a farm near Pretoria. His responsibilities were to 'take out', 'make a plan with', or 'eliminate' enemies of the state, a mission he performed with zeal both inside and outside South Africa's borders. He was awarded the Silver Star, the highest national honour for bravery. He had access to millions of rands in state funds to use at his discretion.

The crimes committed at Vlakplaas were exposed by Almond Nofemela, a turncoat policeman. Nofemela confessed to the murder of Durban lawyer and ANC activist Griffith Mxenge[30] to save himself from the hangman for a murder he had committed outside his official criminal mandate as a police operative. He refused to go down alone and spilled the beans about the deaths of many activists that had remained unexplained, over and above those of Mxenge and his wife Victoria.[31] Nofemela won his freedom in exchange for coming clean. De Kock, renounced by his superiors, became the scapegoat for the system that had employed him to kill.

De Kock took full advantage of the healing process that was made available by the TRC. He made what he claimed to be a full disclosure of the heinous crimes that had been perpetrated with the knowledge and encouragement of the top brass in the police force. He also provided the clearest links to the highest levels in the apartheid government. De Kock's testimony forced many of the top brass to come clean about their roles. The then Chief of the South African Police,

General Johann van der Merwe, and the former Minister of Police, Adriaan Vlok, who had decorated De Kock with medals for his most important killings, had to acknowledge that abuses did occur. However, they put the blame on agents such as De Kock for operating outside the law.

De Kock's testimony raised questions about his label as 'Prime Evil' – a deranged man who went beyond the call of duty because he enjoyed killing. He was hurt by being demonised, but it also strengthened his resolve. He stuck to his story that he was being made the fall guy for acts that had been sanctioned by the state. His demonisation was an attempt by the apartheid state to distance itself from the killing machine it had spawned and sustained over the years.

De Kock went further. He apologised to all those families whose relatives he had killed or whose relatives had been killed on his instructions. Pumla Gobodo–Madikizela, a psychologist who worked for the TRC, gives a moving testimony of De Kock's journey of healing in her account of interviews with him in a book that is intensely personal.[32] He shared with her his agony at having committed horrific crimes in the name of a regime that he now realised had been unjust. He wept over the losses widows, children and others had suffered because of his actions. He wept as he witnessed the generosity of those he had wronged who extended hands of friendship to him to express their forgiveness.

The TRC in this case transformed the fall guy into an instrument for telling the truth about our ugly past. The healing did not just come to De Kock, but to those families who were finally relieved of the burden of the mysterious disappearance of their loved ones. Their faith in themselves and in those who shared their grief and suspicions about death squads was affirmed. At last they could mourn, and then face the future having come to terms with the finality of their losses.

White South Africans could no longer hide behind their ignorance. De Kock's testimony raised fundamental questions about state violence that had been conducted over decades to protect white rule and privilege.

De Kock is still serving two life sentences for his role in the murders for which he was convicted. But the 'Prime Evil' label cannot stick as easily after the TRC hearings. The more appropriate question his testimony raises is: who is not evil? Both black and white South Africans had been engaged in what amounted to a civil war that spilled much innocent blood. De Kock had this to say about being a victim of lost ideologies:

> . . . it's a feeling of loss. Well, the first thing that goes is innocence . . . We killed a lot of people, they killed some of ours. We fought for nothing . . . We could have all been alive and having a beer. And the politicians? If we could put all politicians in the front lines with their families, and grandparents, and grandchildren – if they are in the front line, I don't think we will ever have a war again. [33]

The prospects of warmongering politicians putting their own lives at risk are slim. F.W. de Klerk, the last apartheid president and a member of successive governments during the period these crimes were committed, was still able to say boldly: 'My hands are clean.' He has maintained his innocence in public statements in South Africa and abroad. For years after the fall of apartheid he refused to even apologise for its crimes. When he finally did, it was a lukewarm acknowledgement that apartheid had been wrong and had caused pain and humiliation.

De Klerk asserted that the National Party reforms in the dying days of apartheid needed to be recognised as efforts to make amends for the errors of the past. He had difficulty acknowledging that the ANC or any other liberation movement had played a bigger role than his party. His testimony to the TRC had a similar tone.

De Klerk sustains the same views in his autobiography.[34] He makes an interesting reference to the instructions of his predecessor, P.W. Botha, to the State Security Council in 1986:

> The Third Force must be mobile and must have well-trained ability to wipe out terrorists . . . It must be prepared to be unpopular and even feared . . . and the security forces must co-

operate in the establishment of the Third Force so that the
subversives could be engaged by using their own methods . . .[35]

In De Klerk's interpretation, these words should not be seen as au-
thorisation of the security police to kill, as De Kock was claiming.
They were merely the robust words of a leader confronted with 'a
bitter revolutionary struggle'. Few would share this view. Certainly
few amongst those on the receiving end of Third Force activities. As
De Kock attested, people died brutally as a result of the robust action
ordered by Botha's cabinet of which F.W. de Klerk had been a member.

It is often said that F.W. de Klerk's respect for his forefathers, who
had been key architects of apartheid, makes it difficult for him to
acknowledge that the atrocities were a logical outcome of its policies.
He comes from a long line of prominent establishment Afrikaners –
the Malans and De Klerks – who actively shaped the apartheid project.
Frank acknowledgement of wrong-doing would be tantamount to re-
nouncing what his forefathers stood for. This deference has survived
overwhelming evidence of the brutality of the apartheid project.

In an irony of history, De Klerk's sharing of the 1993 Nobel Peace
Prize with Mandela seems to have vindicated his stance. Mandela's
snub to De Klerk at the Nobel Prize ceremony in Oslo by refusing
to shake his hand in full view of TV cameras was uncharacteristic. It
was a desperate act to show his frustration with De Klerk's failure
to halt the carnage in the townships that was fuelled by the then
security forces bent on derailing the transition. They fomented conflict amongst black people – the so-called 'black-on-black violence'
that claimed thousands of lives.

There are strong views on either side of the question of whether
or not De Klerk deserved the honour of the Nobel Peace Prize for
having made the transition to democracy possible by agreeing to negotiations. His ambivalence about a truly democratic South Africa
under majority rule throughout the transition phase will remain a matter of historical record. Many blame this ambivalence for the loss of
thousands of innocent lives between 1990 and 1994. They argue that
he could have given clearer directives to the security forces to protect

civilians caught between warring factions. But history will judge him kindly for the role he played in ushering in the negotiation process that culminated in the democratic order we enjoy today.

The dilemma of moral equivalence relating to crimes committed by both sides to the conflict during the anti-apartheid civil-war period remains open in the minds of many. Is it fair that the liberation movements were also asked to come clean about the atrocities they committed in the name of the struggle against apartheid? Does the right to defend oneself against an unjust order not make for a just war? Do the combatants in a just war face the same moral test for their actions in engaging the enemy? In the case of accusations of abuse and torture of fellow combatants accused of aiding the enemy, should the liberation movement not be understood to have faced horrendous odds and thus have been justified in using torture to reduce further losses from attacks by a superior enemy?

The unresolved questions posed by the moral-equivalence dilemma marred the publication of the interim TRC Report in 1998. The ANC under its then recently elected president, Thabo Mbeki, sought a Supreme Court injunction to stop the public release of the report. President Mandela, as the head of state, stood firm in support of the TRC. He had failed to persuade his colleagues in the party leadership not to mount the legal challenge. In the end the ANC lost the case, but the damage had been done to the dignity of the TRC ritual process.

The ANC missed the opportunity to take the moral high ground as the initiators of an innovative instrument for dealing with the ugly apartheid past. Some of the dilemmas of moral equivalence could have been dealt with by drawing a distinction between those aspects of the struggle that were part of a just cause and those that were not. There can be no argument that after all avenues for peaceful protest had been exhausted, taking up the armed struggle was a just cause. Oppressed people everywhere have the inalienable right to defend themselves against tyranny. Apartheid was a tyrannical system that violated the rights of the majority.

However, there were acts committed during that armed struggle that cannot pass the test of 'just cause'. These are acts of detention, torture and abuse of suspected traitors that occurred in some of the ANC's camps. Without underestimating the risks that traitors posed in that context, one has to acknowledge that innocent people did get hurt. Abuses of human rights in those camps needed to be confessed and put behind us in the same way as other gross violations of human rights. Equally, targeting civilians in restaurants and churches as happened from both the ANC and PAC cadres cannot pass the test of just cause.

Sadly, in asserting that because theirs was a just cause there was nothing to tell the truth about in the reconciliation process, some ANC leaders allowed themselves to be governed by short-term political considerations rather than the long-term benefits of healing the nation. Unfortunately, ghosts in search of peace do not distinguish between just and unjust causes. They need to be acknowledged and laid to rest. The liberation movements still have work to do to unburden individuals who may still be haunted by those ghosts.

In addition to the ANC's court challenge, the Inkatha Freedom Party (IFP) also objected to the publication of the TRC's interim report in 1998. They insisted that unsubstantiated allegations contained in the report could not be made public without due process. Those sections had to be removed pending the final TRC report in 2003.

The unfortunate reality is that more than ten years after the political settlement, most of those abused and wronged have yet to receive the reparations promised under the TRC Act. They are the unsung heroes and heroines of the reconciliation process.

Filibustering by political parties delayed the reparation process. Adding to the unfairness of the unmet reparation promises is that many abusers are walking free and some are enjoying the benefits of their ill-gotten wealth. They received amnesty for fulfilling their side of the bargain, namely, to tell 'the truth'. Some of the political top brass who refused to participate in the amnesty process have also remained free. In 2007 the former head of police, General Johann van der Merwe, and former Minister Adrian Vlok entered into plea-bargain arrangements with the National Prosecuting Authority and were given suspended sentences. Many others are still unrepentant.

The exclusion from the TRC process of violations of socio-economic rights underlies much of the persistent inequalities in our society. The majority of the population is trapped in structural poverty. The legacy of systemic socio-economic neglect is at the core of the unfinished agenda of acknowledging the impact of colonialism and apartheid that Dave Steward speaks of. Unfortunately, history has no precedents of socio-economic reparations in a situation where there are neither victors nor vanquished. South Africans have to find their own model to make peace with this aspect of the past.

Notwithstanding these weaknesses, many poor people accepted the compromise presented by the TRC and were willing to make their contributions to a united South Africa. They were generous with their forgiveness in return for truth about the fate of their loved ones and the promise of symbolic reparations. The generosity of the many people who participated in the TRC has not been adequately acknowledged. It could be argued that their trust in the TRC was betrayed in two important ways: inadequate attention to payment of reparations and inadequate implementation of the RDP.

The issue of reparations should have been the easiest aspect of the TRC recommendations to discharge. But there was an inherent bias in the TRC Act that tilted the balance in favour of perpetrators of human-rights violations, who received immediate and automatic amnesty upon making a full disclosure. The survivors of human-rights abuses, on the other hand, did not enjoy automatic and immediate payment of reparations on the granting of forgiveness.

The TRC recommended urgent reparations of R2 000 (US$330) to each of the survivors plus an amount of R23 000 (US$3 830)[36] per year for six years after that. The total budget required from the national treasury was estimated to be R2,9bn (US$447m) – hardly the stuff that would have broken the proverbial fiscal rectitude bank. In addition, many well-meaning South Africans, black and white, offered to contribute a once-off 1% additional tax to cover any shortfall in meeting the reparation requirements. This offer has yet to be taken up by the government.

A disappointed Tutu concluded in a newspaper interview in 2003:

Can you explain how a black person wakes up in a squalid ghetto today, almost 10 years after freedom? Then goes to work in town, which is still largely white, in palatial homes. And at the end of the day, he goes home to squalor? I don't know why those people don't just say, 'To hell with peace. To hell with Tutu and the Truth Commission.'[37]

Ambivalence towards reparations on the part of our government remains an impediment to discharging this responsibility. There is a strongly held view that the struggle was not fought with compensation in mind. But that is not the point of reparations. Reparations are by nature symbolic. There is, however, an irony in this ambivalence. Many returning exiles and those who were prevented from setting aside provisions for pensions in their old age are being paid 'struggle pensions'. I am personally a recipient of about R2 800 per month for my troubles as an activist from 1973 to 1984. Many former ANC activists have been rewarded similarly in addition to well-paying public service jobs, comfortable homes and many other forms of patronage from the ruling party.

Many white civil servants who earned their keep by enforcing unjust laws enjoy generous pensions made possible by inflated salaries at the end of the apartheid era. In contrast, black civil servants (especially teachers, nurses and policemen) who served the nation under difficult colonial and apartheid conditions continue to struggle to make ends meet on pitiable pensions. My mother, who had been a teacher for over 40 years (1938-1979), retired with a princely lump-sum payment of R1 104 and a meagre monthly pension of less than R600. She was refused an adjustment to her pension by the Minister of Finance in the late 1990s despite vigorous representations by the public interest advocate, the Legal Resources Centre.

The Legal Resources Centre agreed to this brief as a test case to open the way for a review of teachers' pensions, especially those of women who had been discriminated against in terms of both race and gender. Until the early 1970s female teachers were forced to resign each time they went on maternity leave, resulting in the erosion of their years-in-service credits. As late as the early 1990s no female civil servant was entitled to maternity leave.

The defence by the Minister of Finance was that the government would only act if the teachers' trade union raised the matter through NEDLAC or a similar forum. How my mother of over 70 years could have had the resources to lobby the union to act is difficult to imagine. I am in the fortunate position of being able to transfer my 'struggle pension' to my mother who deserves it more than I do. But what about the thousands of poor black women who have to get by on such meagre pensions after selfless civil service?

It could be asked why the government has dragged its heels in dealing with reparations for people who are most vulnerable and for whom TRC reparations would have made such a difference. Examples of adequate attention to the reparation needs of poor people in post-conflict situations are hard to find. Attention tends to be concentrated on those who have the capacity to destabilise political settlements. The greater the capacity of people to do harm, the more accommodating negotiators tend to be towards their reparation, compensation or demobilisation demands. Poor, powerless people are often treated with little respect for their material needs beyond emergency humanitarian ones.

The divergence of interests between the 'middle orders', who tend to be few in number, and the 'lower orders', who are the multitudinous masses, is a common feature of post-liberation social dynamics.[38] Nineteenth-century Europe went through waves of nationalist revolutions in which the middle and lower orders combined efforts that led to the defeat of aristocrats. Germany, Italy and Romania provide examples of the divergence of interests between those at the lower socio-economic level who seek social power to improve their quality of life, and those in the middle strata whose primary focus is state power. After gaining state power, the middle orders would abandon the lower orders. In most cases the masses would be demobilised to the same poverty and unemployment they had fought against.

The social dynamics of post-revolutionary Europe seem to bear a striking resemblance to those of post-colonial Africa. Basil Davidson's description of 19th-century Europe could well be applied to our own continent: 'The nation states that came eventually to birth were to be the political work of the "middle strata" . . . The breaking of the promise of freedom was the outcome, as is easily understood now, of the victory of the "national" over the "social".'[39]

Chinua Achebe, the celebrated Nigerian novelist, captures his disappointment in the failure of post-colonial political leaders to rise to their social responsibilities in the beautiful but shocking novel *The Anthills of the Savannah*.[40] Achebe ascribes this failure of leadership to 'the failure of our rulers to re-establish vital links with the poor and dispossessed of this country'.

The challenge for our young democracy is whether the political elites will rise to the task of re-establishing these vital links with all those who are poor and vulnerable. Such links are essential for the development of an ethos of civic duty amongst those serving the public that would compel them to put the interests of poor people first.

It is disappointing to hear the mixed messages from our political leaders with regard to reparations. On the one hand, President Mbeki has repeatedly said that the struggle was not fought with compensation in mind. On the other, Smuts Ngonyama, a senior political advisor in the Presidency, is on record as saying that he did not join the struggle in order to remain poor. This was in response to queries about his participation in the Telkom Black Economic Empowerment (BEE) deal that involved millions of rand in benefits to those in the winning consortia.

One can argue that poor people, too, did not struggle for freedom in order to continue to endure poverty. Why should they not be able to access even meagre reparations or the delayed benefits of the RDP? Where is the empathy that bound us together during the struggle for freedom? It is difficult to see how we can continue to claim to be informed by the spirit of *ubuntu* when there is so little empathy with those who are most vulnerable. Our social relationships and the quality of public service need to be re-invigorated through the re-establishment of those vital links that are essential to social cohesion across all levels of society.

Ibbo Mandaza, a Zimbabwean academic and Zanu-PF journalist, argues that 'Reconciliation is the forgiveness of a small elite that inherits state power without fulfilment of social justice for the majority . . . For this reason, reconciliation is neither durable nor sustainable.'[41] Seen from this perspective, it is not surprising that socio-economic justice did not feature in the TRC mandate. It could also explain the lack of enthusiasm for the payment of reparations by the new elites. After all, many activists in the ranks of the ruling alliance obtained their reparations from public-service jobs and other forms of patronage that come with state power.

Mandaza's thesis does not, however, adequately capture the complexities of South Africa's transition arrangements. A major justification for the lack of enthusiasm for significant reparations by government officials was that the legacy of socio-economic disadvantage would be comprehensively addressed through the implementation of the ANC's election commitment to a Reconstruction and Development Programme (RDP). However, the ambitions of the RDP were not matched by the capacity of the state to deliver on its many promises. The fiscal resources were also inadequate, given the inherited weaknesses in the economy.

Despite all the shortcomings, there is much to celebrate in the successes the TRC did achieve. But its mandate to 'lay the ghosts of that past' remains unfinished. Some of those ghosts continue to haunt us as we consolidate our democracy. They are crying out for attention, in the words of Dave Steward and Nkosinathi Biko. How are we to deal with them?

PART TWO

Stubborn
ghosts

CHAPTER 4
Racism

LAYING GHOSTS TO REST IS NOT ONLY ABOUT THE NAME THAT ONE has to call; it is the acknowledgement that comes with the naming that matters. For South Africans, racism represents the most frightening ghost. It cannot merely be viewed as an unfortunate historical phenomenon. Admitting how it has influenced each one of us matters.

Notions of white superiority and black inferiority have significantly shaped the mind-sets of both black and white South Africans. The superiority complex of white people is not a problem peculiar to unreconstructed racists. It has been programmed into those who have grown up in an environment that accorded them higher status than most of their fellow citizens by virtue of the colour of their skin.

The same applies to black inferiority. It is not simply something one shrugs off like a bad cold. It has been branded deeply into one's psyche by doors that have been shut in one's face, resulting in repeated humiliation. Humiliation tends to breed both self-hatred and rage. Both emotions make it hard for one to rise to the challenges of the rights and responsibilities of citizenship. The expectation of humiliation leads to defensiveness in relationships.

Racism is essentially the use of the concept of 'races' to establish a hierarchy of power relationships by assigning value to categories of people defined as inferior or superior. It is a socio-economic and political mechanism that justifies treating fellow human beings as 'others'. This 'othering' is often driven by differences in physical appearance and cultural expression: skin colour, facial features, hair texture, language, beliefs and customs. Like other members of the animal kingdom, humans have a tendency to gravitate towards those who look like them and share their language and culture. But racism makes morphological difference destiny by assigning value to some features over others. White racism assigns superior value to a white skin above all else and imbues it with higher-order capabilities that include morality and ethics.

Basil Davidson speaks of the failure of European historical analysts to appreciate the profound and lasting sense of injury, above all the moral injury, inflicted on Africans by colonial dispossession justified on the basis of the inferiority of indigenous people.[42] The constant humiliation of people over generations through the assigning of negative value to everything that they held dear has inevitably left deep psychological scars.

Racist culture asserts its dominance by humiliating its victims and denying their humanity. Defining people's physique and culture as inferior or as deviations from the 'norm' is at the core of the successful strategy of subjugation. Take the example of Saartjie Baartman, the young Khoisan woman known as the Hottentot Venus whose curvaceous and prominently pear-shaped physique aroused great public interest when she performed in shows in Europe in the early 19th century. After her death in Paris, her body was studied by scientists and her remains put on display in a French museum. It is appropriate that the post-apartheid government repatriated Saartjie's remains to the Gamtoos River Valley, where she was buried on 9 August 2002 with the respect and honour that had eluded her during her lifetime.

As has been mentioned in Chapter 1, Frantz Fanon[43] identified several symptoms of the 'scarring of the black psyche' that result from the experience of colonial oppression. These symptoms sometimes include a defensive romanticisation of indigenous culture. Such idealisation of tradition makes it difficult to adapt to the demands of an evolving socio-economic and political environment. Successful dynamic cultures are those that identify core elements of their cultural endowments that are essential to their self-definition and need to be protected and preserved. Aspects of a culture that have a negative impact on adaptive behaviour and are in conflict with core values of a given society, however, need to be identified and changed. This ensures dynamism in society.

Romanticising archaic practices that are harmful to sectors of the population is a sign of defensiveness and lack of self-confidence. Female genital mutilation, for instance, is a practice with such dire consequences for young girls and women that it cannot be justified on any ground other than romanticisation. African and Muslim cultures that adhere to this custom are coming under increasing international pressure. The responsibilities of global citizenship, like those of national citizenship, include the duty to protect the vulnerable from decisions taken on their behalf that are damaging to their welfare and violate their human rights. Among the Masai people of Kenya, local activists are finding creative substitutes for these harmful initiation practices. Alternative rituals have been introduced to preserve respect for rites of initiation into adulthood without the physical risks.

Ironically, harmful cultural practices that are carried out in the name of tradition are often perpetuated by those who suffered most under such practices. In the case of female genital mutilation, older women who may themselves have incurred unspeakable trauma and disabilities from the excision of the labia of the vagina and the clitoris tend to be the most ardent advocates. They reflect the tendency for victims of abuse to become abusers themselves. Genital mutilation lowers women's enjoyment of sexual intercourse, reducing their role to that of satisfying their husbands' needs.

In our own society, we seem to be torn between the values of our human-rights-based constitution and traditional practices that violate some of those rights. While gender equality is firmly entrenched in the Bill of Rights as part of the inherent equality of all human beings, women are still treated as lesser beings in the name of culture. They are considered minors and possessions of their patriarchal families in many settings, and are denied the right to inherit. Pride in the distinctiveness of African customs is cited as a reason for continuing practices that are in conflict with our constitution.

The myth that racism was, and remains, confined to the operatives of the apartheid system, who now have to change to join the rest of civilised white society, continues to find resonance. It is amazing how many English-speaking white South Africans have woven a web of denial around their role in the dispossession and impoverishment of black people over the centuries of white rule. Many more deny being beneficiaries of the discriminatory system that promoted white prosperity at the expense of black people. It is often suggested that all had been well in the colonial period until the National Party came to power in 1948.

Many of the English-speaking white supporters of the United Party (UP) under General Jan Smuts and Sir De Villiers Graaff conveniently forget this party's fundamental opposition to any notion of non-racialism. Veteran politician Colin Eglin's account of his political career is refreshingly honest in its acknowledgement of the racist politics of the UP. Its unwillingness to move into a more inclusive political space led to the establishment of the Progressive Party in 1959.[44]

One of the ironies of our history is that General Smuts, prime minister at a time when South Africa was part of the alliance that defeated the Nazis in World War II, participated in the post-war drafting of the preamble to the United Nations Charter that affirms the fundamental principle of the equality of all human beings before the law. Yet Smuts could not see his way clear to applying this equality principle at home. Racism trumped post-war anti-Nazi idealism.

Apartheid systematised white racism into one of the most successful social engineering projects of the 20th century. It vested colour with socio-economic and political power that attained a logic that remains deeply embedded in our society. But it is especially the equating of colour with intellectual superiority or inferiority, which predates apartheid, that has left a damning legacy.

Imagine growing up as a black child in a society where black people are the poorest by any measure, the ones most likely to be uneducated, unemployed or employed in the most menial jobs. Add to this the experience of the daily indignities of family relationships framed by anger, frustration and powerlessness, with frequent outbursts of domestic violence. Then take the daily insults such as not being allowed to play in a public park because it is reserved for others. All this while you watch 'the others' thrive in all areas of life.

Imagine seeing, not once but often, your own father being humiliated by white people of your own age or younger and not daring to defend his own dignity. Picture the confusion in your mind as you realise that he lacks the courage to do so, and the doubt you begin to have in his ability to defend you.

In a society with a strongly patriarchal ethos, such failure by fathers to stand up to other men creates cognitive dissonance in children. You begin to ask yourself why your father is not able to defend his territory. Why he looks impotent in the face of challenges to his authority even by younger men? You might be forgiven then for believing the lie that black people are indeed inferior. And you are one of them. This inferiority complex remains real in the lives of many.

Continued unacknowledged white privilege feeds a superiority complex that adds salt to the wounds of racism. Many white people still do not recognise that they are beneficiaries of one of the most successful affirmative action programmes in history. They benefited from universal and almost free education. Job reservation ensured protection from competition for jobs with black people. Access to cheap labour guaranteed high profits. Property acquisition at subsidised rates ensured a firm basis for capital accumulation. All these measures virtually guaranteed success for white people regardless of their intellectual capability.

Few white South Africans admit that their relatively high standard of living was purchased at the cost of the impoverishment of black people. Home ownership is a striking example. Cecil John Rhodes's stripping of property rights from indigenous peoples from the Cape towards Cairo as he built the British Empire, as well as Lord Milner's migrant-labour policies, had far-reaching consequences.

My white friends and colleagues at the University of Cape Town (UCT) who bought their homes in white suburbs in the 1970s received government subsidies paid for by taxes to which black people had contributed, which made their homes affordable. They have accumulated significant wealth over the years. A private home in, say, the Cape Town suburb of Rondebosch that was worth R70 000 then is worth R2 million or more in 2007. The return on investment is huge by any measure. Add to this the many opportunities to refinance their mortgages in order to obtain additional capital for investments elsewhere.

Until the early 1990s, black[45] UCT staff could only buy homes in the townships set aside for black people. Such purchases would not result in much capital appreciation. On the contrary, those who had invested in places such as Langa and Guguletu experienced capital depreciation. In the post-apartheid period middle-class migration into suburbia led to a lower demand for relatively comfortable houses in townships, far from urban facilities.

One of the major dilemmas of our transformation process is how to address the legacy of unjust policies such as apartheid property rights without upsetting the political-settlement applecart. The elite pact that underpinned our negotiated settlement included protection of private property rights. Secure property rights are the foundation for capital accumulation in modern economies. Private property acquisition under apartheid laws was inherently unjust in that it deliberately excluded African people in particular. Yet those same rights had to be accepted and protected under our post-apartheid constitution.

The price of peace included forgoing claims for opportunity costs incurred by black people in missing out on opportunities for wealth accumulation. The unarticulated resentment of this perceived perpetuation of privilege among those segments of the population that remain trapped in poverty should not be underestimated.

The geography of apartheid remains firmly etched in settlement patterns. A drive around cities in Gauteng Province shows how even government-initiated housing projects follow the unwritten rule of apartheid geography that settled poor people furthest away from the amenities associated with urban life. Rural settlements also continue to reflect the contours of the racist order of the past and many still lack proper tarred roads, water, sanitation and waste-removal services. Those previously discriminated against remain in marginal areas where capital accumulation is difficult. Persistent structural inequalities continue to hurt the majority of those who were on the wrong side of the racial divide.

A complex web of factors drives the perpetuation of stereotypes on all sides of the colour divide. Black and white South Africans' views of one another are distorted by their successful separation into different worlds. This is particularly true at the lower socio-economic levels. Many black people have not been exposed to white people as ordinary human beings with strengths and frailties. They know white people only as authority figures. Few have seen white people struggle with the mundane challenges of life – the joys and frustrations that are part of the human condition. Likewise, many white people have little experience of black people as fellow humans with the same capacity for joy and pain. Their experience of black people has often been limited to contact with them as menial workers. Encountering black people as authority figures is novel and disconcerting to some.

Complexities also arise from divisions within the black population. Divide and rule strategies of successive white governments put barriers between black people according to the absurdities of the Population Registration Act of 1950. Hierarchies of privilege and the physical separation of sub-groups in different residential areas led to envy and superiority complexes. Coloured people looked down on Africans as the members of the lowest socio-economic rung. Africans in turn despised Coloured people as rootless and obsessed with identification with whiteness as a source of power and privilege. Indian people had their own prejudices against both Africans and Coloured people who in turn mistrusted Indian people as ruthless merchants. Racial divisions and hierarchies forged over the years continue to undermine solidarity within the black segment of our society.

The ghost of racism should be acknowledged by name. Not in an accusatory manner that may trigger defensive denial, but in the same way in which families come together to acknowledge mutual hurt and make amends. Ghosts need to be appeased and turned into acknowledged ancestors. Ancestors bring blessings and protection to the present and pave the way to the future. Many ordinary people have yet to speak of the experience of racism without either venting their anger or denying any impact on themselves as individuals. It is, of course, hard to find the appropriate language.

Racism needs to be ritualised in the same way that we ritualised closure on brutal political crimes through the TRC process. Black and white people have to confront that past together and agree to set it aside to pursue a shared vision of the future. It is a struggle that will take generations to play out. The generation of South Africans beyond thirty years of age needs to find the tools for transcendence of our racist past to enable future generations to live together in greater peace.

Denial of the impact of racism on our society has been exacerbated by the denial of the role of the Black Consciousness Movement (BCM) in the struggle for liberation by some sectors of the political community. Popular documentaries and literature on the struggle tend to treat the 1970s as a void in our political history. Such revisionism has been fuelled by the tendency of dominant liberation movements worldwide to claim exclusive credit for success in freedom struggles as a prelude to appropriating political power to the exclusion of other role players. It is one of the dilemmas of our transformation that the ANC faced as it sought to reassert its dominance in the political landscape in preparation for the transfer of power to the majority in the early 1990s.

One of the astonishing symptoms of the depth of denial of the role of others is reflected in historical texts. For example, in Nelson Mandela's celebrated *Long Walk to Freedom* there is no mention of Stephen Bantu Biko and the role he played in re-energising the liberation movement in the 1970s. This omission is a powerful political statement. Such revisionist history has contributed to the poverty of language to speak of racism and its impact on individuals as well as on social relationships. We need to remind ourselves that the South African Students' Organisation (Saso) under Biko's leadership had been responsible for introducing a whole new language that challenged the assumptions of our racist society. Terms such as 'non-white' or 'non- European' had been part of our language until the early 1970s. The irony of an indigenous majority being defined negatively as 'non-something else' had not been contested until then. Acceptance of the apartheid system's 'racial categories' – White, Bantu, Coloured and Indian – was also challenged by the BCM's non-racialism that rejected the 'multiracialism' implied by the above categories. The coining of the term 'black' was a political statement against the divide-and-rule tactic embedded in the use of 'racial categories'. Blackness became an assertion of a positive self-definition on the part of oppressed people.

The BCM was a profoundly spiritual movement that understood the importance of the psychological dimension of freedom. The 'human face' that Africa could bestow on the world, as Biko said, could only emerge from a deeply spiritual ethos that went beyond conceiving human rights in legalistic terms. Value-based freedom, as defined in the BCM formulation, transcended the trappings of materialism.

Activists who experienced the rebirth of the BCM in the 1970s empowered themselves to address both the psychological impact of racism on the self-concept and the reality of living in an oppressive racist society. They tend to carry themselves very differently from those who have yet to confront the enemy within that leads to self-doubt and self-hatred. Self-doubt gives others permission to denigrate one. Confronting the enemy within is a major and essential first step to psychological liberation from the oppression that comes from believing racist myths. One cannot claim the right to freedom unless one believes that freedom is an entitlement that is inherent in being human.

The youth revolt that started on 16 June 1976 marked the beginning of the end of apartheid. It signalled that young people had chosen freedom over safety and comfort. The momentum generated by their hunger for freedom and demands for an education free from the dictates of the apartheid agenda became unstoppable. Trade unions joined in, women's groups added their voices, and civic associations swelled the ranks of freedom fighters. Many faith-based organisations also threw in their lot on the side of those in the struggle: Christians, Hindus, Muslims, Jews. It became a cross-party mass liberation movement spanning class divisions that kept its eye on the prize. Nothing short of freedom would do.

Some, however, were left out: non-unionised workers as well as poor rural people who remained under the thumb of chiefs, many of whom were collaborators of the apartheid system. Many people were too timid to venture into what they regarded as risky behaviour. Significant numbers of those who were in exile or in prison at the time also missed out on the liberating impact of this mass psychological liberation movement. Even today in the post-apartheid period many have yet to free themselves from the traps of the inferiority complex that is the legacy of apartheid. Until they name the problem, the racism ghost will continue to haunt them.

The denial of the BCM's role in the liberation process is complicated further by the articulation of its tenets by some of those claiming its mantle today. Some proponents of Black Consciousness today have difficulty in adjusting to the reality that to be conscious of one's blackness is a means to enabling one to live in a society with a diversity of people and cultures to which one contributes as an equal. Solidarity politics today need to be framed within the context of more inclusive politics in a pluralistic society. Too many of those claiming the BCM mantle cling to the notion that all white people are racists and should therefore either be shunned or excluded from participating in the new South Africa.

Many black people still feel vulnerable in interactions with white people, fearing that their trust would be betrayed by racist responses or innuendo. Those with such vulnerabilities need to be supported to confront their self-doubt and to explore safe interactions. They should be helped to free themselves from the fear of failure that holds them back from taking ownership of the freedom offered by their country and its institutions.

There are, unfortunately, also a significant number of black people who exploit the injustices of the past to claim benefits for themselves. They cast themselves in the role of perpetual victims with unending claims on society to redress historical wrongs. They have no hesitation in driving a wedge between black and white people. Nor do they shrink from sowing divisions among black people by focusing on who is blacker than whom and thus most eligible to the spoils of freedom.

As vice-chancellor of UCT from 1996 to 2000 I had to contend with tensions between historically black institutions (HBIs) and historically white institutions (HWIs) in the higher-education sector. Many of these tensions were driven by colleagues who saw benefits in claiming privileged access to public resources. They demanded that historical disadvantage rather than what they could contribute should be the paramount criterion for resource allocation. One could not but be supportive of redress measures for HBIs to create an equitable high-quality environment for teaching, learning and research in all higher education-institutions. But at the same time there has to be institutional accountability for efficient and effective use of public resources.

Colleagues driven by a redress agenda often undermined any effort to present a united forum for the government to deal with in planning and implementing transformation in the sector. It was as if the promotion of a shared vision by South African institutions would undermine the victim status that entitled HBIs to preferential treatment. This tendency to cling to victimhood is not confined to the higher-education sector. Wherever it is found, it has to be acknowledged and addressed in a manner that weans its proponents from their dependence on victim status.

It is also important to acknowledge the unintended consequences of policies aimed at redressing the injustices wrought by racism. The continuing resistance by some white-led institutions to promoting greater equality of opportunity and more inclusion has strengthened the arm of those urging stricter compliance-driven approaches. On the other hand, those bent on extracting maximum personal benefits from the process would stop at nothing to play the victim card, without any regard for the impact of such actions on greater equity and better outcomes in society.

White senior managers who resist change often justify their inaction by claiming that they cannot find qualified black people to fill important positions. As Saki Macozoma, the deputy chair of Standard Bank, aptly remarked: 'When they see a black person enter the corporate space, they see a training opportunity!' The assumption is that a black person cannot be qualified for the position he or she is filling. The idea that there are black people with sophisticated skills is outside the frame of reference of some white people. More training is prescribed for aspirant black senior management as a mechanism of postponing the moment of truth where they have to deal with black people as equals or seniors.

Those playing 'the victim game' also stop at nothing to get their way. Some lie about their qualifications in order to qualify for jobs and to benefit from the income attached. They have no qualms about putting the institutions in which they work at risk by being unable to discharge their responsibilities. It is amazing how tolerant the post-apartheid government at all levels – local, provincial and national – has been of this fraudulent behaviour in the public sector.

There are local authority managers with no competence in the core functions for which they are responsible. The Auditor General's reports of 1996 to 2006 on the performance of the management of the public sector indicate a severe crisis. For example, in the 2005/2006 audit process only 2% of local authorities had unqualified audits.

Capacity building has become the answer to problems that are created by the tolerance of false claims of qualifications and competence by public officials. But one cannot build the capacity of people who lack even the basic requirements of numeracy and literacy for the jobs they hold. The national government's Project Consolidate, aimed at technical support for local authority managers, is a good intervention. However, its effectiveness will depend on the determination of decision-makers to stop practices that undermine the recruitment, retention and promotion of competent managers in local authority structures. Sustainable competent management of service delivery at grass-roots level is critical to making the promise of freedom come alive in the daily lives of ordinary citizens.

The legacy of job reservation and the exclusion of black people from high-level positions in the economy and political decision-making is being addressed through the Employment Equity Act, 55 of 1998 (EE Act). The focus of the Act is to promote more equitable employment opportunities for all South Africans without undermining efficiency and effectiveness.

Under the rubric of affirmative action – called *regstellende aksie* (corrective action) in Afrikaans – specific measures have to be taken by employers to ensure that 'suitably qualified people from designated groups have equal employment opportunities and are equitably represented in all occupational categories and levels' in their workforces.[46] The 'designated groups' specified in the EE Act are all those previously discriminated against and put at a disadvantage: black people, women, and people with disabilities. Such affirmative action includes recognising prior learning as a complementary source of valuable experience. Providing training opportunities to fast-track talented people in the workplace is an essential part of affirmative action to promote employment equity.

Many perversions have been introduced in employment practices in both the public and private sector resulting in unintended consequences in the implementation of the EE Act.

There is a major dilemma in the continuing use of racial categories as a basis for redress. The EE Act defines black people as including 'Africans, Coloured and Indians', and in their workforce profiles, employment equity plans and reports to the Department of Labour employers have to subdivide black employees into these categories. These are the apartheid racial categories, with the only difference that the category 'black' (previously 'Bantu') of that era has been replaced by 'African'. The Act stipulates that affirmative action measures that should be instituted to the benefit of designated groups include preferential treatment and numerical goals, but exclude quotas.

Some zealots have resorted to the use of demographic quotas of the apartheid-style 'population register' categories to allocate employment opportunities. This has led to complaints about people feeling that they are treated as if they are 'not black enough' to qualify for the benefits of employment equity. Comrades who fought side by side in the anti-apartheid struggle find themselves pitted against each other in divisive competition for positions that are seen as the route to personal wealth and power. The solidarity that characterised the struggle is being shattered by the increasing application of the apartheid population categories to assign priority rankings to beneficiaries of redress policies.

There are also cases of white people being denied the right to employment in jobs for which they are qualified even where there are no black candidates competing for the same positions. Concrete examples are to be found in the public health sector in some provinces where a 'racial quota' for certain specialist jobs is in place. These practices have led to the bizarre situation that South Africa continues to suffer skills shortages while young white South Africans are forced to emigrate in droves in search of employment opportunities. Such practices amount to a denial of the rights of white people as citizens – a situation no different from the very racism we are trying to consign to the dustbin of history. This sense of being unwanted in one's country has led to an increasing number of young white people not even trying to apply for jobs locally. They make themselves available to the growing international labour market for skilled workers instead, to the benefit of the economies of countries where their talents are welcomed.

South Africa is inflicting a double injury on itself. It is losing sorely needed essential skills in engineering, medicine and the humanities. It is also throwing away the significant investment made by taxpayers in educating those young people. We behave like a person who is limping from an injured foot who then shoots himself in the other foot to even the score.

Crude use of demographic data to construct employment equity targets risks making demography destiny. Demographic profiles of particular regions are a guide to what is possible. The probability of finding candidates to fill the skills gaps in line with those possibilities depends on the complex dynamics that shape career choices. For example, academia as a career involves a sacrifice of material benefits. The rewards of academic excellence lie in higher-order intellectual and emotional satisfaction. In our transitional context, those under pressure to meet significant family obligations are unlikely to settle for higher-order non-financial rewards. It will take two or more generations for the majority of South Africans to have the luxury to make decisions that are not driven primarily by material need.

The increasing numbers of graduates in various fields do not necessarily translate into their availability for public-sector jobs. The maturation from graduate to specialist in a given field – a pre-condition for world-class scholarship – takes five to ten years, depending on the field of study. Appointing freshly graduated PhDs in senior academic posts is unfair on the inexperienced and also undermines the quality of teaching and learning. Black students who often have complex support needs would suffer most from such practices. In addition, the government will have to rethink its approach to conditions of service for the public sector to be able to attract the best brains into academia and key public-sector jobs, and retain them.

The unintended consequences of policies aimed at redressing the past injustices of racism are wreaking havoc in our society. The capacity to deliver public services to poor people who have no other recourse has been sorely lacking in most instances. Redress benefits for political elites who do not deliver undermine redress for poor people, whose needs are greater. Freedom for poor people is access to quality education, health care and decent housing. Redress that is focused on elites gaining access to state power bears within it the risk of a disarticulation between the interests of the majority at the lower levels of the socio-economic ladder and those in the middle and higher strata.

The post-apartheid transformation process has been interpreted in some quarters as one of replacing the white men who dominated the ranks of the public sector with black people. This blinkered approach neglects key considerations behind the whole project.

First, a transformed South Africa should be a country that is both more equitable and more prosperous, with the benefits of prosperity shared by all as envisaged by our national constitution. Second, the process of transformation has to proceed within the realms of possibility. One cannot immediately have the desired equity in the high-skills employment arena when South Africa in the past has not invested in the development of high skills among all sectors of the population. Equity in such areas would have to be established over time as equal opportunities are created to draw on a wider pool of talent to enhance our base. Third, skills inherited from the apartheid era represent investments made by all taxpayers (willingly or unwillingly) and should be harvested to improve the delivery of essential public services and South Africa's competitiveness as an economy.

The shortage of essential skills to manage public utilities and deliver services is real across our society. A 2005 study by the South African Institute of Civil Engineers (SAICE) established that of the 231 local municipalities, 79 had no civil engineers, technologists or technicians. Of the 47 district municipalities, four had no civil engineers, technologists or technicians. In addition, those municipalities that had civil engineering staff reported 35% vacancies and the freezing of many posts owing to budget constraints. Provincial government structures also have acute shortages of skilled staff, with some positions reported to have been vacant for seven or more years.[47]

Many of these vacancies resulted from the zealous enforcement of early retirement of experienced white male engineers and technicians who had occupied important positions as town planners and managers of complex urban systems. The hoped-for influx of competent black people to replace them did not materialise, leaving our urban systems at great risk. The parlous state of local infrastructure, outbreaks of water-borne diseases and failure to provide homes for poor people reflect these skills gaps.

An additional cost to the taxpayer of the overzealous application of affirmative action that forced white people into early retirement is the extraordinary reliance on outside consultants. Many former public sector white experts are enjoying both the benefits of early retirement and pension payouts and extraordinarily lucrative consultancies to government at premier rates. Poor people are the real victims of this short-termism that undermines the quality of essential public services to which they are entitled.

The Western Cape Province and Cape Town Metropolitan City have become crucibles for the struggles around 'race-based' redress policies. The legacy of the 'Coloured labour preferential policy' of the apartheid era is poisoning relationships between and within political parties. In 2004, the province had a total population of 4,6 million of which white people constituted 18,4%, Coloured people 53,9% and Africans 26,7%.[48] The struggle between 'Africanists' and those supporting 'Coloured' candidates has degenerated into an appalling mess both within and outside political-party structures. Within the ANC, accusations and counter-accusations continue to fly as different segments position themselves for leadership stakes. These struggles have seen provincial premier Ebrahim Rasool ousted as chairman of the Western Cape Provincial ANC and replaced by James Ngculu in 2005.

Outside the ANC there are also tensions. The election of the new leader of the Democratic Alliance (DA) in 2007 raised major issues that had less to do with the competence of prospective candidates than with the colour of their skin. Political analysts who have become apologists of 'politically correct' approaches to diversity debates even went as far as dismissing Helen Zille's appointment as irrelevant to the fortunes of that party in strengthening opposition politics be-cause 'politics does not work that way in South Africa'. Zille was dismissed as a credible candidate for the leadership because she is white, not because she is not competent. One of her competitors was recommended as more appropriate not because he was more com-petent, but because he was black. I am passing no judgment on the relative merits of the two candidates, but simply commenting on the debates surrounding the selection process.

At the heart of the dilemmas we face is our acceptance of the no-tion of 'races' despite scientific evidence that there is only one race, namely, the human race. In this we are not alone. Countries such as the US and Britain, with strong racist histories, continue to adhere to the concept of 'races'. The social construct of racial categories has permeated our discourse at all levels. We speak effortlessly of 'race relations', of 'different races living in harmony' and of 'multiracial schools', while in the same breath professing our commitment to a 'non-racial' South Africa. Our continued use of the discredited apart-heid-era 'population register' is a sign of the unresolved conflict between the benefits of moving away from that painful past on the one hand, and those of using these 'racial categories' in the implementation of redress policies on the other.

Settling old scores in the name of employment equity is detrimental to society as a whole. The increasingly public debates on affirmative action are to be welcomed, as the dilemmas inherent in corrective action have to be acknowledged and addressed. For how long should this practice continue – for another ten, twenty or how many more years after 1994? Why are class and socio-economic status not additional markers for candidates for redress measures? Should different markers be used for different areas of redress? Our continued reliance on a discourse informed by apartheid categories makes it difficult for us to embark on a transformative re-imagining journey. When are we unselfconsciously going to be able to call ourselves South Africans? What can we learn from other societies in this respect? Learn we must, or we will remain stuck in the past, haunted by this race ghost.

CHAPTER 5
Ethnic chauvinism

WHEN SOUTH AFRICANS WERE SPARED THE ETHNIC BLOOD BATH predicted by our detractors in the 1990s, those who cannot conceive of Africa without ethnic conflict were disappointed. The violent conflict in KwaZulu-Natal in the run-up to the transition to democracy was not between AmaXhosa of the ANC and AmaZulu of the IFP. It was a struggle for dominance between two political parties. Both sides in that conflict comprised members of the AmaZulu ethnic group. This was a contest for the political control of KwaZulu-Natal Province, not an ethnic war.

Basil Davidson, informed by careful study of many African countries, takes the view that 'tribalism' has always been used to express the solidarity and common loyalties of people who share a country and a culture. 'In this important sense, tribalism in Africa has always existed as a force for good, a force for creating a civil society dependent on laws and the rule of law.'[49] With regard to traditional leadership, Davidson quotes the work of the anthropologist Max Gluckman among the Barotse people in Zambia that documents the evolution of a way of balancing the power from inheritance with power from appointment. Entitlement to inherited leadership was constantly tested against appointability on the basis of the competence of the candidate. Those in line for succession were assessed for competence and if found wanting, a regent would be appointed to take care of the business of the tribe.[50] The form of tribalism we see today is a product of the perversion of traditional systems resulting from colonial 'divide-

and-conquer' politics that have created disorder, destroyed civil society and openly flouted morality and the rule of law.

It would be foolhardy to imagine that more than three hundred
years of divide and rule along ethnic lines would not have left cleav-
ages among the people who today make up the South African nation. Tribal and ethnic consciousness is often heightened by the lack
of other focal points for solidarity. This is particularly the case among
uneducated and marginalised peoples. Ethnic consciousness is also
reinforced where access to resources are framed along ethnic lines.
All successful democracies seek mechanisms to ensure that access to
decision-making and resources is untied from tribal and ethnic identities. Even a highly industrialised country such as Canada continues to face the challenge of Anglo/French tensions in the Quebec
province.

Colonial governments applied their own notions of nationalism and
bureaucratic administration to Africa. Ethnic chauvinism and tribalism as we know them today are largely products of Africa's colonial
legacy. They were 'invented' by colonial administrations in order to
divide African populations into more manageable ethnic units. This
was done on the basis of common language and cultural practices of
people as observed, recorded and often invented by anthropologists
and missionaries. Pre-colonial notions of ethnicity and tribalism had
been more flexible, being influenced by environmental factors, wars
and intermarriages.[51]

Rwanda is an example of a colony that was organised along ethnic
lines. Rwandan society was divided into the two main groups of Hutus and Tutsis. (The indigenous Twa people were a third and very
small component of the population.) Tutsis were favoured by the
Belgian government and put in positions of power, which afforded
them access to resources, education, wealth and opportunities. These
divisions were based on notions of the Tutsi constituting the aris-
tocracy of Rwandan society. Colonial officers rated their features and
mannerisms as more akin to Western norms, and access to modern
comforts by Tutsis reinforced this perception. Collectively, these factors contributed to feelings of ethnic superiority amongst the Tutsi.

Hutus were regarded as barbaric and denied access to resources, which in turn perpetuated perceptions of Hutu inferiority.

A vicious circle of inferiority/resentment reinforced by superiority/entitlement set in, with devastating long-term consequences. These ethnic identities were internalised by both Tutsis and Hutus and contributed to tension that resulted in ongoing conflicts after independence in 1959, culminating in the much-publicised Rwandan genocide in 1994.

In the 1990s, the post-colonial Hutu government found itself under increasing pressure due to an economic crisis triggered by the declining coffee price (Rwanda's chief export) and stringent structural adjustment programmes mandated by the World Bank and the International Monetary Fund (IMF).[52] In the view of many observers, the Hutu government used the colonial legacy of favouritism towards the Tutsi as an opportunity to target them as scapegoats for the dire economic situation. The Hutu government incited anti-Tutsi sentiment through propaganda that projected Tutsis as collaborators with past colonial governments. The shooting down of a plane carrying President Habyarimana was blamed on the Tutsi, sparking the 1994 genocide.[53]

It is important to note the irony in the coincidence of the Rwandan genocide with South Africa's own 'peaceful' transition to democracy in 1994. South Africa and the world were so caught up in the 'miracle' of the transition process that the Rwandan genocide went by with little public comment in our own country. The lessons from Rwanda must not be glossed over. We should also not fail to recognise how close we ourselves came to a fully fledged civil war which could have evolved into genocide. The Rwandan example emphasises the need to address the persistent ghosts of racism and ethnic chauvinism lest they come back to haunt us.

Rwanda also presents a success story of how to lay the ethnic ghost to rest. The post-genocide government tackled the trauma of genocide head on. They did not hide behind the legacy of colonialism, but admitted their own responsibility for having failed to tackle divisions and tensions that had led to the bloodshed. They also acknowledged the contributory role of competition for scarce resources to the crisis. Rwanda has set itself a 2020 vision as a knowledge economy and has been systematically implementing coordinated strategies towards that end since 2000. It recruited the diaspora to join government and operates efficiently by harnessing the power of information technology to create a truly wired government. The president, Paul Kagame, actively drives the agenda and tolerates neither incompetence nor corruption from his cabinet colleagues.

The genocide museum in Kigali makes a harrowing and unforgettable statement about what the Rwandese did to one another. The skulls, broken bones of victims from babies to adults, and personal effects are on permanent display. There is also a cemetery on the museum property where victims are buried as their remains are discovered all over Kigali. Denialism has no place in Rwanda today as it powers towards its 2020 vision.

The roots of the current crisis in Darfur, in western Sudan, can also be linked to in the ethnic divisions between 'Arabs' and 'Africans' that had been amplified by the British colonial government, who favoured Arabs. Resources were concentrated around Arabs living in the Nile Valley region while Darfur remained underdeveloped. Feelings of ethnic superiority among Arabs were enhanced while indigenous Africans experienced feelings of ethnic inferiority, leading to tensions and resentment between the two groups.[54]

In Uganda, the colonial government favoured the Buganda and regarded them as ethnically superior. The Buganda chiefs were put into positions of power in the colonial administration. In exchange, the Buganda received payoffs in the form of money, weapons, education, jobs and land. The denial of access to these resources and opportunities to the Bunyoro reinforced their sense of ethnic inferiority. The Bunyoro were recruited as cheap labour, soldiers and policemen for the Buganda. This situation created tribal tensions and resentment that led to the conflicts characterising the independence and post-colonial era.[55]

In South Africa, ethnic identities have been shaped by the institution of the Population Registration Act of 1950 that classified people according to their 'racial' category. This classification was used to determine who had access to what resources and provided the foundation for the introduction of the 'homelands' policy intended to 'advance Bantu culture and independence'. Today ethnicity continues to influence access to resources in South Africa. Divisions within the ruling ANC (between supporters of President Thabo Mbeki on the one hand and those of recently elected ANC president Jacob Zuma on the other) are framed in ethnic terms by some of the contestants. Mbeki's detractors play on the dominance of AmaXhosa in leadership ranks and the need to give other groups a chance. His relatively privileged background as a trader's son and his access to good education in exile is also used to discredit Mbeki as elitist. In contrast, Jacob Zuma is portrayed by his supporters as 'a man of the people' who boasts about crediting no one but himself for his ability to read and write.

As solidarity forged in the struggle for freedom recedes into the past, the ethnic ghost may start strutting about in South Africa with greater confidence. Ethnic tensions are currently held in check by the federal system of government that provides space for various concentrations of ethnic groups to wield power and influence within the nine provincial governments. The Eastern Cape, for example, is dominated by AmaXhosa and KwaZulu-Natal is predominantly home to AmaZulu, while Limpopo Province comprises mainly Ba-Pedi, BaVenda and BaTsonga. Members of different ethnic groups experience their sense of 'belonging' in different regions of South Africa.

The constitutional complications of traditional leaders co-existing with elected leaders have been managed in different ways in post-colonial Africa. In Tanzania, President Julius Nyerere abolished their formal role in the interest of national unity. The outcome seems to have been a success – Tanzanians see themselves as Tanzanians and nothing else. Mozambique also abolished the formal role of traditional leaders in the post-1975 democracy. Their collaboration with the former colonial powers and the potential divisiveness of tribal politics were cited as justification for doing away with the system. Again the outcome appears to have been satisfactory. Mozambicans speak of themselves as a nation, not as ethnic groups.

The role of traditional leaders in a democracy such as ours presents major dilemmas. The compromise reached during the negotiations to include them in the governance system was driven more by the imperatives of managing the risks of revolt on their part than by a proper definition of their roles. Those arguing for downgrading the role of traditional leaders cite the risks of perpetuating fragmented tribal/ethnic politics that had been promoted by colonial and apartheid governments. In addition, 'traditional leadership' was reinvented over the years to reward loyalists of old regimes, while authentic leaders were in some cases exiled or demoted. The question of the authenticity of traditional leadership is not an uncomplicated one.

Another difficulty of promoting traditional leadership lies in the contradiction between the equality clauses of our constitution and the tenets of male-dominated traditional leadership. Gender equality is often violated by the practice of customary law. Some of its provisions have been corrupted by collusion between successive colonial powers and male leaders, and practices that were intended to be flexible have become more rigid over time. Thandabantu Nhlapo[56] identified a list of notorious provisions that need urgent review:

- The levirate, which is the continuation of the deceased husband's marriage through a brother or male relative
- The sororate - a practice where a younger sister bears children for an older one in the case of barren marriages
- Polygyny - a practice that allows a man to marry more than one wife
- Child betrothal and forced marriages linked to family obligations
- Inheritance laws that follow patrilineal patterns through which family wealth passes from father to son
- Women's status as minors that deprives them of rights to land and economic decision-making
- *Lobola* or *bohadi* that exchanges women and cattle between families.

These weighty matters need to be resolved to enable us to align customary practices with the precepts of our constitution. Failure to do so puts the most vulnerable women and children at risk of having their human rights violated without access to any recourse. It is especially rights relating to land and property ownership and gender equality that are being compromised in the name of traditionalism. Equality before the law is yet to have meaning for the most vulnerable among us.

There are some who argue for strengthening the institution of traditional leadership as a sign of pride in indigenous African culture. They concur with Basil Davidson's view that 'tribalism' or 'ethnic solidarity' has always existed in Africa as a force for good. Davidson argues that the neglect of this rich heritage may explain the continuing challenges that democratic governance faces in Africa. The introduction of an alien system of governance without rooting it in the cultural milieu of the African continent has undermined the consolidation of democracy in post-colonial Africa. Davidson, however, recognises the perversions the colonial enterprise introduced into traditional leadership practices and customs that undermine civil society and principles of good governance. Romanticising traditional leadership without acknowledgement of these perversions would threaten the very foundations of our democracy.

Some of the protagonists of traditional leadership cite the co-existence of the monarchy with a democratic order in European countries such as the UK, Sweden and the Netherlands.[57] What is often neglected in such arguments is that each of these societies has over many centuries found a modus operandi to enable the respective roles of the monarchy and elected representative. It is also significant that the monarchies in these societies are a unifying force. There is only one British monarch. Likewise, Swaziland and Lesotho have one monarch for the whole country.

The dilemma for us in South Africa is how we can strengthen national unity while at the same time promoting fragmented ethnic leadership comprising at least nine sets of leaders at the top and many more layers underneath for each of the indigenous ethnic groups. What are the costs of staying this course in terms of both material and societal value? The strengthening of traditional leadership could encourage ethnic divisions and worsen conflicts over scarce resources. And how would one manage the vested interests some would have in perpetuating distinctions that accentuate the differences between groups above shared national interests?

The persistence of the urban/rural divide may be detrimental to the very people whose interests are supposed to be protected under traditional leadership. There are ironies in the continuing relegation of rural people to traditional leadership regimes that may be disadvantaging them. What if the traditional leaders are corrupt? What if nepotistic practices lead to poor people being neglected in favour of relatives closest to the leaders? There are also complications resulting from relics of landownership laws of the past.

Communal landownership, which is often romanticised, has not been properly incorporated into the post-1994 property-rights regime. For example, a section of my home village in the Bochum district of Limpopo has been left out of the reconstruction and development plans of the post-1994 government. The rationale is that it is an autonomous area with communal landowners who have to take responsibility for their own development. These communal landowners are among the poorest segment of our population. How are they to foot the bill for their own infrastructure development?

My mother (88 years old in 2007) saw her house by-passed when electricity, water and other amenities were established for those above the fence that divide landowners from the rest of the villagers. We had to find family resources to install public-service amenities that should be the entitlement of all citizens. Poor rural folk in these communal land areas who are less fortunate than my mother continue to battle with no end in sight. How can they be so easily defined out of the entitlement of citizens in the name of respect for custom?

Indigenous laws and practices can only enrich our democracy if they are properly reviewed and aligned to the values we aspire to in our national constitution. Otherwise tradition will continue to be a source of disadvantage and division.

CHAPTER 6

Sexism

SEXISM MAY WELL PROVE TO BE ONE OF OUR MOST TENACIOUS ghosts. Discrimination against women is a common feature of all South African cultures, and all the various cultural strands that came together in 1994 brought the legacies of their own versions of sexism. It is deeply embedded in our social relationships and shapes notions of power in our society. Transforming our social relationships in line with the gender equality and anti-sexist precepts of our constitution requires a radical change in attitudes and practices at the personal, family, community, institutional and national levels. Radical change poses major dilemmas for a society that is significantly conservative.

Sexism as practised today has also been influenced by the legacy of colonialism. Colonialism changed the power structure of gender relations. Colonial administrations transferred their own notions of female domesticity onto African women, making them housebound. Working the land was considered male work by colonial powers. Indigenous women who previously took pride in working on the land as a source of independent livelihoods became dependent on their husbands and fathers, migrant workers who earned money on the mines, on farms or in factories.

Land dispossession deprived women of the source of their independent economic base. This undermined the position of African women in a society in which they were previously held in high regard as mothers and workers of the land. The imperatives of divide and rule reinforced patriarchal control within the tribal/ethnic authority structures that became tools of the colonial administration. Desperation led women to resort to illegal practices such as beer brewing and prostitution to sustain themselves and their children.

Former President Mandela was very clear about the indivisibility of the freedom delivered in 1994 when he said: 'Freedom cannot be achieved unless the women have been emancipated from all forms of oppression . . . the objectives of the Reconstruction and Development Programme will not have been realised unless we see in visible practical terms that the conditions of women in our country have been radically changed for the better, and that they have been empowered to intervene in all aspects of life as equals with other members of society.'[58]

Our society is struggling to live up to that commitment. Women are still treated as second-class citizens. This is tied to traditional notions of them as 'mothers' whose proper role is to nurture and be subservient to men. Women continue to be socialised into roles that mark them as submissive, passive and emotionally driven. Men, on the other hand, are encouraged to be rational thinkers and to be assertive, competitive and aggressive. Women are still largely seen as belonging to the private sphere of the home while men occupy the public domain of work, politics and community influence.

On a radio talk show during Women's Month (August) in 2007, an African man in his twenties was emphatic that he would never work for a female boss:

> Women are too emotional and illogical. They do not have the intellectual wherewithal to run organisations or companies. They can't make sound decisions unless there is a man they can use as a crutch.[59]

It is disconcerting that the speaker was a young person from whom one would expect less resistance to change. Moreover, this was a student, not an uneducated person unexposed to the discourse of transformation of our society. The young man does not seem to realise just how much he has internalised the very arguments that were used to justify denying African people rights as full citizens in their own country. Research[60] on gender, race and power dynamics has identified reasons for the continued undermining of women in post-apartheid South Africa and violence against them in particular, to which we will return later in this chapter:

- Embedded patriarchy reflected in gender identities in South Africa, the economics of gender identities, and gendered constructions of female and male sexuality
- The intersection of race and gender in relation to violence against women dating back to slavery and indentured servitude
- Militarisation, conflict and a culture of violence that is sanctioned by the state
- Thwarted gender identities within a conservative social ethos
- Changes in the social order that have led to historical shifts in gender relations
- The legitimisation of violence against women is often based on interpretations of Roman-Dutch law and traditional African customs and customary law.

The media worldwide play an important role in shaping public opinion that impacts on social relationships over time. A two-phase study by the South African National Editors' Forum (Sanef) reveals that the South African media have not yet transformed themselves to promote gender equality as entrenched in our constitution. The second phase of this study, *Glass Ceiling Two: An Audit of Women and Men in South African newsrooms*,[61] released in 2007, provides evidence of a host of barriers to the advancement of women in the media. Discriminatory practices, structural inequalities, cultural factors, prejudice, patriarchal assumptions and sexual harassment are still alive and well in our newsrooms.

In the first phase of the study, the terms 'old boys' club' and 'network' featured repeatedly in explanations as to why women are overlooked for senior posts. They are simply not seen as equals by the vast majority of men, who still hold the reins of power in all media houses. Women's opinions do not appear to be taken as seriously as those of men. For example, jokes are often made at their expense when they give their opinions, or they are teased mercilessly. Some of these subtle undermining tactics seem friendly and even affectionate, but they are actually demeaning. They serve to discourage women from putting themselves in a position where they pose a competitive threat to men.

While governments in southern Africa have committed themselves to achieving gender parity in all areas of decision-making by 2015, none of the media houses in the Sanef study could point to specific targets for ensuring gender equality. A frequently asked question within the media fraternity is why the preoccupation with these numbers: what difference would more women managers really make to the newsroom?

More women decision-makers in newsrooms will not necessarily lead to more being written for and about women. However, *Glass Ceiling Two* establishes a positive correlation between having women in senior and top management positions and hiring higher numbers of women journalists. The Global Media Monitoring Project in which South Africa participated in 2005 showed that women journalists are more likely than their male counterparts to consult female opinion in their reporting. This study found that women constituted 21% of news sources globally. In South Africa, the figure was 26%.

The continued stereotyping of women in our public media reflects the male-dominated decision-making structure. Television adverts continue to foster racial and gender stereotyping. A pertinent example was an advertisement for Joko tea aired on SABC TV that showed a black woman wearing a domestic worker's uniform, broom in hand, cleaning the floor of a big building. She is shown shaking and twitching her big bottom to signal her delight at the invigorating cup of tea she has just had! It is unlikely that a liberated black woman manager would have made the decision to air such an advertisement.

The public sector has led by example in placing women in decision-making positions in government. Forty-three per cent of South Africa's cabinet ministers are women and four of the nine provinces have female premiers. Women are also well represented at the level of deputy ministers and directors-general. At the local-government level female representation stands at 40%, while 32% of our parliamentarians are women. The South African Parliament is ranked tenth out of 130 parliaments in the world in terms of advancing women in governance[62]. This is a dramatic change from the 2,8% women in Parliament towards the end of the apartheid era.[63]

The private sector is lagging behind on this score. A 2007 Business Women's Association Report found that only 16,8% of chief executive officers of companies listed on the Johannesburg Securities Exchange (JSE) and 11,5% of directors of JSE-listed companies are women.[64] In addition, the Companies Act of South Africa, a relic from apartheid days, continues to treat women as minors. Women who are invited to become directors are asked to submit proof of consent from their spouses. This is clearly in violation of the equality principle of our 1996 constitution. A new Companies Act is likely to come into effect in 2008, but that it took so many years speaks volumes about our priorities with regard to legislative reform.

Notwithstanding the progress that has been made since 1994, the domination of men in the socio-economic and political spheres continues in the post-apartheid era, perpetuating the image of women as inferior and the dependence of women on men.

Public leadership roles for women are important in both symbolic and material terms. Many women remain in dysfunctional and abusive relationships for economic reasons only.

Sexism is expressed in its most extreme form in violence against women. South Africa has the unenviable record of having the highest recorded prevalence of violence against women. In most cases, the perpetrators of violent physical or sexual abuse to which women are subjected are their intimate partners or people known to them. A national study of this tragedy, conducted in 2004 by the Medical Research Council (MRC),[65] found that in 1999, one woman was killed every six hours by an intimate partner.

Racial category and class position were found to be important factors. The rate at which Coloured women were killed by their intimate partners was more than double that for African women, and more than six times that for white women. Men who kill their intimate partners are likely to be employed as blue-collar workers, farm hands and security workers. Perpetrators of non-intimate female homicide are likely to be unemployed, students, self-employed or of unknown occupation.

Guns and alcohol play a key role. According to the MRC study, women killed by intimate partners are likely to be killed at home, be younger, work as domestics, be killed by a firearm or blunt instrument, and be killed by someone with an alcohol problem. A history of domestic violence commonly precedes the fatal episode.

The intersection of race, class and gender disadvantages places women at risk from the very people who are meant to protect them. Intimate partners who turn into killers are themselves victims of a system that has made it difficult for them to be effective in exercising their roles as providers as defined by a male-dominated society. To be a man who is humiliated by racism, undermined by poor education and training, unable to access high-paying jobs, mocked by inadequacy that forces one's wife or partner to work to put food on the table, is to be a wounded man. Alcohol and drugs become a temporary refuge from the painful reality of daily humiliation. Anger and resentment turned inwards find an outlet in the closest target.

The current spate of domestic violence and killing of women by their intimate partners can be traced to the tensions generated by the inability of vulnerable men to accept women as equal partners in relationships and in the home. Uncertainty that comes with social change can produce unusual behaviour, which tends to be directed at those closest to the vulnerable person.

South Africa also has a high rate of family murders where a man kills his wife and other family members and then commits suicide. Psychologist Ilse Terblanche makes the important but frightening point that

> a family murder can be described as an 'extended suicide'. The killer does not fear the anger of society, because he plans to die . . . he already feels rejected or discarded by society. A common feature of family relationships prior to a killing incident is pathological possessiveness over the wife and children, in-

cluding sexual jealousy over the wife. The family killer believes that these people are his property and is unable to see
that they have rights and lives of their own. This is not really
a feature of individual mentality, but rather of participation
in a culture or tradition that does not allow equality.[66]

Terblanche's observations reflect her understanding of Afrikaner patriarchal culture, but they could just as well be directed at any other
patriarchal cultural setting. The extent to which the possessiveness
towards the wife and children is expressed and ultimately triggers the
'extended suicide' depends on the level of insecurity and desperation
of the patriarch. But such an explanation takes us back to the extent
to which we pay attention to spiritual and psychological matters in
our transformation processes.

How can we build a strong nation anchored on a value system reflecting the human-rights principles enshrined in our constitution
if some men and their families are caught up in identity crises that
preclude equality between men and women? Those trapped in the
vicious circle of poor self-image and vulnerability are more likely than
not to cling to the idea that their tradition is rigidly set against gender equality. The sense of entrapment contributes to the desperation
that might end in the horror of domestic violence and even murder.

Social change with its unsettling consequences creates levels of
vulnerability for those at the lower end of the social ladder who are
desperate to make it or hold on to what they have. But it is the sense
of being abandoned that should be a concern for us as a society. What
do we need to do to be present in the lives of young and vulnerable
families as they struggle with the demands of modern materialistic
environments in which success is measured by what one owns rather
than what one is? The macho culture that permeates all our diverse
communities discourages men from acknowledging and dealing with
their feelings. Seeking help tends to be regarded as a sign of weakness.
These factors set the scene for some men getting sucked into a vicious
circle that might lead to disaster for themselves and their loved ones.

Black men at the lower- and middle-class levels are particularly vulnerable, given the fear of failure linked to the legacy of racist stereotypes of black inferiority. The opening up of opportunities for black people and women in general, while presenting exciting possibilities, also triggers fears of failure. How can one fail as a man in a world that defines the man as protector and provider while women, including one's own wife or partner, succeed?

Akin to Ilse Terblanche's thinking, some criminologists suggest that in the case of family murders, the killer does not intend killing 'other people' at all. In his mind, his wife and children are part of the self he is killing. 'He plans to kill himself, but for him to be fully dead, they too must no longer live. Alternatively, he may have become convinced that they cannot survive without him.'[67] Unaccountable as this might seem to some of us, there are still men who subscribe to the notion of women as inferior and helpless beings who cannot survive without them.

We also face challenges in documenting these aspects of our reality in our national statistics. It is hard to know just how many of these family murders have occurred since 1994, let alone the individual circumstances of those tragic families. Surviving family members often do not speak about the details, given the pain and shame. In my own extended family there have been at least two such cases. Fortunately in both cases the children were spared, but their mothers perished. Family murders are a cancer in our society that requires radical preventive action at many levels.

Rape has also become a major epidemic that blots our post-apartheid track record as a society. While rape is the ultimate weapon of domination by men over women, it is increasingly being recognised as a weapon of subordination of men by men. Rape is an expression of powerlessness and lack of self-respect. It is a perversion of the gift of sexuality that defines us as humans. In the human species sexuality is not just about procreation; it is also an expression of mutual celebration of the body. Sexual intercourse is the ultimate act of making oneself vulnerable to another. It is an intimate act of trust.

Rapists are like bullies who, because they feel inadequate and are unable to form meaningful relationships, prey on unsuspecting vulnerable victims instead. The bully in rapists is most evident when they rape children and frail people. Such acts are the ultimate expression of self-loathing that comes from the loss of that which defines us as human and enables us to draw boundaries between right and wrong. The same applies to incestuous sexual violence. A man who can rape his own daughter or a child entrusted to him has lost his humanity.

The rising levels of gender-based violence and rape involving not just women, but children as well, make a mockery of the human-rights foundations of our constitution. South Africa has the highest recorded rape incidence in the world: 121 per 100 000 in 2001/02 and 111 per 100 000 in 2006/07. From April 2001 to March 2007, 322 108 cases of rape were reported to the SAPS.[68] These figures are, sadly, a gross underestimate of the real incidence. Not only are women and children discouraged from reporting rape because of fear of stigma, the police seem to have a vested interest in under-reporting in order not to embarrass their political masters. Many individuals, community activists and NGOs cite examples of victims being discouraged from reporting incidents to police. Equally worrying is the failure to secure convictions of rapists even when evidence is presented.

What causes even greater concern are reported incidents of law enforcement officers committing rape or acts that expose women to the risk of rape. One of the most outrageous cases in Mpumalanga involved a woman who was raped while locked up in a police cell with male prisoners. The police officer concerned claimed that he could not distinguish between the male and female cells because it was a dark night and the lights were off. The underlying attitude at work in this policeman's mind is one that should see him dismissed from public service. But there is no evidence of intolerance for such dereliction of duty in our law enforcement system to date.

Given the risks of HIV/Aids, rape can be seen as another way of killing women and children. The striking gender disparities in HIV/Aids prevalence attest to the risks that women face in our society. Mortality rates from Aids among young women aged from 20 to 39 years more than tripled between 1997 and 2004, whereas for men from 30 to 44 years old deaths more than doubled. Over the same period, deaths from Aids-related conditions such as tuberculosis in the age group from 25 to 29 years increased sixfold among females and tripled among males. UNAIDS estimates that women make up 58 percent of the adult population (15 years and over) who are HIV positive in South Africa.[69]

There is a frightening level of tolerance of violence against women and children in our society. Even our highly regarded judiciary has far to go in sending out a strong message about the rights of women. In one case, the Appellate Division upheld an appeal by a 29-year-old man against his life sentence, converting it to 16 years' imprisonment. The appellant had virtually kidnapped a woman, locked her in his hotel room and raped her. He then left her locked up in the room and went to the bar to drink. When she tried to flee, he assaulted her and raped her four more times. The lower court appropriately took the view that this man was a danger to society and not likely to be rehabilitated. However, when his appeal was upheld on the grounds that he was employed and had young children, the judiciary failed to send a clear signal that women's bodies are not to be violated and that men who break the law will forfeit their right to freedom.[70]

Transforming a patriarchal society into one aligned to gender equality requires a radical shift from traditional comfort zones. At the political level, the government and most political parties are making efforts to enforce the spirit of the constitution that mandates equality between men and women. But the disgruntlement at the grassroots levels continues as women candidates are seen as competing unfairly with men for scarce leadership positions with material benefits attached. Reports of sexual harassment within the corridors of power reflect unresolved conflicts between public positions on equality and personal conduct.

The most visible recent example is the 2007 case of sexual harassment of a female Parliamentary staff member brought against the then ANC Chief Whip, Mr Mbulelo Goniwe. The act of harassment was an outrage from one entrusted with leadership of the ruling party in Parliament – the very body that is responsible for upholding the national constitution.

Even worse, the complainant received little support from senior managers in Parliament in trying to lay a complaint. It is noteworthy that both the Speaker and Deputy Speaker of our Parliament are women. Yet it took extraordinary efforts by the victim with the support of one senior female parliamentarian to bring disciplinary action against Goniwe.

Even after a guilty verdict by the ANC Disciplinary Committee and dismissal from his powerful position, Goniwe showed little remorse. He appealed against the committee's verdict and sentence, succeeding in getting the party leaders to overturn his expulsion from the ANC. The ANC Appeal Committee subsequently confirmed his guilt and his dismissal from parliament.

Other evidence of Goniwe's disregard for the rights of women and children has also emerged. For years he avoided child-support subpoenas under the protection of Parliament, as the Speaker had to give permission for the serving of subpoenas on members on Parliamentary premises. Parliament faces a credibility problem if it is seen to be undermining the very laws that it enacts. It is charged with the watchdog role of ensuring that laws are respected.

Addressing the legacy of sexism requires holistic approaches to help both men and women redefine themselves. Women have to assert their rights to equality as citizens. But they also need to approach their relationships with men in a manner that enhances the transformative process. Women as mothers have a major role to play in nurturing their sons and daughters in a manner that prepares them for equality between the sexes. This does not imply a world of sameness, but one that celebrates the best in women – the feminine instincts – and the best in men – the masculine elements. It is when women and men play to their strengths and complement each other that relationships thrive at the personal, family, community and social levels. Diversity enriches all participants in the long term.

The dilemma for our young democracy in this regard is how to respect traditions and customs while protecting human rights. The particular vulnerabilities of women and children make the dilemma all the more urgent. Core values and rights that should be paramount in all relationships, trumping whatever traditional practices some cultural groups may hold dear, should be spelt out. For example, child abuse in any form should be outlawed. In addition, the violation of the bodies of children, such as under-age girls forced into virginity tests or genital mutilation, should be prohibited whatever the claims of traditional custom. Children have a right to the protection and respect that the state and society owes them. Dangerous practices such as widow inheritance are a virtual death sentence for vulnerable women and children in an age of HIV/Aids, and should have no place in our democracy.

Men have a major role to play in helping young men and women define themselves for the roles they are to play in society. Male initiation is still a widely practised custom in South Africa, and older men have always played a critical role in initiating younger men into manhood. But the manhood of yesterday is not necessarily relevant to today's realities. There is a need for the redefinition of what it means to be a man so as to enable young men to meet the challenges of a social context of equality. Older men have to redefine and reshape the ancient custom of initiation to better prepare young men for the demands of today. This is most critical for young men in households headed by women who grow up without positive male role models.

To borrow Hillary Clinton's words about the role of communities and government in supporting families and children, it will take a village[71] to raise tomorrow's men and women to enable them to live the values of our constitution. All of us have to develop a greater consciousness of the trappings of sexism and work together to overcome them.

CHAPTER 7

Authoritarianism

THE GHOST OF AUTHORITARIANISM NEEDS TO BE ACKNOWLEDGED as a dominant facet of our traditional political culture. Colonial culture is by its nature authoritarian. Its success depends on imposing its will on the colonised. The colonial project is about extracting maximum benefit for the coloniser regardless of the cost to the victims. Authoritarianism resulting from centuries of colonial exploits has coloured most political cultures across Africa, and South Africa could not have escaped it.

White minority rule sustained itself by flexing its authoritarian muscle not just against subjugated black people but also against acquiescent white people. Afrikaner nationalism added a particularly harsh Calvinistic streak to the authoritarian British colonial culture that it replaced in 1948. Those in powerful positions called the shots. The rest of society had to follow or face severe consequences.

The African traditional system of governance is also authoritarian at its core. Despite the romantic notion of accountability of chiefs and kings through the *lekgotla*[72] system, hereditary leadership is inherently non-democratic. As indicated earlier, some tribes have over the years evolved a system of balancing inherited entitlement to leadership with appointability to leadership to align the interests of the tribe to those of the chief's family.

The *lekgotla* system also excluded women from decision-making in most instances. Most hereditary leadership follows the dominant patrilineal system common to most African regions. Traditional leaders tend to be male. Notable exceptions are the queen mothers in Ghana and the queens of the Balobedu ethnic group. Balobedu leaders are descendents of Queen Modjadji, the famous rainmaker of the Limpopo Province. Nonetheless, the Balobedu are neither necessarily less authoritarian nor less sexist than the rest of society.

Organisations leading the anti-apartheid struggle over the decades inherited strands of authoritarianism from African traditional systems, European traditions and the sexism pervasive to our political culture. The South African Communist Party (SACP) added its own heritage from international communism, including centrism and Stalinism. Silence on the excesses of Communist allies especially in the Soviet Union that included brutal repression of dissent in Eastern Europe created a climate of silence and a fear of voicing dissenting views within the ANC in exile.

Mass mobilisation from the late 1970s to the early 1990s injected a greater focus on grass-roots democratic participation. The 'broad church' cutting across political ideologies that came together under the umbrella of the United Democratic Front (UDF) allowed for debate and the forging of common strategies across communities. The need for unity made a diversity of opinions on tactics acceptable. Religious leaders, trade union leaders, student activists, civic leaders and others all joined in the pursuit of freedom.

It was not surprising that authoritarian excesses showed their ugly face in sectors of the anti-apartheid movement, including the UDF. The same strands of authoritarianism that infected the ANC in exile were also embedded in the UDF. Under pressure from the apartheid regime, the ideals of democratic participation were compromised in favour of stringent enforcement of solidarity. Brutal assaults on suspected agents of the state culminated in the gruesome necklace murders that surfaced in the middle of the 1980s. Campaigns such as consumer boycotts, strikes, school boycotts and other protests assumed strong elements of intimidation and intolerance for individual choices.

Even without these excesses, it is unlikely that a decade or so of post-apartheid experimentation with democracy would have been enough to exorcise the ghost of authoritarianism. All South Africans are newcomers to democracy. We must acknowledge our authoritarian political heritage. It will not simply go away in the face of a democratic national constitution. It should be called by name and put to rest.

Building a participatory, inclusive democratic culture is a long-term process of cultural change. Schools, homes, communities and the workplace have distinctive and mutually supportive roles to play in this.

It is vitally important that we define what kind of democracy we want in our society and what values we would like to see underpinning our social relationships. The human-rights foundations of our constitution will become a lived experience for all citizens only to the extent that the whole society works tirelessly for the progressive realisation of those rights. But rights without responsibilities become entitlements without the ethos of deep respect for the self and others as well as the commitment to guarding the basic tenets of our democracy.

We have devoted inadequate attention to what kind of society we envisage ourselves becoming. How does one live the values of non-hierarchy, non-racialism, non-sexism and greater egalitarianism? Our constitution demands non-discrimination on the grounds of religion or beliefs. How do we build a secular state that avoids the rule of religion or ideology yet protects the right to practise religion and to enjoy intellectual freedom? How do we honour freedom of expression without promoting the imposition of dominant views that undermine the rights of others to hold theirs?

A democracy that takes the spiritual, intellectual and human values in our constitution seriously as central to quality of life beyond material needs cannot avoid confronting those aspects of our past that undermine these values. The transformation of authoritarian relationships needs to be tackled simultaneously in key spaces: the home, educational institutions, political parties, government-citizen relationships, the public service and the private sector.

The home is the cradle that nurtures children. Being brought up in an authoritarian home makes becoming a respectful democratic parent very difficult. The pressures of modern life where both parents are working or women are single parents add to the challenges. 'Do as I say' becomes an easier approach than responding to questions about decisions adults make. Although corporal punishment is frowned upon and outlawed in our schools, the temptation for parents to resort to it in the face of discipline problems remains strong. Parenting is a daunting responsibility. Yet societies globally pay little attention to helping young adults prepare themselves for responsible parenthood.

Child abuse is the worst outcome of an authoritarian culture. The rising tide[73] of child abuse in our midst is a sign of the pressures in our society. The Child Welfare Society of South Africa has registered its alarm at this epidemic, including sexual abuse and abandonment.[74] Our high figures of reported child-abuse cases are a window into the sick souls of families across the country. The actual figures are probably much higher, given the widespread underreporting of such crimes. In the Western Cape, the province with the highest incidence, many of the problems are alcohol and drug related in communities with few resources and whose social capital is in shreds.

Children are at risk of abuse in authoritarian societies where adults take out their frustrations on the most vulnerable among them. Recognising the importance of the family as the foundation of any society has to be accompanied by active measures to identify those most vulnerable and provide urgent psychological and material support to stabilise them. Protection of women and children needs to be at the heart of such interventions. Men should not be neglected and further alienated in the process, but the safety of vulnerable children has to be paramount whilst remedial action is taken to help those wanting to change destructive life styles. We are not investing enough in providing adequate social-work support to troubled families.

The school is another site of struggle with the authoritarian ghost. Many of our teachers are products of authoritarian homes as well as authoritarian schools. Many are also graduates of higher-education institutions where brutal initiation programmes shaped their entry into academia. Even elite private schools carry the stamp of the authoritarian cultures that go back to their founding. Neither the governing bodies of schools nor the provincial and national education authorities appear to recognise the urgency and the level of support needed to help teachers create a more enabling educational setting.

The laudable step of outlawing corporal punishment in schools needs to be accompanied by initiatives in the school system to transform its authoritarian culture to one of respect and trust. Such initiatives should include learning how to manage and resolve conflict without resorting to violence and humiliation. Teachers should also be assisted to confront their own development deficits as products of an authoritarian society. Transforming school culture is a prerequisite for a high-performance teaching and learning platform across our nation.

Given the lack of transformative interventions such as those suggested above, it not surprising that authoritarianism continues to permeate all levels of our society. It expresses itself in hierarchical social relationships, high-handed leadership styles, intolerance of alternative viewpoints, and disrespectful treatment of the most vulnerable members of our society. Hierarchical relationships are defined by seniority in terms of the positions people occupy as well as by age. Despite public statements about the role that young people have played in the liberation struggle, those in authority tend to be dismissive of young people's capacity to add value to decision-making.

Political parties across the spectrum fare no better. Young women are most at risk of being discounted, given the dynamic interplay between sexism and authoritarianism that defines leadership as the prerogative of adult males. One needs to look no further than the ANC Youth League to see how marginal young women are to its leadership, programmes and priorities. One would be forgiven for assuming that the ANC Youth League is an exclusive young men's organisation. I have not once seen or heard of a woman leader of the ANC Youth League in the thirteen years of our democracy.

Authoritarianism permeates all political parties and frames relationships in the public sector. The characteristics of this culture are hierarchies that privilege leaders as the source of ideas and initiatives; rewards for loyalty to the party line rather than for encouraging vigorous debate within the party; and the predominance of the seniority principle when it comes to attaching weight to different views within institutions. In our political culture, party loyalty trumps loyalty to the state and the citizens it is meant to serve. The privileging of party loyalty over civic duty undermines civic-mindedness and responsiveness to fellow citizens and is at variance with the desired egalitarian democratic culture.

Authoritarianism also frames government-citizen relationships. Our political culture is characterised by acceptance of the view that government leads and the people follow rather than that of government serving the public within an agreed national framework. The enormity of the transformation challenges at the political and socioeconomic levels has put the government under pressure to deliver on its promises. This has in some cases led to impatience with consultative processes that are seen as delaying urgently needed programmes.

There are limits to consultative decision-making in any setting otherwise there is a risk of paralysis. In the best of worlds it is difficult to reach full consensus about turn-around strategies, but many critics argue that more effort could have been made to reach sufficient consensus on the new macro-economic framework now known as the Growth, Employment and Redistribution Strategy (Gear). The assumption that the public would not have been able to understand the need to change gear from old-fashioned public-sector-driven economic development to a more liberalised model with sufficient safety nets is indicative of a lack of faith in the capacity of citizens to engage with policy choices.

Such a lack of faith within the Tripartite Alliance between the ruling ANC, the SACP and the trade-union federation Cosatu may well have been justified in light of how the trade unions have conducted themselves over the last decade or so. Take the reluctance of the South African Democratic Teachers Union (Sadtu) to negotiate agreements to implement incentive-based pay that could help the teaching profession to attract and retain mathematics, science and other highly valued skills. The logic is that differentiation is necessarily bad for solidarity within the union. Tensions within the Tripartite Alliance are likely to continue to reverberate in our politics for the foreseeable future and undermine the emergence of a respectful political culture.

The public service is also framed within the same authoritarian political culture. Seniority is linked to both position and age in rather rigid terms. It is quite unnerving to see how easily the new elites have embraced the bureaucratic culture they inherited from apartheid. The pecking order is defined not just in terms of decision-making but other markers of power and status such as office size, type of car, and support staff. Top officials vigorously defend their turf even when collaborative efforts would deliver higher-quality outcomes for service delivery.

The poor quality of public services reflects our failure to confront the legacy of disrespectful public-service approaches under apartheid. Public servants in all departments across all levels of government should be assisted to confront their authoritarian heritage from their homes, schools, communities and activist experiences. It is not enough to say *Batho Pele* (people first) and assume that public officials would translate that into day-to-day conduct as they serve the public. The pressures of delivering service with little experience and, in some cases, inadequate training, bring out the worst in people.

Good intentions are not enough. An empowering set of transformative initiatives to change the culture of public service is needed across all sectors: nurses, teachers, police, clerks, and other senior personnel. Authoritarianism should be confronted systematically and be rooted out of our social framework. We need to recapture the civic-mindedness that characterised those who served their people under the tough apartheid conditions, yet managed to produce excellent results. Examples should be held up for younger generations to learn from: teachers such as the mathematics enthusiast Thamsanqa Khambule, social workers such as Ellen Khuzwayo and nurses such as Albertina Sisulu.

Much has been made of *ubuntu* as a uniquely African ethos hinging on the acute consciousness of the interconnectedness and interdependence of human beings as a basis for the *Batho Pele* approach to

public service. This ethos reflects the reality that we are human because others recognise us as such. The reference point of our own
humanity is the humanity of others. The claim to the uniqueness of
this ethos in human history can be easily challenged. Other cultures
over the ages have come to the same conclusion. The nomenclature
may be different but the essence is the same. What we have to be proud
of is that Africa has from time immemorial embedded this notion in
the conduct of social relationships. It is our heritage that we should
bring to life in our society.

It is hard to recognise any reflection of *ubuntu* in some areas of the
public service where one is confronted with the abuse of power by
officials, from the most junior to seniors. Of particular concern is the
callous disrespect shown by some to the most vulnerable citizens: the
elderly, the disabled and children. It should be easier for our government to insist on all officials living up to this widely recognised principle of treating others as one would like to be treated.

One of the manifestations of authoritarian political culture is the
ambivalence towards civil society on the part of many members of our
government. There seems to be a view that the government has to be
seen to be in control. This ignores the complexity of the challenges
of transformation which no single party, however powerful, can
address on its own. Recognition of the importance of tripartite cooperation between government, labour and the private sector resulted
in the establishment of the National Economic, Development and
Labour Council (Nedlac) as a negotiating forum to tackle all major
economic policy issues. Yet today Nedlac has become marginal to
policy-making.

The control focus in government was particularly pronounced in
the early stages of the post-apartheid era when the new elites felt
anxious to establish their authority over the state. There was a systematic demobilisation of the massive NGO infrastructure in order to
make room for the government to exercise state power and entrench
itself. Replacing funding support for independent NGOs with the
centrally controlled National Development Agency (NDA) came at a
huge cost to implementation capacity that had been built over the

years of struggle for freedom from the 1970s to 1994. The scandal-prone NDA has added little to help the government implement its laudable policies on the ground.

The same control impulse demobilised a huge intellectual-capital base in the Independent Development Trust (IDT)[75] that could have made the Reconstruction and Development Programme (RDP) run like a well-oiled machine. Pushing out the top management that had expertise in many sectors was unwise. Accumulated experience over the five years of IDT operations involving planning and implementing nationwide projects in education, health, low-income housing, water-resources management and financing for development was lost. Party loyalists with little development expertise were put in positions beyond their level of competence, with predictable outcomes. The cost of delayed social development is ultimately borne by poor people in whose name control is exercised.

At the centre of the development model of the IDT and most NGOs that honed their skills in the 1970-1994 period was the belief in self-reliance. Self-reliance was one of the principles of psychological liberation advocated by Black Consciousness as a prerequisite to enabling black people to become active agents of history. The self-doubt, dependency and sense of worthlessness that had paralysed people during the period of brutal repression after the banning of the ANC and the PAC in the 1960s had to be rooted out by projects that engaged people as agents of their own development.

The amazing energy that was unleashed in rural and urban areas as poor people became part of the solution to their problems contributed in no small measure to the self-confidence to take on the mighty apartheid system. People built their own homes with the help of subsidies in the site-and-service programmes that were run across the country. Schools were built and revitalised, and protected from vandalism by proud communities. Clinics, vegetable gardens and hospital upgrades were all part of community-development efforts.

The unintended consequence of the demobilisation of community-based and non-governmental organisations in the quest for control by the new government has been the re-creation of a dependency culture and an entitlement mentality. The RDP approach to building homes, clinics, schools and other public amenities has backfired. There is a crisis of expectations, created by the legacy of neglect, exacerbated by the election promises that were made but not kept.

We should revisit the development model we have used thus far and re-establish a culture of self-reliance and pride. The government's role should be one of creating an enabling environment for citizens to engage in their own development and that of their communities. Such an approach would go a long way to breaking the current impasse between demands for services by poor communities and the government's lack of capacity to meet these demands. Importantly, facilities built by and with the cooperation of communities are more likely to be protected from vandalism because of a greater sense of ownership.

Authoritarianism in our society has taken on some comical aspects. Comrades in the struggle who were proud of being on first-name terms have become quite particular about titles. The use of Doctor for recipients of honorary degrees is most striking. Conventional practice is that only medical doctors or those who have earned an academic doctorate are entitled to refer to themselves as Doctor. In the pre-1994 era, only a notable few used their honorary degrees to assume the Doctor title; today many do. The authoritarian nature of our political culture is showing in a most embarrassing way in this addiction to titles.

The private sector is also marked by hierarchical structures that stand in the way of efficiency and innovation. Decades of white-male dominance has left many private-sector leaders unable to conceive of a scenario where someone who does not look like them is in a top position. The unwritten rule of the private-sector hierarchy is white males at the top of the pyramid, a growing sprinkling of black males, white women, and then black women at the bottom. Age also matters in the private-sector hierarchy. Younger leaders are often held back while older men stay at the top beyond their prime. Transformation in the private sector is weighed down by a failure to embed meritocracy into the system.

This is also reflected in decades of failure to invest in a wider pool of talent, which has robbed our economy of the creative impulses that come from the richness of diversity. Competitive pressures are compelling more and more companies to abandon authoritarian management styles. The global knowledge economy is also forcing many old-style leaders to yield to younger, more nimble people who are open to innovation. Yet the authoritarian pecking order lurks underneath.

Common to all the stubborn ghosts we have explored - racism, sexism, ethnic chauvinism, and authoritarianism - is a notion of power as finite. Other people are seen as competitors for this scarce and limited resource. Such an understanding of power leads to intolerance of people with different views.

This notion of power is predicated on the idea of 'power as a right to do what one wants' rather than 'power as capacity to act'. Power as 'right' is an entitlement that excludes others. It is more about control of others than about enabling participatory decision-making. Such an approach to power requires a hierarchy to allocate rights in accordance with its logic. The logic of the pecking order frames social relationships and access to resources on an 'us and them' basis. Racism, sexism, ethnicity and authoritarianism are used to define who has a right to resources. It is not surprising that thirteen years after the formal end of apartheid, South Africans still see themselves in terms of 'us and them'.

Power understood as capacity to act is limitless. In fact, the more citizens have the capacity to act, the more power society would have to tackle its challenges. A democracy built on the values informed by power as the capacity to act would be one where empowerment becomes the outcome of each human interaction: at home, at school, at work and in government's relationships with citizens. One would see children nurtured in homes where their potential is explored enabling them to become the best they can be. Schools would become platforms for intellectual and personal development and the wider community would provide an enabling environment for citizens to add value to society.

Understanding power as 'capacity' shifts us from the need to compete for a limited resource to a focus on creating an enabling environment for all. This understanding of power as capacity lies at the heart of Amartya Sen's notion of development as freedom.[76] The capacity of individuals to add value to their own lives, to their families, their communities and the larger society is a measure of development. Such enabled persons become agents of their own destiny, free to exercise choice and to participate in the society for the greater good.

The combination of the legacy of racism, ethnicity, sexism and authoritarianism makes establishing a democratic culture reflecting the values of our national constitution hard work. We have grossly underestimated the efforts required. We shall return to the challenges of consolidating democracy in the next chapter.

PART THREE

Ready to
govern?

CHAPTER 8

Challenges of citizenship

POST-APARTHEID SOUTH AFRICA ASPIRES TO A VALUE SYSTEM THAT IS reflected in its national constitution, inspired by the United Nation's 1948 Universal Declaration of Human Rights. Our constitution also embraces the view of the ANC's 1955 Freedom Charter that 'the people shall govern'. This aspiration provides the young democracy with a compelling vision:

We, the people of South Africa,
Recognise the injustices of our past;
Honour those who suffered for justice and freedom in our land;
Respect those who have worked to build and develop our country; and
Believe that South Africa belongs to all who live in it, united in our diversity.
We therefore, through our freely elected representatives, adopt this Constitution as the supreme law of the Republic so as to –
Heal the divisions of the past and establish a society based on democratic values, social justice and fundamental human rights;
Lay the foundations for a democratic and open society in which government is based on the will of the people and every citizen is equally protected by law;
Improve the quality of life of all citizens and free the potential of each person; and

Build a united and democratic South Africa able to take its rightful place as a sovereign state in the family of nations.

The themes highlighted in this preamble to our constitution affirm our commitment to democratic practice, the promotion of human rights, and the ordinary person's role in active citizenship, expressed through the verbs 'recognise', 'honour', 'respect', 'believe', 'heal', 'improve' and 'build'.

But major dilemmas arise from the gap between the rights and responsibilities of citizens as envisaged in the constitution, and their capacity to assume their new status. Different sectors of the population face different challenges in the transformation they have to undergo to be able to take up their appropriate roles as participants in the democracy.

For previously disenfranchised people actively or passively opposed to apartheid, the dilemmas relate to owning the freedom they have won and acting as responsible citizens. For those who were active participants in a system that privileged them as citizens while denying the rights of the majority, it is about adapting to a shared citizenship with a value system that promotes equality before the law.

All South Africans are newcomers to citizenship of an inclusive democracy in their own country. It is important to establish what is understood by citizenship in a democracy if we are to rise to the challenge of assuming our responsibilities. Common to a variety of definitions[77] of citizenship is the reciprocal relationship between rights and duties.

In a democracy, these rights accrue to individuals as civil rights, which include equality before the law, liberty of person, and freedom of speech, thought and faith. There are also political rights (to take part in elections and serve on political bodies) and social rights (the right to social and economic welfare, to share in social heritage, and the provision of public institutions such as courts, political bodies and social services). Citizens must discharge their duties to the common good through allegiance to the state in return for protection of their rights by the state.

An example of citizenship (*burgherskap*) is the evolution of landownership under the Dutch colonial regime. The *Vereenigde Oostindische Compagnie* (VOC) released company workers and allocated land to them for farming, to make more produce available for the company's refreshment station. This first occurred in 1657, and these farmers were called free burghers. They accepted the duties of *burgherskap* in return for its benefits, seeing themselves as guardians of the land they were allowed to occupy.

Their descendants in the Cape Colony, including the Boers who later migrated north in search of greener pastures, honoured this understanding of citizenship. They sustained the livelihoods of those who depended on them, and ensured that future generations would continue to enjoy the rights and privileges. The irony of *burgherskap* arising out of dispossessing others of citizenship, however, seems to have escaped them.

Citizenship as stewardship in the post-apartheid era starts with taking ownership of the gift of freedom from those whose sacrifices made freedom possible for all South Africans. Stewardship has been defined as 'the mantle under which operate all progressive causes: human rights, conservation, economic welfare, government reform and oversight, education, health care, disaster relief, animal welfare, mental health and peace'.[78] Citizenship as stewardship seen in this way conforms to the obligations (values, rights, ideals, way of life, laws) that South Africans, their government and institutions of democracy have committed themselves to uphold.

In Aaron Sorkin's film *The American President*, the fictional US president Andrew Shepard says:

> You want to claim this land as the land of the free? The symbol of your country cannot just be a flag. The symbol also has to be of its citizen exercising his right to burn the flag in protest. Now show me that, defend that, celebrate that, in your classrooms. Then you can sing about the land of the free.

Sorkin's film explores the difficulties the USA faced in defining citizenship beyond the symbolism of unity after the Civil War. The challenge facing our young democracy is for its citizens to go beyond the symbols of citizenship, be they the flag or national anthem, to defending our core constitutional values.

For example, how willing are South Africans to defend the right of fellow citizens who question the abuse of state power that threatens the basic rights of some citizens or their socio-economic welfare? Why were South African citizens silent for so long while the government undermined the rights of poor citizens to access comprehensive HIV/Aids treatment that would have reduced fatalities? What about our inaction in the face of our national epidemic of abuse of women and children? Have we as citizens gone beyond singing about the beloved country to defending its values? Civic-mindedness means we have to go beyond doing no harm to doing good.

We have a long way to go, as illustrated by the 2006 security guards' strike, in the course of which 69 non-striking guards were killed. As the *Sunday Independent*[79] put it:

[N]o one has been convicted in connection with any of the deaths of the 69 security guards who were murdered throughout the country during the security guards' strike.

They died like animals because many of their names are simply not known. Police and security companies could not or would not give the names of the victims' families and the Security Industry Employees' Provident Fund did not want to do so due to 'reasons of privacy' or – said Kevin Derrick, the chairman of the Fund – 'it's not even certain that some of the victims were properly on the books of the companies for which they were working. They might have been temps.'

Many died in the killing fields of the network of railway lines that connect Pretoria and the East and West Rand with Johannesburg. They were flung from trains. But many were also shot or severely assaulted, and it happened in Durban and Cape Town as well as on the Reef.

Neither the office of Charles Nqakula, the Minister of Safety and Security, nor any provincial police spokespeople could give details on what had happened to the murder investigations. They were also unable to give details of any court cases or appearances.

Some elements in this strike and its aftermath highlight the failure of the state and its citizens to protect the rights of those most vulnerable. The rights of the victims of this strike to life, livelihoods, dignity and family life were extinguished by the violent actions of their fellow security guards and inaction on the part of many citizens. First, the security industry paid pitiful wages and must take responsibility for what happened.[80] The right to work for a decent reward was violated by its exploitative practices. The demands of the South African Transport and Allied Workers Union (Satawu) indicated a need for major reforms of the security industry to strike a better balance between the rights of workers and those of firms.

Second, regulators failed to question and enforce reform of the industry's practices within the framework of the law, permitting exploitation to continue.

Third, the labour-relations machinery failed the workers by letting the situation deteriorate into a protracted strike that led to increasing desperation on the part of its leaders.

Fourth, Satawu must accept responsibility for failing to protect the rights of workers who elected not to strike. The brutality of the actions against non-striking workers made a mockery of the claim that trade unions are committed to protecting workers' rights. Those rights should not be conditional on following the leaders' injunction to strike. The right not to strike, like the right to burn the flag, is an inherent right that comes with freedom.

Fifth, the law-enforcement process failed to protect the strike victims' rights. Whether the police have been unable or unwilling to track down the perpetrators, no one has yet been brought to book. Responding to enquiries by the media, the Minister of Safety and Security's spokesperson, Hangwani Mulaudzi, said: 'Following the strike all dockets were taken to individual police stations. At least eleven suspects were arrested in Gauteng. All investigations were handled provincially. There is no reason for the Minister to intervene as police are progressing well in their investigations.' Confronted with information that none of the provincial police contacted knew of any ongoing investigations or charges laid, Mulaudzi remained unfazed: 'According to our knowledge, everything is above board to [bring] those involved to face the music. Hence I am reiterating . . . that everything is progressing well.'[81] The duty to protect citizens has not been discharged by the Minister and his team.

Finally, those victims' rights continue to be violated as a result of our silence as citizens. We have chosen to be silent about the exploitative practices of the security industry that protects our homes, workplaces and businesses. Satawu's general secretary need not fear being held accountable for acts of intimidation by striking workers he organised because citizens who witnessed the crimes have chosen silence. We have also chosen to be silent in the face of the failure of the police and the Minister of Safety and Security to discharge their responsibilities to protect innocent people and uphold the law. Our silence is creating a culture of impunity in which criminals go free and innocent people's rights are violated.

South Africa has traditionally exhibited different understandings of citizenship. Two main variants of citizenship dominated our pre-1994 landscape: republican and liberal. Republican citizenship emphasises self-governance and active participation in the affairs of state as a sacred duty. Many adherents of this view either defended or actively opposed the injustices of apartheid. Liberal citizenship, on the other hand, emphasises individual rights and government responsibility for the welfare and rights of citizens. In this view, the responsibilities and obligations of the individual citizen stop at payment of taxes, after which each individual is free to pursue his or her personal interests.

During the long struggle for freedom, many white South Africans took the liberal view of citizenship to the extreme by becoming 'free-riders'. They were passive beneficiaries of a system that protected their material interests, while pleading powerlessness to influence the direction society was taking. Lamenting the opportunity costs of apartheid from the safety of their dinner-tables, they were unwilling to stand up and be counted in public debates.

Many captains of industry fell into this category. They did not even push the boundaries in the running of their businesses, where they could have made a difference. For example, there was no law prohibiting investment in the education and training of workers except in the formal apprenticeship system, yet few companies invested in upgrading work-ers' skills. That we still have illiteracy among people who have been in formal employment for decades speaks volumes.

This extreme form of liberal citizenship poses a danger to our young democracy, as illustrated by the silence of citizens during the security guards' strike. Many white citizens are guilty of being free-riders, as afraid of speaking out now as they were in the apartheid era. The argu-ments for silence have changed, but the substance is the same. People often say: 'As a white person, I can't be critical of government policy for fear of being called a racist.' Such a position assumes classes of citizen-ship defined by colour. They are denying themselves a voice in the life of their own society and allowing themselves to be defined by racist for-mulations in post-apartheid South Africa.

Both black and white South Africans need to learn how to be citizens of a democracy. Black people, previously excluded from citizenship rights, face a particularly challenging task. How does one exercise a role one is unfamiliar with? Should there be a process of enabling 'the people to govern', or will it happen on its own as people try and err? We need to critically evaluate the performance of our democracy thus far against the stewardship role that was accepted freely in the new democratic order.

Ownership of our democracy entails asserting rights guaranteed to all citizens and discharging the reciprocal responsibilities embedded in the Bill of Rights. But systematic education for democracy is needed to en-sure that the commitments we made in our constitution are familiar to all citizens and used to guide interactions between the state and citizens.

Social scientist Ivor Chipkin challenges us with his definition of citi-zenship in his book *Do South Africans Exist?*

> . . . the citizen is such when called upon to act socially in the public domain; in other words, the public space is a domain of normative action . . . the conditions of the public domain are twofold: firstly, a set of institutions and practices that allow for social interests to be expressed politically; and secondly, a politi-cal space that captures and holds persons to social, i.e. ethical standards of behaviour.[82]

The redefined public domain in our country demands that we express our social interests in accordance with the ethical standards to which we have committed ourselves. We have established the institutions that allow social interests to be expressed politically, but we have yet to embed the practices that are rooted in a democratic culture that holds each of us to standards of appropriate behaviour.

Chipkin suggests that the emergence of the citizen as subject occurs when he or she says: 'Yes, I really am a citizen. I have the same rights and responsibilities as those around me and I will respect them as citizens like me.'[83] Encounters between citizens in which their equality and solidarity are enacted happen in both ritual settings and everyday practical acts. Our history offers many examples. But the legacy of negative encounters holds us back from embedding respect for fellow citizens and sharing the deep solidarity essential to a functional democracy.

The struggle for freedom has left many citizens with highly developed activist skills honed in campaigns to mobilise 'people's power' to challenge the apartheid state. Commitments were made in UDF documents to inculcating 'discipline', 'commitment' and 'comradely' behaviour to pave the way for the 'ethical' citizen, and many activists' civic-mindedness remains exemplary in the post-apartheid era. For others, however, activism focused on opposing what was wrong rather than on setting the foundations for a value-based society. Moving from negative opposition to constructive criticism is proving difficult.

Ironically, negative opposition re-enacts the tactics used during anti-apartheid activism to make the country ungovernable. Civil disobedience, destruction of property and enforcing solidarity action all put the apartheid system under pressure. Those considered collaborators were ruthlessly dealt with, culminating in the horrors of necklace murders. Violent settlement of scores became a vicious circle. It is unnerving to see images of violent protests today that evoke memories of that era. Ownership of the democracy has not yet occurred for many of those destroying the few public resources they have in the desperate hope that their own government would pay greater attention to their views and needs.

Of relevance here is the legacy of violence and its impact on social relationships. Amilcar Cabral, Guinea–Bissau's liberation leader, warned about what he termed 'infections of violence', saying that the tolerance of violence that may result from armed liberation struggles could spread into the post-colonial period.[84] There are too many examples of former liberation leaders who show all the signs of 'infections of violence'. Once in power, some have turned the state's machinery of war against their own people. Examples include Liberia, Nigeria under military rule, and Zimbabwe over the last decade.

In the mid-1980s, Desmond Tutu condemned the increasing use of coercive violence against perceived collaborators and necklace murders in particular, and warned of the long-term impact. We are seeing some of the chickens of that wanton brutality coming home to roost in the growing use of extreme violence to settle disputes at many levels in our communities.

South Africans are also struggling with the legacy of disrespect for the law. Apartheid criminalised normal behaviour, such as the desire of families to live together in urban areas. African women and children were arrested for exercising their right to family life. Who would respect such a legal system? Law-enforcement agents themselves acted in a criminal way in defence of 'national security', as reported to the TRC, discrediting the police in the eyes of ordinary people.

The dilemma now is how to instill respect for the law and trust in the police in the face of the many reported cases of ongoing police brutality and corruption. This is complicated by the growing desperation of un-employed young people, some of them former activists, who resent being marginalised in the economy. Freedom for them has yet to deliver the promised fruits.

The mismatch between jobs being created in the 21st-century know-ledge economy and the lack of skills among many young people has cre-ated a crisis. Many bright youngsters are unemployable except in the lowest levels of the economy. The majority are unskilled, yet have higher expectations from the job market than is possible. Many are angry. The struggle cry of 'Freedom now, education later' has come back to haunt them: freedom without education is proving to be a nightmare. Many of these angry young people are in car-hijacking rings and other organised crime syndicates.[85] Perpetrators of these crimes have nothing to lose in a society that in their day-to-day life has failed them.

Violence is communication by other means. It signals a breakdown in relationships. Communication skills are essential to democratic discourse, but the legacy of the past has left us ill-prepared for effective communication. Many young South Africans grew up in a political culture characterised by violent standoffs. Debate and transparency were also hampered by security considerations. For many rank-and-file activists the war chant and dance of the toyi-toyi became a weapon to intimidate opponents.

Although democracy acknowledges the voices of all citizens, the degree to which each citizen is heard still depends on socio-economic status. Our authoritarian culture continues to silence the voices of those at the bottom of the hierarchy. Unsurprisingly, some take to the streets to demand to be heard. The nature of the struggle to make South Africa ungovernable nurtured anarchist, anti-authority, non-transparent and short-term strategies that are antithetical to good governance. Unlearning those survival skills remains a challenge.

Institution building requires tolerance for different viewpoints. Our political practice has yet to reach the level of maturity that nurtures debate and mutual respect even when dealing with those holding different viewpoints. There is still too much insecurity within the political process to allow the free flowering of ideas. Citizens are still unsure about the boundary between patriotism and disloyalty. Bottled-up emotion tends to spill out as public violence.

The dispute about the township of Khutsong being reassigned to the North West Province from Gauteng demonstrates how much work must still go into shifting gear from the politics of destructive protest to those of ownership of our democracy. Khutsong residents, angry at the government's decision, have made their township ungovernable in the old anti-apartheid way: burning councillors' houses, closing schools, destroying public property, burning tyres and setting up blockades. The government has thus far been unable to respond to this anger in a creative way.

In contrast, residents of Matatiele, who have always fallen between the provinces of KwaZulu-Natal and the Eastern Cape, have chosen to challenge their incorporation into the Eastern Cape Province through dialogue and court action. They have acted as citizens entitled to be heard and to seek a settlement of the dispute in a less confrontational manner. They are more likely to gain support from others because of their dignified manner. At the heart of the different responses is the quality of leadership and the choices leaders help residents to make.

Helping young people develop communication skills to enable them to assert their rights as citizens is key to consolidating our democracy. An essential part of such skills is listening. One cannot listen while chanting and dancing. Not enough is being done yet to focus on essential skills development. Re-channeling anger into creative energy is also important. Many activists grew up in violent environments, learning to settle scores violently. The blurring of the line between criminality and activism has left many young people confused about what is right and what is wrong.

As a former activist, I am conscious of the learning process involved. My journey was made easier by the nature of my professional background. A medical practitioner has to respect rules and practise modern management techniques to run institutions. Moving into academia in the 1980s helped me to moderate my activist tone further. I learned to discipline my arguments and listen to other views. But still the basic activist instincts remain: to question, to challenge conventional wisdom, and to take risks.

These activist instincts can be valuable assets in building a more innovative and dynamic citizenship. Questioning is vital to keep those in authority on their toes. Challenging authority and conventional wisdom is important. Leaders perform better if they anticipate having to justify their policies and actions to those whom they represent. Passivity invites arrogance from leadership.

But these traits can also turn into obstacles to progress. Questioning that does not end in accepting that one might not necessarily be right can paralyse public policy and implementation. Challenging authority even when all the issues have been aired and agreed can also be counterproductive. For example, student politics in the heady mid-1990s often degenerated into anti-authority action that paralysed higher-education institutions. Arguments lost at negotiation tables were restated in disruptive protests that undermined the purposes of scholarship and the pursuit of excellence in education.

Those who have come late to activism face the greatest challenges in adapting to responsible citizenship. Many of today's young generation of trade unionists, especially teachers, caught the tail end of the activist wave. Some new activists sound and act more radical than those of our generation who value the freedom so many of our colleagues died for. Many of today's activists seem to take freedom for granted without recognising its responsibilities, such as the need to guard it jealously and defend the rights of others with whom they may disagree.

Between 1994 and 2000 many teachers took to the streets at the slightest sign of disagreement with education authorities. 'Chalk-downs' became a way of delaying or stopping reforms. For example, resistance against the re-introduction of supervision as part of performance management is motivated by the fear of being held accountable. The continued underperformance of our education system results partly from the deep-seated negative attitudes among teachers who refuse to be held accountable. Their disruptive actions undermine the right to education by poor pupils who have few choices.

The 2007 strike by public-service workers also demonstrates how far we still have to go. Each of the parties – government, strikers and the police – can benefit from self-reflection.

The government could have been more proactive in restructuring conditions of service over the last thirteen years as it became clear that there was a growing gap between the salaries of different classes of public servants. A cursory look at the haemorrhaging of professional nurses and teachers of mathematics, science and English from our country should have warned of the unsustainability of our public service. Attaching higher value to the professional work of nurses, teachers, social workers, doctors and other health and educational workers would have prompted early intervention. Ensuring satisfactory conditions of service for essential workers on whom the delivery of socio-economic rights depends is a central part of good governance.

Furthermore, the conduct of striking professionals left much to be desired. No level of anger against the government can justify the abuse of the rights of others. Denying the right of those teachers who elected not to strike, as well as the right of children to learn, is reminiscent of the 'Freedom now, education later' strategy that has left us with a generation of unskilled young people. Denying sick patients life-saving treatment is criminal by any standard. What right do strikers have to put sick poor people's lives at risk to press their own demands for better conditions of service?

Violent coercion of non-striking professionals reared its ugly head. In one case, a woman teacher in a Johannesburg school was whipped by male teachers for 'failing to listen'! What kind of free society is it that gives permission to some to physically violate the rights of others in order to assert theirs?

Policing methods also came under the spotlight again. The right to public protest and their role in protecting both protesters and non-participants seems foreign to many law-enforcement agents. They have neither the experience nor the training to act appropriately in such situations. Crowd-control methods that do not rely on brutal force must be introduced to all those in the front line of conflicts between citizens. Law-enforcement officers must act in an exemplary manner to win public trust. Unfortunately, the model of policing our law-enforcement officers know well is to use physical violence to assert authority. Meeting violence with violence simply takes us down a spiral of public violence.

We need radical change in our value system in order to align practical action with our democratic commitments. This can be achieved through civic education that nurtures the roots of civic-mindedness and equips people with the knowledge and skills necessary to active citizenship.

Our democracy will be judged by the quality of life of the least among citizens. As stewards of this democracy we all need to share responsibility for promoting the greatest good for the largest number of people. Enabling citizens to contribute actively to the common good beyond the minimalist liberal citizenship levels is essential; the state alone cannot succeed in tackling the legacy problems we face at so many levels. We need social movements, involving youth in public service; we need philanthropic ventures and trans-generational support networks to help realise the potential of each citizen to contribute positively to society.

A good place to start is by including an abridged version of our national constitution among the school books issued to each pupil each year. Civic education should also be incorporated in the Life Skills Programme that is already part of our school curriculum, but treated as a free period in many schools. Civic education could become a joint learning programme for both teachers and pupils and could promote a culture of debate on civic matters.

As part of civic education, we need to redefine patriotism and loyalty to the state to enable citizens to distinguish between constructive critical comment and treasonable utterances. The legacies of both struggle-era activism and the repressive apartheid state have distorted our understanding of loyalty. Both demanded absolute loyalty and solidarity within the in-group.

For the apartheid state, state security as defined by the dominant party, justified the violation of individual rights. For example, state security was cited as the reason why, as a banned person, I was not entitled to know why I was designated 'a communist' under the then Suppression of Communism Act of 1950. My right to information was trumped by the security considerations of the state.

Within the ranks of anti-apartheid struggle activists, loyalty was elevated to a creed. The party line was stringently enforced to promote coherence in a fragile movement under constant threat from a brutal state system. Debate about different options was stifled. In the liberation movement in exile, security considerations were paramount. Disagreements over strategy and tactics frequently raised suspicion about the trustworthiness of those asking questions. One tended to follow the line that leaders regarded as appropriate for fear of being seen as disloyal.

Both the anti-apartheid struggle and the apartheid state bred a tendency of intolerance of critical comment. The apartheid experiment was at such odds with the flow of history that zealotry was required to live with it and promote its agenda. Any attempt to question its sustainability was seen to be strengthening the hand of state enemies. The apartheid state was also over-sensitive to critical comment from inside our national borders, partly because it felt the pressure of external criticism from a growing body of international opinion. Labelling any critical comment as 'communist inspired' silenced many who did not want to be associated with communism. Even within the National Party, criticism of public policy was regarded as betrayal, leading to the silence or withdrawal of those holding different viewpoints.

The notion of 'respect' also needs to be interrogated more. The authoritarian strands in our heritage put leaders on too high a pedestal for citizens to feel comfortable about questioning them on important public-policy issues. Questioning leaders is seen as disrespectful in the same way that for many South Africans older than thirty-five years questioning their parents was out of the question.

Many of our political leaders were socialised in a culture that reveres leaders. Party loyalists continue to shy away from raising questions about policies and strategies that shape decision-making. There is a need for a deliberate reframing of respect so that it does not exclude critical comment, otherwise we run the risk of rage boiling over at inappropriate places and moments.

Discharging our stewardship role in our democracy requires radical inner transformation. Such a process is by its nature psychological and spiritual. It requires a consciousness of the self as an individual within a wider context that encompasses our families, our community, our society and the wider universe. It speaks to a definition of the self and a consciousness of what it means to be fully human. This requires an inner spiritual journey. Our sensitivity to criticism makes us vulnerable. Our tendency to label whatever we disagree with as hostile speaks to the incompleteness of our journey to become fully what we can be. We need to acknowledge the woundedness of our psyche and mindset that comes from the legacy of our past.

We are only thirteen years into the journey towards our envisaged self as a society. South Africa is but a teenager in democracy terms. We like to think of ourselves as one of those child prodigies who are performing ahead of their peers on many fronts. In those areas where we do well we excel, but where we have capacity constraints we struggle to come to terms with our own failures. As in the case of many over-achieving teens, psychological and mental stress is a major risk as we wrestle with the challenges. We have underestimated the challenges of migrating from our divided past towards a united nation.

None of the segments of our population that came together on this journey to South African nationhood has had any experience of citizenship in a democracy on our own home ground. In addition, all citizens have come into this new democracy with deeply fragmented identities, not just relating to race, class, gender, sexual orientation, language and beliefs, but also to political affiliation within and between political parties.

The challenges of identity as a nation are not necessarily related to the multiplicity of fragments, but to the willingness to accept that multiple identities can co-exist with our identity as a united nation. There are still too many instances where 'them' and 'us' are cast in immutable terms. The idea of one single human race is hard to accept for many. There are still both black and white people who deeply believe in irreconcilable differences between black and white people, in essentialist differences that are unbridgeable.

Differences - perceived or real - would not necessarily pose insurmountable difficulties in forging a united nation. What is critically important, however, is acceptance of multiple identities in people with whom we share citizenship of our nation. Such acceptance is widespread among South Africans. What is a challenge is the depth of that acceptance. Acceptance often turns into rejection if opinions on key issues differ.

Another manifestation of our continued wrestling with multiple identities as a nation is the tendency to silence others by labelling them as racist or agents of racists. For example, white people are regarded as great South Africans as long as they do not criticise black people in leadership positions. Even constructive criticism and fair comment on public issues are often dismissed as racist attacks.

There are also dangerous tendencies among some public commentators who deny fellow black people the right to disagree with government policies or to criticise officials in the private and public sectors. There is an unstated assumption that as a black person, one should hold views that are aligned to those of the dominant political establishment. Christine Qunta, deputy chairperson of the board of the South African Broadcasting Corporation (SABC), went as far as stating that black people who criticise a black government are agents of destruction:

Their willingness to be deployed to discredit African people is not only motivated by material gain or flattery. Like black policemen and askaris during apartheid, there seems to be a genuine belief deep within their consciousness of the omnipotence of white power and, conversely, the inherent powerlessness and inferiority of Africans.[86]

There are interesting assumptions here. First is the notion that black critics of the government are unable to act as independent people with views that happen to differ from hers and those of the government. This reflects her own inability to imagine that some black people could have autonomous and diverse views on affairs of their nation without being 'deployed' by white people to express those views. Qunta's statement also reflects a lack of confidence in the intellectual capability of black people to form opinions independent of white people.

Second is the assumption that those in government embody everything that is to be identified with 'African people'. What about black people, African or not, who hold different views and express them in their membership of political parties that are in opposition to the dominant ruling party? Are they not 'African people' too? What about white people who identify themselves as African – are they not 'Africans' if they hold different views from the dominant political party?

Third is an implied understanding of critical comment as condemnation. There does not seem to be room in this view for citizens to express their social interests in the public domain in a manner that might be at variance with the views of political leaders. Qunta's seems to be an all-or-nothing law. It cannot be true that criticism of a majority black government is equivalent to rendering them powerless. Is our government so fragile that it cannot take constructive criticism? Nor should we accept that criticism of a majority black government implies an affirmation of 'white omnipotence'. It is strange logic to equate criticising a black government with praising white power. A majority black government, like any other government in the world, can and will make mistakes. It is the duty of citizens to engage in constructive criticism of their governments to ensure that we learn from mistakes and do not repeat them.

Finally, of greater concern to the values of our nascent democracy is Qunta's suggestion that criticism amounts to treason. The reference to 'askaris' is ominous. Askaris were former liberation-movement operatives who were arrested, tortured and turned into agents of the dreaded intelligence services of the apartheid state. It is dangerous to use such language in our young democracy; we should be encouraging, not discouraging, critical comment on the affairs of state by all citizens. If critical comment becomes synonymous with treason, we weaken the democratic foundations of our society.

We should resist the temptations of classifying people into irreconcilable categories in a country where diversity is our biggest strength. There are black and white people who support our majority black government but are critical of some aspects of its policies. They are as loyal as any other South African. There are also black and white people who never criticise our government but who may be betraying our national constitution through inaction. Support for the government, whether public or silent, is not necessarily a measure of good citizenship. It is the discharging of our stewardship responsibilities as citizens by acting in the public domain to express our social interests that should be a measure of our patriotism and loyalty to our democracy.

Central to active citizenship is the politics of the public interest. Concerns about the quality of politics and the extent to which the promotion of the common good finds expression are reviving public debate in the USA. *Daedalus*, the Journal of the American Academy of Sciences, devoted a whole issue to this topic.[87] Michael Tomasky's approach to the public interest has relevance for us here. He argues that decent forward-looking governance is only possible when citizens are called upon to 'look beyond their own self-interest and work for a greater common interest . . . [T]his idea of citizens sacrificing for and participating in the creation of a common good has a name: civic republicanism.'[88]

South Africans need robustly to debate how we define the public interest, to discuss how all citizens can practise 'civic republicanism'. Apartheid's divisiveness makes the emergence of civic republicanism difficult. We have to invest in civic republicanism by mobilising resources for mass civic education. The quality and consolidation of our democracy depends on how much effort we are prepared to devote to the critical task of enabling citizens to govern in the public interest.

A discussion on the challenges of citizenship would be incomplete without a look at the role of middle-class citizens. There has been much debate about the impact of the growing black middle class on our economy. Estimates by market researchers, including the UCT Graduate School of Business, of the numbers of the so-called 'black diamonds' vary between just under 400 000 and 2,9 million, depending on the definition of what constitutes 'middle class'. Whatever the estimate, there is no doubt that this group is fuelling our economic growth through high levels of consumption of goods and services as its income levels increase. What has not been sufficiently explored is the impact of this group on the quality of our democracy.

There is strong historical evidence of the importance of the middle class in any society in shaping and strengthening democratic systems. Societies with significant middle classes benefit from their tendency to demand better-quality public services and to exercise their rights and hold public officials and political leaders to account. Unlike poor and vulnerable people, middle classes tend to be independent of political patronage. They also usually have higher expectations of their governments and are more likely to demand freedom of expression and respect for human rights.

Post-colonial Africa has suffered from the lack of a significant middle class as a cushion between the new political elites and the large base of poor people. The absence of the voice and professional contributions from this class that could strengthen democracy is a crucial factor in the weakness of many young democracies. Development support by donors has reinforced the marginalisation of the middle class. Most development assistance is government to government and tends to ignore indigenous professionals and nascent private-sector actors in newly independent countries. This marginalisation compounds what is often a numeric minority status of middle classes, given the colonial legacy of under-investment in local human and intellectual capital.

Even in cases where the middle classes are a significant force in post-colonial Africa, they have tended not to exercise their roles as independent political actors. Their identification with post-colonial political leader-ship has often led to their reluctance to express constructive criticism. In addition, many are constrained by being recipients of political patron-age in the form of high-level public-sector jobs or lucrative government contracts. South Africa's black middle class faces additional challenges. The unintended consequences of Black Economic Empowerment (BEE) policies have created disincentives for critical independent voices. Ac-cess to preferential procurement and other BEE benefits is often heavily influenced by public officials who might withhold approval of competitive bids for goods and services from those seen to be too critical of the powers that be. Citizen action in the 'public interest' is trumped by short-term personal interests focusing on maintaining patronage relationships with those in decision-making roles in government.

The quality of our political discourse is undermined by the reticence of many black and white middle-class people. There is fear that any criti-cal comment might be interpreted as disloyalty, but acquiesense in such silencing tactics would be a betrayal of our constitutional ideals. The middle class is a beneficiary of unprecedented prosperity. It has a respon-sibility to assert its rights and to use its strong voice on key public inter-est issues.

We need look no further than Zimbabwe to see just how costly silence by middle classes in the early phase of democracy has been. When atroc-ities against the people of Matebeleland occurred, many did not ask the appropriate questions. When the first land grabs happened, many lauded the move as poetic justice against minority white landownership. By the time Zanu-PF excesses visited them and the country went into free fall, it was too late.

Ibbo Mandaza, one of the Zimbabwean middle-class now living in South Africa, has cautioned us about our post-1994 excitement.[89] He warns against uncritical support for the new political elites, given his own experiences in Zimbabwe. Ugandans, Nigerians, Ghanaians and many others can trade war stories about being let down by politicians. The question history will ask each of us is how active we have been as citizens in raising our voices against actions and words that undermine democracy.

CHAPTER 9

State capacity to govern

SOUTH AFRICA'S TRANSFORMATION COULD NOT HAVE OCCURRED AT a more challenging time. The competitive international environment of the 21st century is not kind to those who cannot compete in the marketplace of skills, ideas, goods, services and positions of power. Even former allied countries and supporters of the anti-apartheid struggle have turned out to be fierce competitors.

Yet it is also important to acknowledge and exploit the opportunities that globalisation presents to our young democracy to leapfrog development stages and become a sustainable and prosperous economy. The key to success in the global knowledge economy is the quality of a country's human-, intellectual- and social-capital base.

State capacity to govern relates to three critical elements: the state's institutional framework, its values framework, and its human and intellectual capacity.

In South Africa's case, the institutional framework is the most developed and is enshrined in our national constitution and the legal and judicial system. We have also elaborated a proportional-representation governance system based on a three-tiered co-governance model between the national, provincial and local levels of government. Innovative institutions established in terms of Chapter 9 of our constitution are intended to act as independent watchdogs to ensure that the founding principles of our democracy are upheld. These institutions provide space for the public and individual citizens to hold public officials to account.

Our values framework is the least developed, despite our acclaimed human-rights-based constitution. There is, however, a rich heritage of value-based conduct in the struggle for freedom that we are not sufficiently drawing on in our public life. Selfless public service by the likes of Nelson Mandela, Oliver Tambo, Walter and Albertina Sisulu, Robert Sobukwe, Stephen Bantu Biko and others provides models for practising a value-based politics.

Václav Havel, former dissident who became president of Czechoslovakia and later of the Czech Republic, gives insight into how ideals of freedom can be lived through 'politics as morality in practice'. He sees politics as selfless service to fellow human beings based on conscience and truth.[90] This echoes Mandela's speech at the Rivonia Trial. Facing a possible death sentence, he said he was committed to living for the ideal of a democratic and free society but also prepared to die for it. 'Politics as morality in practice' resonates with Michael Tomasky's notion of 'civic republicanism' mentioned before.[91]

Our challenge is to recapture the idealism that fired our freedom struggle and to inject it into the daily practice of politics. Such ideals would enable public servants to serve in a manner that is right and just, as measured by the outcomes for the least among us. Adam Wolfson reminds us, 'Government is not simply about securing individual rights and interests but some more substantial and transcendent good.'[92] Transcendent good is the common good that enables all citizens to develop their full potential and contribute to the public interest.

Mahatma Gandhi put it even more eloquently: 'Democracy must in essence, therefore, mean the art and science of mobilising the entire physical, economic and spiritual resources of all the various sections of the people in the service of the common good for all.'[93] Gandhi reminds us of the importance of integrating the spiritual dimension in the practice of politics and economics to enhance the quality of democracy as a system of governance.

Human and intellectual capacity is critical to the practice of politics in the modern globalising world. Yet the human capital to run a modern economy is in short supply in post-1994 South Africa. Skills shortages are both technical and attitudinal. The failure of past governments to invest in educating and training the majority population has left us with severe technical-skills shortages. There are also gaps in professionalism and appropriate attitudes to public service. Years of exclusion from professional jobs and a lack of professional role models in their family or community circles have left an experiential gap in the lives of many people now occupying positions of authority.

In addition, struggle activism was not necessarily a good place for young people to learn how to be professionals. Anti-authority behaviour was essential to challenging the oppressive system successfully, and was widely celebrated. By contrast, respect for rules of conduct, procedures and accountability are at the heart of professionalism. Many of the new political elites in public service have yet to make the transition.

The difficulty of making this transition is compounded by the fact that most black South Africans' experience of the public service during the apartheid era was consistently negative. The stark contrast between the dignified treatment of white citizens, no matter how poor, and disrespect for black people, left a deep impression.

Our state's capacity problems are exacerbated by the choice of a Rolls Royce model of governance. It would have been challenging enough recruiting skilled people to run our public service at the national level. But our decentralised model has to find additional personnel for nine provinces, 47 district municipalities and 231 local municipalities. Each deals with challenging responsibilities to deliver on the promises of freedom for ordinary citizens. Both the legislative and executive functions have to be staffed with competent people. There are also the nine watchdog institutions mandated under Chapter 9 of the constitution, in addition to the Constitutional Court. All must be run by people with technical and political skills to ensure their effectiveness.

There is a saying in my language – *O se ke wa re o bona e hlotsa, wa e nametsa thaba* – one cannot force a limping animal to walk up to the top of a mountain. We seem to have defied all wisdom in going for the toughest policy assignments in the face of weak state capacity.

Post-1948 and post-1994 state capacity compared

Many former activists in positions of power today overestimate the capacity to use state power in the post-apartheid era to meet national goals. Reference is often made to the National Party (NP)'s post-1948 use of state power to meet its objectives. The success of the NP between 1948 and 1994 in getting poor whites, especially Afrikaans speakers, out of poverty remains a notable example of a successful targeted anti-poverty programme. White poverty practically became history. Afrikaans-speaking white South Africans moved from the margins to the centre of society and wielded power in the political, social and economic spheres until 1994.

Often neglected in such discussions is an understanding of the radical difference in complexity between the post-1948 and post-1994 contexts. The former followed World War II, when South Africa enjoyed a special place as a war ally and part of the British Commonwealth, with strong personal and economic ties to Europe. Post-apartheid South Africa had no special position in geopolitical terms. After the collapse of Soviet Union communist hegemony, Africa has become marginal to the strategic interests of the sole super power, the USA, except for Nigeria and Angola as sources of mineral and oil resources.

A second difference is the quality of human capital among white people that had improved significantly after the publication of the report of the Carnegie Commission of Inquiry into the poor-white problem in South Africa in 1932. It had recommended establishing institutions and programmes, and led to anti-poverty initiatives that laid the foundations for better education, health and employment opportunities for poor white people.[94] The State Bureau of Social Welfare was a key instrument in coordinating education, vocational and health programmes to enhance the quality of human and social capital. Universal compulsory education introduced in the 19th century for white children was enforced and expanded. Better public-health services were provided and access was improved. Public-works programmes and other employment opportunities in both the public and private sectors were created and promoted to absorb those on the margins of the economy.

The benefits of free compulsory education over many generations before the NP victory enabled the post-1948 government to deploy a large pool of educated Afrikaners to take the reins of state power. What they lacked in experience of running the country was made up for by the willingness of the majority of white people already in the public service and the private sector to provide support.

The leaders of the post-1948 NP government were unashamed in their pursuit of affirmative action for Afrikaners. The period is captured persuasively in Shaun Johnson's novel *The Native Commissioner.*[95] It describes how a committed English-speaking public servant was driven to depression and suicide by being passed over for promotion and good posts. It was a case of affirmative action that paid scant attention to equity considerations, let alone excellence of performance. Afrikaners felt their time had come to replace English-speaking South Africans, who had dominated the public and private sectors, with their own people.

Affirmative action in a post-1994 democratic society is more complex. Our constitution does not permit unfair discrimination other than for redress purposes to serve the public interest. Affirmative action in the 21st century must also be driven by the realities of the demand of the highly competitive knowledge economy for a skilled public service.

The mismatch between the desire to change the profile of the public service to reflect the diversity of South Africa's people and the legacy of the skills base that overwhelmingly resides in white people creates major dilemmas. Affirmative action is essential to ensure that the fruits of freedom are reflected in the opening up of opportunities for those previously excluded. But affirmative action that sacrifices skills to achieve greater diversity has major implications for the state's capacity to deliver on the promises of freedom. There are real risks that in the quest to empower elites, poor people's rights to public services are being undermined.

There was a stark contrast between the positive response to the first Carnegie report and the NP government's negative response to the Second Carnegie Inquiry into Poverty in 1989. The second report[96] was denounced as mischievous by President P.W. Botha, and largely ignored by the then government that insisted that black people were happy and better off than their counterparts in other parts of Africa. The glaring inequities caused by deliberately dispossessing black people of the means to get themselves out of poverty – land, education, quality health services, employment opportunities – were dismissed.

The third difference between the post-1948 and post-1994 contexts is that poor white people in the post-1948 period were a minority cushioned by a large base of poor disenfranchised black people. According to a review by the Carnegie Corporation of New York in 2004, poor white people, estimated at 300 000 at the time, comprised one third of the total white population in the 1930s.[97] Whatever limited resources the state had could be devoted to this minority and protests from the majority population could be dismissed and brutally suppressed. Job reservation, segregated amenities, discriminatory social services and other affirmative action programmes could be applied with maximum benefit for the targeted minority. The post-1994 government has to contend with much higher expectations from all citizens for fairness and respect for their rights.

The fourth difference is the global economic context after 1994 compared to that after 1948. Closed economies were the order of the day until the 1980s. The post-1948 public sector was enlarged to provide jobs for poor white people without much concern for how the international markets and rating agencies would react. Financial markets were less sophisticated. The South African economy was largely based on primary commodities and heavily reliant on the mining industry. It was one of the world's fastest-growing post-war economies,[98] providing a strong base for expansionary anti-poverty programmes.

The post-1948 government could use agricultural subsidies from the Land Bank and the Agricultural Credit Board to enable white farmers to own land, often without putting personal capital at risk. Many absentee white farmers could farm recklessly in the knowledge that they would be compensated for crop failures. They received nearly R350 million in annual subsidies from these two institutions, and the Land Bank charged negative interest rates for loans until 1990. Towards the end of the apartheid era R3,5 billion in debt was written off to provide debt and drought relief to white farmers.[99] Cheap, practically bonded black labour added to the benefits white commercial farmers enjoyed under apartheid.

The final critical difference is that apartheid created new separate institutions that provided huge employment opportunities for poor white people. These institutions were part of the grand design of separate development in public service: education, health and other social services. As the social engineering advanced, more institutions were added in line with the policy of fragmentation of the black sector of the population along 'population group' and ethnic lines[100]. Each ethnic group was to be developed into an 'independent nation' in its own homeland, thus providing plenty of opportunity for the employment of white officials to 'support and guide these nations'.

At tertiary-education level, separate colleges[101] were set up under a cynically named law, The Extension of Universities Act of 1959. These became known as 'bush colleges' among black people who regarded them as part of the 'separate and unequal' policy in higher-education provision. Many of the academics and administrators at these colleges would not have qualified to compete at the level expected of university staff elsewhere within the system, let alone internationally. For example, the Registrar of the University of the North in 1966 had no higher-education qualification. When challenged, he used to proclaim: *'My vel is my graad.'* ('My skin is my degree').

The contrast between the many opportunities of the closed economy outlined above and the risks and challenges of the global economy could not be greater. The post-1994 democratic government is severely constrained from using state power to redistribute opportunities and benefits. First, the views of international markets on how well a country is run are critical to attract and retain private-sector investments. Second, the size of the public service has to be managed carefully to promote the sustainable budgets essential to macro-economic stability. Third, the challenges of effecting redress for previously disadvantaged groups within a constitutional dispensation that respects the principle of equality and the rule of law are considerable.

Critics of the government's Growth, Employment and Redistribution (Gear) policy and its focus on macro-economic discipline tend to underestimate the quandary that the post-1994 government faced in meeting the needs of redress without undermining long-term economic growth and stability. The discipline imposed by Gear enabled the post-apartheid government to do what analysts suggested could not be done – turn a weak economy into a vibrant one after democratisation. Gear was critical to creating the sustainable resource base for greater investment in human and social capital in the form of education, health and social safety nets.

State institutional and policy framework after 1994

Eradicating poverty remains a stated focus of the post-1994 government. Political freedom without economic justice is widely regarded as untenable in the new democracy. The Poverty and Inequality Report (PIR) of 1997 was the most comprehensive study into poverty since the second Carnegie report.[102] Its recommendations took South Africa's budget and infrastructure constraints and realities into consideration. A committee was formed to take responsibility for the coordination of poverty- and inequality-related activities. It established a system for monitoring the impact of government policy on poverty and inequality reduction that included collection of data and analysis through Statistics South Africa, national household surveys and state expenditure reviews. This report formed the basis for the change in focus of the post-apartheid government's development strategy from the Reconstruction and Development Programme (RDP) to Gear.

The 1994-1996 RDP was directed at ensuring the basic needs of all South Africans were met – job creation, land reform, provision of housing, clean water, electricity, telecommunications, transport, environmental programmes, nutritional programmes, health care and social welfare. Although the RDP set its aims too high and the ambitious promises (e.g. a million houses per year, jobs for all) could not be fulfilled, much was achieved over the first decade of democracy in providing water and electricity, land redistribution, health care, housing and school nutrition programmes.[103]

The development model behind the RDP was that of a paternalistic state delivering political goods to passive citizens, who become loyal and dependent on the state. But it underestimated the capacity of poor people to be agents of their own development. It ignored the strong self-reliance and resourcefulness that had been part of the anti-apartheid struggle. What was needed instead was to create public space for citizens and civic bodies to work with government to ensure the sustainable development of all citizens and communities.

According to some analysts, the motivation behind the RDP approach to development came mainly from trade unions and SACP members of the Tripartite Alliance who saw the RDP as the peaceful route to socialism as envisaged in the National Democratic Revolution.[104] Whatever the motivation, the unintended consequence of a paternalistic state has been demobilisation of communities that had been accustomed to helping themselves with the support of community-based and non-governmental organisations (see Chapter 7). Loss of this capacity has further burdened a state that is experiencing severe capacity problems.

Gear replaced the RDP when it was realised that greater focus on macro-economic stability was essential to sustainable economic growth. One of Gear's key pillars is more efficient state expenditure. Gear has come in for severe criticism, especially from the trade-union federation Cosatu and the SA National Coalition of Non-governmental Organisations (Sangoco). They felt that the post-apartheid state had 'sold out' on its socialist vision as elaborated in the 1955 Freedom Charter. In their view, Gear paid too much attention to the demands of the global capitalist agenda at the expense of providing for the basic needs of poor people.

The government has repeatedly reiterated its commitment to meeting the basic needs of all people. Critics seem to ignore the real achievements over the first ten years of democracy.[105] South Africa has had unprecedented and sustained economic growth over the last decade. The 4,5% average GDP (gross domestic product) growth rates since 2004 have created the fiscal space for sustained investments to promote shared growth promised by the government. Inflation has been tamed, putting more money into the pockets of ordinary citizens. There have been sustained investments in RDP-targeted areas such as housing for poor people (2,3 million as at 2006); potable water (10,8 million of the 13 million total households); access to electricity (9,5 million households out of a total of 13 million); and sanitation (9 million of 13 million total households).

The failures are also notable. Unemployment remains high at 25% in the narrow definition and 37% in the broad one that includes discouraged job seekers. Despite growth in job creation between 2001 and 2006 from 11 million to 12,8 million jobs, prospects remain bleak for the unskilled and those with inappropriate training. Inequality has grown over the last decade or so as the growth process has spawned winners and losers. For those in the poorest 10-20% of the population, social grants have become the only source of income. The increase in social assistance to cover 12 million people on social grants, representing 3,2% of GDP, is a double-edged sword. The potential to entrench dependency with all its negative social consequences is real.

These failures reflect dilemmas that the government has yet to confront. Passive delivery of political goods without enabling citizens to participate meaningfully in their own development undermines sustainable development. It is creating a culture of dependency. Weak state capacity to meet rising expectations effectively is increasingly likely to create a social crisis.

Lessons from Latin America point to the need to link the provision of safety nets, especially child grants, to socio-economic development. Such a link depends largely on designing conditional social grants to provide incentives for recipients to participate in their own personal and family development. An example is *Progressa*, developed in Mexico with World Bank support, and adapted for use by Brazil and Chile.

Child grants in these programmes are tied to mothers getting their children immunised and attending regular under-five health clinics, and satisfactory school attendance. Mothers receive adult basic education and training so they can become employable and productive citizens.

South Africa can benefit from lessons from these programmes to break the growing cycle of dependency. There is mounting evidence that teenagers are deliberately falling pregnant in order to access child grants. There are also abuses of disability grants by local and foreign citizens taking advantage of an inefficient, sometimes corrupt, system.

The most significant failures of delivery on promises by government are in the provision of social services. Much of this is due to the ANC's underestimation of the scale and complexity of social-service provision in the aftermath of apartheid's wanton neglect of the majority. Most ANC leaders who returned from exile in the 1990s were unfamiliar with the strengths and weaknesses of our social services at the time. Public policies adopted by the post-apartheid ANC-dominated government took insufficient cognisance of these aspects, and tended to throw the baby out with the bath water.

The education system, the ladder out of poverty, still fails to produce the high-quality outcomes for the majority of poor young people. Health services are in a parlous state, with reversals of gains made in previous decades in key areas. The failure to manage our health system properly, both nationally and provincially, is reflected in the worsening health indicators, especially infant and maternal mortality.[106]

The underperformance of the health system is aggravated by the impact of HIV/Aids.[107] The scale of the pandemic and its devastating effects are the consequences of a failure by government to leverage the knowledge residing in our scientifically and technologically proficient society. The HIV/Aids challenge is discussed in more detail in Chapter 13.

The underperformance of the public service reflects a lack of human and intellectual capacity rather than a lack of fiscal resources. President Mbeki's stated focus since taking office in 1999 has been on transforming the governance system from a 'bureaucratic model' towards one that strives for greater 'goal-orientated fulfilment of public tasks'.[108] His approach has been characterised by centralising accountability of the cabinet, provincial premiers, directors-general and other key public officials in the Presidency. He has set targets around key performance areas and focused attention on achieving these over specified time frames.

Mbeki's 2005 State of the Nation address acknowledged that targets have not been met, that the capacity to meet them is in doubt, and that mechanisms to deal with bottlenecks obstructing delivery are not in place. He singled out three main problem areas:

- Weaknesses in the governance system mean plans to build school infrastructure 'are unfolding at a much slower pace than envisaged'
- The misapplication of policies of free basic electricity which is 'accruing mainly to those who are relatively well-off'

- Slow transfers of Municipal Infrastructure Grants to municipalities, reflecting 'lack of all-round capacity particularly in technical areas with regard to water, sanitation and public works projects'.

The focus here is on *why* we have persistent problems in meeting our goals notwithstanding public commitments to address them.

Delivery problems in the public sector reflect fundamental structural bottlenecks. We must confront these by openly identifying their nature and committing ourselves to tackling them systematically, while transparently monitoring and evaluating our performance. There is a growing consensus that the Accelerated and Shared Growth Initiative for South Africa (AsgiSA) aimed at sustainable 6% economic growth by 2010 is achievable, provided we address skills shortages, labour market rigidities, a volatile currency, and crime.

Surprisingly, despite underperformance in many areas of delivery of political goods, President Mbeki has yet to dismiss any public official for incompetence. The only dismissals have been justified on the basis of breakdown in relationships or insubordination.[109] The tolerance for underperformance in the public sector flies in the face of the President's stated intention in 1999 in centralising the appointment of key leadership positions to effect better performance management.

Human and intellectual capacity

A major dilemma confronting any post-liberation majority party is how to reward its cadres with the 'spoils of victory' while also delivering on the promises of freedom to ordinary citizens. The post-1994 ANC had to constitute a government to promote national unity yet also reward those who had sacrificed their professional lives for freedom. A further complication is that freedom in South Africa's case was not won by the storming of the capital by ANC freedom fighters, but through the effort of exiles who were active in the struggle from outside the country, and so-called inziles, who were active inside South Africa. Acknowledging this collective effort is essential to remobilising the energy to tackle the development challenges confronting us more than a decade after the birth of our democracy.

In addition, South Africa's sophisticated economy demands highly technical skills that for obvious historic reasons lie predominately with white people. The desire to see black people in charge has to be tempered by this reality.

There are opportunities that could have been, and can still be harnessed through courageous leadership to address the state's human and intellectual capacity problems. These include utilising more inzile capacity to augment exile skills, leveraging migration as a source of strength to recruit and retain the African diaspora, and leveraging South Africa's science and technology proficiency to tackle socioeconomic challenges.

First, utilising both exile and inzile leadership would create complementary strengths to bolster state capacity. Evidence over the last decade indicates that former exiles have been favoured above inziles. A better balance between those who understood the functioning of the country's key public-service systems and political appointees would have produced better outcomes.

The underperforming social-service ministries could have done better under the leadership of inziles who had a more sophisticated knowledge of the legacy systems in terms of what worked and what did not, which could have led to entirely different public-policy choices. The first post-apartheid Minister of Education, Sibusiso Bhengu, a former high-school principal, was hampered by his absence from the country for more than a decade and lack of knowledge of policy debates in the run-up to 1994. The choice of education-reform strategies demonstrated the lack of a reality check with practitioners on the ground. Our failure to match new ideas with working models, or to build the capacity of teachers and parents to assume new roles under the reformed system is at the heart of persistent quality problems.

The same is true of our health-system reform. It could have benefited from building on the sophisticated tertiary and quaternary services inherited from the past while increasing access to primary health care for the majority. The overzealous shift of resources from the tertiary and quaternary sectors has weakened the health system and disabled what was working in the referral chain. Activists who recommended these radical shifts took an almost punitive approach to redressing past imbalances in resource allocations. Too little attention was paid to making the transition to a more equitable system less disruptive to service provision for poor and vulnerable people. Primary-healthcare clinics established with inadequate attention to staffing and other resources have become white elephants in many rural areas.

Social development has also paid the price of exile leadership that undermined the strengths of our individualised family-based and community social work. The role of social workers was not adequately understood by the new political elites. Many frustrated social workers have left the service, some emigrating to countries that are using their skills and rewarding them adequately. We are now in a tragic situation where the growing needs for social development owing to the impact of HIV/ Aids and other social disruptions are outpacing the availability of social workers. Training institutions are finding it difficult to recruit young people into this profession, which is seen as a dead end.

Second, in the first post-apartheid government too much attention was paid to rewarding political leaders and activists for their commitment and sacrifices during the struggle. The question of balance between political-appointee imperatives and practical realities of effective delivery of political goods to the rest of society needs to be raised. For freedom to mean something in the lives of citizens, it has to be accompanied by tangible gains in key areas of public services: education, health, safety and security, human rights and the rule of law. From the ANC's own public commitments to its voter base one would have expected that capacity to deliver would have been a priority in key public services from which many of these voters stand to benefit.

The focus on political appointments in the first democratic government has come at great cost to the poorest among us. The poorest provinces such as Limpopo, the Eastern Cape and KwaZulu-Natal continue to pay a high price for rewarding political loyalties. Some portfolios were overburdened with loyalists at the expense of technical appointees who could deliver. For example, education as the route out of poverty did not receive the technical support it needed to ensure a smoother transformation. Political equity and redress was emphasised at the expense of improving the system's quality and performance. Health-system reform also suffered from the over-politicisation of appointments at the expense of enhancing performance. Our post-apartheid government placed insufficient emphasis on promoting the substantial and transcendent good.[110]

Third, mistrust of the old established civil service, dominated by Afrikaners, led to under-utilisation of the accumulated experience in public service. Government departments that managed the transition well encouraged experienced civil servants to commit themselves to the new-era goals, but many skilled civil servants left, taking invaluable wisdom and institutional memory with them. Among these were unreconstructed racists, but many ordinary white public servants with a desire to contribute to the future of their country also left because they felt mistrusted and unwanted. We have effectively thrown away the investments we have made in the development of white skills that should have been harnessed to enhance our capacity to deliver public services to poor people who need them most.

Capacity problems are monumental in safety and security. Unlike the management of our economy where political imperatives to govern were matched with technical capacity building, the safety and security of citizens seems to be driven mainly by political considerations. Given President Mbeki's own focus on crime in his 2005 State of the Nation address, one would have expected a step change in law-enforcement capacity. South Africa could benefit from lessons from global experience that point to the importance of leadership of the police force by top-class senior police officials or senior strategic managers with technical knowledge of the safety and security area.

We face a number of dilemmas as we confront the rise in crime. First, criminals are adept at asserting their rights under the constitution and getting the best legal backup. Freedom from repressive policing without retraining the police in human-rights law has led to ineffective law enforcement. Policing in a climate of respect for human rights is a skilled job that requires systematic training and the harnessing of information technology to track and accost criminals.

Second, providing resources to law-enforcement officers has not received the priority it deserves. Cases of police stations without vehicles or computerised records are not uncommon. The imbalance between the capabilities of criminals and those of law-enforcement officers further erodes public trust.

Third, we have been less than vigilant in the face of globalisation that has made South Africa vulnerable to international crime syndicates, which have taken advantage of the weak law-enforcement culture. Making law enforcement a skilled and valued profession is central to success.

The credibility of the police has been tarnished by the drawn-out saga of allegations of wrongdoing and connections with the criminal underworld against police chief, Commissioner Jackie Selebi, who is facing charges of corruption, fraud, money laundering and racketeering. He has been placed on extended leave, but questions remain about the President's tardiness in responding to the allegations. His earlier suspension of National Director of Public Prosecutions Vusi Pikoli instead of taking action with regard to Selebi has sown confusion.

Worrying trends regarding the use of force by police came to light in a 2001 Institute for Human Rights and Criminal Justice Studies study.[111] An additional source of concern is the poor response of the Department of Safety and Security to these incidents. Disciplinary charges were laid in only 66% of the cases, the state prosecutor took on only 35% of them, and the conviction rate was an abysmal 13%. Focus-group discussions revealed a view shared by the public and the police that criminals had more rights than the police and suspects deserved whatever force was used against them. The study concluded that the police needed more human-rights education and better technical training.

Not surprisingly, the 2007 Ibrahim Index of Good Governance in Africa[112] places South Africa third from the bottom of 48 sub-Saharan countries measured in terms of safety and security for its citizens. Only Somali and Burundi fared worse – both in the throes of civil war. This is an indictment of a country with the largest fiscal resource base in Africa.

The 2005-2006 Report of the Auditor-General on the performance of government departments makes for disturbing reading. In addition to failure to deliver public services of the requisite quality, there are too many cases of wasteful expenditure and irregularities. These findings point to the squandering of state resources that could have been used to address the pressing needs of poor people and for investments to enhance our economy's productive capacity.

Even more disturbing is the tolerance citizens seem to have of the reported severe problems with financial management in our government at all levels. Only 12% of national departments, 4% of provincial departments and 2% of local-authority entities could be given a clean bill of financial-management health. Any country with such a scorecard would go into crisis-management mode to correct the problems identified. No private company would get away with such an audit outcome. Yet South African citizens are looking the other way.

Despite these skills challenges, some departments have performed well by harnessing inzile capabilities and using the experience of those who served in the old government. The distinguishing features of successful departments are identifiable. First, acknowledgement of skills gaps and adoption of strategies to deal with them is crucial. For example, the post-1994 government recognised its lack of financial-management skills and recruited NP member Derek Keys as its first Finance Minister. Chris Liebenberg from Nedcor succeeded him and steps were taken to train successors in Alec Erwin and Trevor Manuel. Manuel has become a successful Minister of Finance and an icon of propriety in fiscal management. Central to his success is admission of his own skills gaps, a commitment to work hard to close them, and professionalism. The partnership with his director-general from1996 to 2005, Maria Ramos, brought together technical and political skills. The tone set within Treasury and Revenue Services is one of excellence in performance at all levels.

Kader Asmal also set a new benchmark in Water and Forestry by leveraging South Africa's science and technology proficiency to tackle development challenges. He turned his lack of knowledge of the field into an opportunity to create partnerships between the academic sector and government. His department ran the most successful public-works programme between 1994 and 1999. Asmal brought the same thoroughness in policy-making into the Education Ministry, but was trumped by political correctness within the ANC. Moves to review and radically reform the Outcomes-based Education (OBE) school curriculum introduced in 1995 were blocked.

South Africa has also failed to leverage its comparative advantage to recruit and retain skills in a globalising labour market. Post-apartheid South Africa is a magnet for many in Africa, offering us the opportunity to recruit the African diaspora both inside and outside the continent to fill skills gaps. Instead, we have allowed xenophobia to take root. Africans from the rest of our continent are targets of racist attacks by the same black South Africans who were victims of apartheid. Xenophobia is evident in our communities and in the disrespectful manner in which Home Affairs officials deal with African refugees and asylum seekers. Reports of assaults of refugees and others seeking public services around our country abound, in violation of our obligations under UN treaties.

Moreover, many refugees with high-level skills are not being identified and encouraged to help our struggling public service. We are failing to use the reality of being a haven for economic and political refugees to our advantage. Mathematics and science teachers from the Democratic Republic of the Congo, Somalia and, more recently, Zimbabwe could be deployed to fill the gaps in skills in our under-performing school system. Endless, costly attempts to arrest and repatriate migrants with irregular status is a 'lose-lose' strategy. Courageous leadership is needed to get us out of this bind.

Politics as morality in practice?

The eagerness to use state resources to reward those loyal to the ruling party has spawned a culture that is further undermining our government's performance. The value system championed by Václav Havel of 'politics as morality in practice' is alien to many of those who have made corruption a way of life in the public sector.

The corrupting influence of the 1996 arms deal continues to reverberate. Worldwide experience points to the inherent corruption of the arms industry. Even more tragic in our society is the role of those who had supported us in our struggle for democracy in pressing our new government into purchasing arms we did not need. The UK, Sweden and Germany speak with forked tongues as donor countries that champion good governance on the one hand, and promoters of their arms industries on the other. We are saddled with an escalating multi-billion-dollar bill, and a cancer of corruption that has tainted many in political office.

Andrew Feinstein, former ANC MP and member of the Standing Committee on Public Accounts (Scopa) that probed allegations of corruption in the arms deal, details the extent to which this deal undermined transparency in our young democracy.[113] 'Hard-wired for corruption' is an apt metaphor for the nature of the arms industry. It could be argued that the arms deal did more to undermine the nascent watchdog role of Parliament than anything else. The interventions of the Executive in preventing an independent investigation into the deal violated the separation of powers between the Legislature and the Executive. It will take courageous leadership on both sides to restore the integrity of that relationship.

Once corruption is introduced into the body politic, it tends to lead to 'state capture' at many levels. Of particular concern is the abuse of public-service positions that deprive poor people of services to which they are entitled. The Social Development Department acknowledged in 2004 that for the first five years, R1,5 billion of the R56 billion allocated for social-assistance grants had been abused. A special investigation unit established that approximately 41 000 government officials were fraudulently registered as beneficiaries of social grants. By April 2005 only 194 officials had been prosecuted and 38 were convicted, with potential recoveries from this intervention estimated at at least R2 billion.[114] Those who pleaded guilty were treated leniently, being allowed to hold their jobs and repay the money on unusually favourable terms over a long period of time.

The so-called Travelgate scandal involved 40 members of parliament. Parliamentarians earn over R500 000 per year and enjoy pension and travel allowances, yet these members of an institution that is meant to enforce good governance helped themselves to more public money by colluding with travel agents to make false travel claims.

Even more disturbing has been the embarrassing tardiness in dealing with this matter over the last five years or so since the scandal broke. Political parties, with the notable exception of the Democratic Alliance (DA), have failed to demonstrate their abhorrence of fraud and corruption by expelling those involved. Instead, many have been assisted to enter into plea bargains and repay the money on favourable terms. Others were shifted into more senior party jobs elsewhere without being held to account for their fraudulence. In the 2006/2007 floor-crossing sessions in parliament, some of those expelled were allowed to form new parties and continue to feed at the trough of public resources. Some crossed the floor from smaller parties and were welcomed by the ANC. By the second half of 2007, only two MPs were facing criminal charges.

Corruption on the scale suggested by these examples and others reported in our media suggests that our society is ensnared in a political culture that tolerates corruption. This is not surprising, given the legacy of apartheid, an inherently corrupt political system that promoted the use of state resources to pursue the interests of a minority.[115] But our democracy is based on the ethical values inherent in human-rights foundations. The standard by which we measure ourselves has to be higher.

In his autobiography *Let My People Go*, the late Nkosi Albert Luthuli expressed his fears about the impact of the legacy of materialism he observed in the 1960s among the power elites on the value system that might emerge in post-apartheid South Africa:

> In South Africa the majority of whites have gone far along the road to the worship of material prosperity . . . Materialism is rampant . . . And the contempt for true religion is taken a stage further by white South Africa's growing state worship, comparable already to that of the Nazis. It is a sad heritage that we should acquire if we modelled ourselves on the whites.[116]

The temptations of materialism are everywhere. Success is defined not by what one accomplishes, but by what one owns. Many young people know no other motivation for developing their talents than to be able to make money. The use of state resources to feed this materialism is worrying. The NP government used 'state capture' to enrich their constituency at the expense of the rest of the population. Post-apartheid South Africa cannot afford to allow 'state capture' by the new elites. It would undermine everything we yearn for in a free, democratic society.

International experience demonstrates that corruption is a function of the nature of the political culture and institutions within a given political system.[117] For example, Finland has consistently been ranked as the most globally competitive society and the least corrupt. Researchers have demonstrated a correlation among globalisation (an open economy and society), freedom, and good governance without corruption. Finland is an egalitarian society with good welfare services. Its legal and administrative system promotes a culture of transparency, accountability, individual autonomy and meritocracy. There are no political appointments such as a political cabinet system and state secretaries. Civil servants are adequately paid and have attractive careers regardless of changes in the political party in government.

Finnish political parties have been receiving public funding since 1967, reducing the risk of special-interest pressures on governments and the temptation to corruption by governing parties. Finally, Finland's administrative culture embodies the idea of continuous checking of the limits of corruption in practice.

All these elements promote a civic-mindedness that enables Finnish society to develop with integrity, and leave no one behind. We must learn from our own ugly legacy and derive lessons about appropriate radical transformation from countries that have successfully transformed themselves into prosperous, egalitarian democracies.

In particular, we should embrace opposition politics as part of our democracy. In some cases, the majority party, the ANC, uses charges of racism levelled at opposition-party members to undermine the voice of opposition parties. The idea of the ANC seeing itself 'ruling until Jesus Christ comes back', as ANC president Jacob Zuma said during his campaign for the leadership of the party in 2007, should send a chill down any democrat's spine.

Ethical politics is not an option in a democracy; it is a requirement. In a democracy governed by ethics one need not fear opposition party victories or changes in leadership. What would matter would be the extent to which those standing for public office are able to advance the common good.

Turf battles: The lack of coordination

Poor coordination within and between different levels of government is another capacity challenge facing our government. For example, the success of the government's Joint Initiative on Priority Skills Acquisition (Jipsa), a programme aimed at addressing shortages of critical skills, depends on the coordination of efforts by all players. But how that can be accomplished in the face of inadequate coordination between Education, Labour, Home Affairs and provincial governments? Apart from turf battles between Education and Labour, Home Affairs has failed to rise to the challenges of an interconnected world. Our competitiveness continues to be undermined by our tardiness to come to terms with the reality of the scarcity of highly mobile skills across all sectors, making it difficult to educate, train, retain, recruit and attract talent from all over the nation and the world.

Teamwork within and between departments and between different levels of government is the only way to improve efficiency. This requires consistent messages from top leadership, accompanied by an alignment of incentives that reward teamwork. Without leadership vision, focused management, monitoring and evaluation, the cultural change from individualism to teamwork will not occur. The seriousness of state-capacity constraints is such that intervention at this level is our only hope.

Those who suffer most from ongoing weaknesses in state capacity are poor people who rely entirely on public-sector services for their survival. Socio-economic rights of the poorest people are being violated daily not because of lack of resources, nor failure to allocate them appropriately, but a failure on the part of government to implement the laudable policies it has enacted and adopted.

It remains to be seen how the Accelerated and Shared Growth Initiative for South Africa (AsgiSA) under Deputy President Phumzile Mlambo-Ngcuka can bring better capacity, coherence and coordination to governance. It is critical that the capacity to govern be enhanced to restore ordinary citizens' trust in the government. She is certainly giving it all the attention it needs, but consistent messages need to come from all leaders, especially the President. Performance management as promised by

President Mbeki at the beginning of his 1999 term is an essential tool for monitoring, evaluating and improving state capacity to govern.

A key element in effective government is respect for and promotion of expertise. Our government has done well in areas where expertise was sought and utilised. For example, the transformation of our stagnant economy into a dynamic one was made possible by the willingness of the post-1994 government to harness national and international expertise to establish firm foundations for growth and development. We have enjoyed uninterrupted growth over the last decade or so thanks to this wise approach. The spillover of a well run Finance Department on the rest of government is also significant. We have more resources to accomplish our objectives of rooting out poverty. The systems and policies are in place. What is missing is the political will and management capacity.

The contrast between the above approach and the government's handling of HIV/Aids and energy generation and management is striking. Expert advice was rejected in both these domains, with disastrous consequences. At the end of 2007, President Mbeki acknowledged that government had been presented with the case for expanding our power generation capacity as far back as 1998 and again in 2004, but had not heeded that advice. Acknowledgement of the refusal to accept expert advice on HIV/Aids has yet to come.

In both these cases, failure to heed expert advice puts the government's success in promoting economic growth at risk. Confidence in the country's capacity to sustain investments is undermined. Uncoordinated responses to the power crisis from Eskom officials and government spokespersons are creating confusion in the market place. Politicians and bureaucrats need to understand that political power does not bestow expert knowledge. Great leaders succeed by drawing on the expertise of others.

PART FOUR

Human
and intellectual
capital

CHAPTER 10

The school system

ONE OF THE BIGGEST CHALLENGES IN POST-1994 SOUTH AFRICA IS the state of the education and training system. The social engineering of Hendrik Verwoerd, who in the 1950s formalised and refined apartheid as a system of governance with deep socio-economic ramifications, reached its zenith when as Minister of Education he imposed Bantu Education on African people. In 1953 he justified the new policy: 'Education must train and teach people in accordance with their opportunities in life . . . The Bantu must be guided to serve his own community in all aspects. There is no place for him in the European community above the level of certain forms of labour.'[118] A clearer commitment to education for servitude one could not find.

The markedly inferior education imposed on African children from the 1950s has had a devastating and lasting impact on the capacity of the majority population to free themselves from the shackles of the apartheid past.

Capacity constraints pose a major challenge to successful transformation of the educational and training system that is vital to sustainable development. Its transformation is hamstrung by weak capacity in the state, the teaching profession, the governing-body system, and in parents to hold the system accountable for delivery of high-quality education to their children.

African children now have a right to aspire to the greener pastures from which Verwoerd excluded them, yet they lack the capacity to do so. It is difficult to function effectively in the knowledge-driven economy of the 21st century without the basic language of mathematics and science.

A closer look at the school system shows how the legacy of the past still impacts on pupils today, especially with regard to mathematics and science.

For example, in 2001 27% of African pupils were taught mathematics by teachers with no mathematics qualifications, and 38% were taught science by teachers with no science qualifications.[119] The minimum requirement for teaching at the primary level according to the International Standard Classification of Education (ISCED) is a tertiary qualification. At the international level 74% of respondents met this criterion, compared to only 50% tested in South Africa in 2000-2002. Among sixth-grade teachers of reading in South Africa, 32% had primary or junior secondary qualifications, while 19% had senior secondary qualifications.

Although a 2005 Department of Education (DOE) study[120] indicated that the levels of unqualified and under-qualified teachers had been much reduced, these statistics should be approached with caution. The proportion of unqualified and under-qualified teachers is higher in primary schools than in high schools, higher in rural schools than in urban schools, and higher in Coloured schools than in white schools. These statistics also do not take into consideration teachers with inadequate training in Outcomes-based Education (OBE) and the new curriculum (RNCS) who continue to struggle to meet the high expectations placed on them.

The low outputs especially in higher grade hamper the capacity to produce qualified maths and science teachers. A study conducted by Edusource in 1997 found that most maths and science teachers were not qualified to teach their subjects.

An estimated 8 000 maths and 8 200 science teachers needed to be targeted for in-service training to address the lack of subject knowledge, according to a DOE 2001 report.[121] Maths and science teachers were also found to have a low level of teaching experience. Such teachers fail to inspire learners who graduate in maths and science to choose teaching as a career. In addition, these subjects provide a basis for much better opportunities and pay in the private sector.

Many secondary schools do not offer maths and science. They lack even unqualified or under-qualified maths and science teachers. There is an urgent need to attract, recruit and select learners with the potential to excel in maths and science to train as teachers at higher-education institutions. Unqualified and under-qualified maths and science teachers need to be upgraded.

The results of planned under-development of human capital over generations are predictable. Denial by white people of their advantaged position owing to this history only fuels an equally dangerous denial of lack of skills from those disadvantaged by the same discriminatory investment pattern. Verwoerd continues to triumph from the grave.

Many black people have difficulty in coming to terms with gaps in their mathematics, science and technological knowledge base. They feel ashamed of admitting to these gaps because of the dangerous conflation of lack of knowledge (a product of lack of access to learning) with lack of intellectual capacity to learn (a problem of intellectual endowment). Denial by black people of the gaps in their knowledge base stems from the unspoken fear of being regarded as intellectually inferior. This fear has been partly responsible for policies and practices that inadvertently vindicate the Verwoerdian logic by perpetuating poor performance by black pupils in mathematics and science.

The legacy of racism was given a twist by Verwoerdian logic that preached that 'Bantus' were inferior to white people in all aspects including in their intellect, while creating conditions designed to prove his ideology correct.

Since 1994 there has been resistance among unionised teachers to a skills audit to assess the match between teaching assignments and skills. An audit would lay a better foundation for focused training to fill whatever skills gaps are identified in individuals and in the profession as a whole. Ironically, resistance to this audit perpetuates the mismatch between skills and teaching assignments that undermines the future of the pupils who are entrusted to under-qualified teachers.

In the 2003 Third International Mathematics and Science Study in which the HSRC tested 9 000 Grade 8 learners for maths and science proficiency at the appropriate level, South Africa came last out of 50 countries, and our scores showed the widest distribution of all countries tested. Disaggregation of the scores by categories of former departments in the apartheid era shows that African schools performed the worst whereas former whites-only schools performed the best, with a mean score closer to the international mean. The legacy of discriminatory education lives on in the under-qualified and unmotivated teachers who teach pupils in most poor former Bantu Education schools.

Denial of the need to honestly face up to skills gaps undermines the foundations of transformation of our society by perpetuating mediocrity among poor black people unable to afford excellent education in the private sector or in suburban areas. The South African Democratic Teachers' Union's (Sadtu) protection of unskilled teachers from public scrutiny undermines the right of the majority of black pupils to quality education. By shielding under-qualified teachers, Sadtu is inadvertently completing the job Verwoerd could not finish.

There is a real dilemma for those in political leadership in acknowledging the realities of the impact of Bantu Education. Part of the ambivalence about acknowledging its impact on the capacity of black South Africans to run a modern economy stems from the fundamental question it raises about the readiness to govern.

The nature of the anti-apartheid struggle after 1976 added to the burden of poor education. In sacrificing education for freedom, many of the activists who are now in their thirties and forties sacrificed their youth and the opportunity to prepare for a future in which they could govern effectively. South Africa has yet to deal effectively with generations of its prime talent pool that missed out on school for three successive decades. The heavy price paid for political freedom has not been adequately factored into public policies to support those facing personal risks in the knowledge economy. Denial of the impact of this sacrifice makes it harder to tackle it.

History provides numerous examples of post-war reconstruction programmes that enabled those who had made sacrifices to support their nation's war effort to establish successful civilian careers. South African soldiers returning from World War II were enabled to enter higher education or apprenticeship programmes to develop skills essential for success in the job market. The dilemmas of the post-1994 transition flow partly from the non-conventional nature of the civil conflict that preceded the changeover. Young people who were the foot soldiers of street battles between 1976 and 1993 were not conventional soldiers. They were not included in programmes established for the demobilisation and integration of veterans into post-apartheid society, but expected simply to go back to being children and return to school.

Those generations of young people not only missed out on education in the formal, technical sense, but on personal development that enables one to reflect and think critically about oneself and one's environment. Education enables one to navigate complex systems and tackle problems in a logical and rational manner, using tools gathered along the path of growing and learning. This extra-curricular element of education is especially important for first-generation entrants into the school and tertiary-level systems. Their parents and relatives are in most cases unable to help them navigate the complexities of choices they have to make.

The legacy of bad education goes beyond the opportunity costs of poor technical and professional skills at the personal level. The wider social impact is reflected in a weak science culture. The values of science centre on analytical approaches to problem solving, evidence-based policy making and action, openness to alternative explanations to observed phenomena, and learning from others.

The values of science form a basis for trust relationships in societies that have come to take them for granted. The empowering knowledge about how and why things happen as they do is often taken for granted by those with a good education. For example, an understanding of the laws of physics and the dynamics of natural phenomena such as lightning allows one to act prudently to manage the risks of injury or death from lightning. In contrast, villagers without the benefit of such knowledge remain imprisoned in the fear of witches who are supposedly able to ride mysteriously on the wave of the energy generated by thunder and strike dead their targeted enemies.

Social capital built on trust relationships cements and enhances the development of foundations for stronger human capital and social institutions. Instead of suspecting one's neighbours of being responsible for the destruction of one's home by lightning, much could be gained by working together to invest in lightning conductors. Social capital is also enhanced by an understanding of power as the capacity to act. The *ubuntu* ethos African people boast of can only work in an environment where the approach to power is one that enables everyone to become the best they can be. The more educated and confident individuals are, the higher the benefits for everyone in society.

Societies built on trust relationships function seamlessly. Systems and institutions are presumed to operate on articulated logical frameworks. Train and airplane schedules, medical procedures and treatment protocols are taken at face value. Science and technology promote the generation, dissemination and application of knowledge that enhances transparency and empowers citizens in their daily lives. Science and technology have benefits that spill over into enhancing the quality of life of citizens and the nature of governance itself. A science culture empowers citizens to exploit the power of information and communications technologies to spread knowledge and promote transparency to hold their leaders to account.

Unintended consequences

The unacknowledged capacity problems in our society and in the post-1994 state have led to unintended policy consequences in transformation of the school system. We have been too fearful to acknowledge the binding constraints of the inherited system and the need for a measured, properly sequenced reform process that does not overburden an already weakened system. We have allowed ideological rigidities to dictate both the policy choices and the people resources to drive change.

The post-1994 government has done a good job of transforming the fragmented, discriminatory and wasteful system of education from 14 departments into one national department with nine provincial ones. Sadly, less attention seems to have been given to undoing the legacy of cognitive under-development by the apartheid system. The promotion of mediocrity and inequity was accomplished through deliberate de-emphasising of mathematics, science, language development, creative arts and critical thinking. It is surprising that a framework for the transformation of apartheid education would not emphasise the promotion of cognitive development and excellence in its principles.

The adoption of an Outcomes-based Education (OBE) system referred to as Curriculum 2005 (to signal the date by which it would be fully operational) was intended to make a clean break with apartheid education. Ironically, it has led to a further weakening of the education system.

Cautionary notes sounded by educationists were ignored by the DOE under Minister Sibusiso Bhengu. OBE includes proposed interactive processes between pupils and teachers (renamed learners and educators) that assume capacities that simply could not be expected to come out of our education history. The focus is on what learners should know and be able to do (knowledge, skills, attitudes and values). Cooperative learning is emphasised, and the goal is to produce lifelong learners with a thirst for knowledge and love of learning.

Notwithstanding country-wide training programmes, widespread implementation problems have dogged the introduction of OBE since 1998. A lack of understanding of the subject matter and poor grasp of the teaching methods required have brought teaching and learning to a crisis point in poor school districts. Teachers in poor schools, who in most cases are under-qualified, cannot make the transition to this new curriculum despite numerous attempts at training. As noted in Chapter 9, a revision of Curriculum 2005 in 2002 under Minister of Education, Kader Asmal, was curtailed by objections from ideologues. There seems to be a hardline view that post-apartheid education has to be as radically different as possible to qualify as a legitimately transformed education.

The new curriculum requires extensive reading and extended writing in all subjects. It requires learners to think critically and develop strong conceptual skills. There is a high expectation of learners to have an awareness of the social, economic, moral and ethical issues facing their country and the world at large. These requirements and expectations are a cultural revolution for many learners and teachers in most poor areas of our society. Given the poor levels of qualifications, the lack of access to libraries in most poor residential areas, the lack of a culture of debate and critical thinking even among teachers, it is not surprising that major implementation problems remain.

Critics of Curriculum 2005 suggest that it is suitable for middle-class schools in which both parents and teachers are able to support the cultural change envisaged in its formulation. How could one expect teachers and learners who have been brought up in an authoritarian cultural setting to switch into interactive, cooperative learning mode after only a few training sessions?

Feedback from teachers concerned about the outcomes of the widespread mismatch between goals and capacity within the system suggested that educational standards are at risk. There were fears that lower requirements would be set under the newly introduced OBE. Although OBE itself does not require setting of low standards, its introduction was seen as being a conduit to 'dumbing down', especially in schools where limited human and intellectual capabilities would hamper innovative learning.

According to unhappy staff at Alexander Sinton High School in Cape Town, the rules introduced in 2003 for pupils in Grade 8 and 9 allowed pupils to proceed to the next grade even though they had failed English and mathematics. The required pass mark had also been lowered from 50% to 35%. The then headmaster of the school and a dedicated teacher, Fazil Parker, complained that the department was imposing OBE without adequate consultation with educators. 'They are bringing outside consultants for what is an African problem. We have a different socio-economic background to the UK where OBE is used and where they have fewer children in each class. Now we are beginning to feel the effects.'[122]

According to Matseleng Allais, national research director of Umalusi,[123] the statutory body charged with quality assurance in the school education system, outcomes-based qualifications are 'a worse than unnecessary' addition to the South African education system. It is an educational model criticised in every country in which it was implemented. Allais argues that education's purpose is to provide students with access to codified knowledge because the information taught is not easily gleaned in the course of everyday life. 'Educational institutions are necessary because specialised knowledge requires sustained, carefully sequenced study. Learners are socialised into a discipline, a field, a content area, or a way of operating.'[124] The fragmented nature of the National Qualifications Framework (NQF) into unit standards, in her opinion, undermines the essence of education.

Nick Taylor, respected educationist and executive director of the Joint Educational Trust Services, shares these views. He quotes a Human Sciences Research Council (HSRC) study which in 2005 found that teachers spend on average 3,2 hours a week teaching, with many hours spent on activities such as 'continuous assessment'. Analysing the results of the annual Senior Certificate examination showed that nearly 80% of our 6 118 schools are essentially dysfunctional.[125] There are only 414 schools (7%) in the top-performing rank, producing 66% of higher-grade mathematics passes. The bulk of schools (4 877, or 79%) are poor performers, contributing only 15% of higher-grade mathematics passes. The good news is that 600 schools serving African pupils are classified as top or moderately performing. These star performers countrywide are producing excellent results despite their disadvantaged history and the fact that they serve poor communities.

Performance in the 23 000 primary schools seems to be mirroring this pattern. Hundreds of thousands of children leave school every year without the skills to benefit from further education or to secure anything but the most menial jobs. Even more disturbing is that dysfunctional schools are unable to socialise young people into the attitudes required for citizenship in a modern democracy. School leavers from these dysfunctional schools are likely to swell the ranks of those who remain mired in poverty or become involved in crime and other social disruption.

Lessons from successful schools in poor areas show that dysfunctional schools can be transformed into positive learning and teaching environments. The leadership and management qualities of the principal are vital, as is time management including punctuality by teachers and pupils. Critical-focus areas of leadership by the principal are: guiding teachers in delivering the curriculum; planning, monitoring and evaluation of performance; provision of stationery, textbooks and other learning aids; and support to teachers to improve their knowledge base.

South Africa's performance in mathematics and science in both national and international tests has been consistently poor. According to the HSRC's 2005-2006 State of the Nation report,[126] the 2002 Department of Education's evaluation of Grade 3 learners found a national average numeracy score of 30%. A Unesco assessment of Grade 4 learners found an average numeracy score of 30% (Mauritius 59%, Senegal 40%, Malawi 43%). In the 2003 Third International Mathematics and Science Study in which the HSRC tested Grade 8 learners for mathematics and science proficiency, South Africa came last of the 50 participating countries. This poor performance was consistent with the 1999 study in which South Africa was last among 38 countries. It is noteworthy that Asian countries (South Korea, Hong Kong, Singapore) are consistent top performers in mathematics and science.

The higher performance of poorer countries like Senegal and Malawi is evidence that resources are not the only constraint. As analysts in the Department of Education acknowledge, '[I]t is also clear that the worst problem, at least from the quality point of view, is the historically-driven lack of practical and serious pedagogical and cognitive skills in the majority of teachers.'[127]

Experience in poorer countries such as Uganda shows that where parents are provided with information about resource allocation and performance, including attendance of teachers in class, and empowered to hold teachers accountable through governing bodies, performance improves significantly. In contrast, teachers in many parts of South Africa are often absent without leave, and some moonlight regularly. Some are full-time members of municipal councils.

What other country with such a gigantic educational challenge would allow teachers to be elected to another full-time position while retaining their jobs in the school system? I was astounded when an education official said the department cannot stop teachers from exercising their right to hold elected office. This is an extreme case of abusing individual rights to undermine the public interest.

Which other country would tolerate the refusal of a teachers' union to have a skills audit in the face of the crisis in quality performance? Surely the primary rights here are the rights of children to education that is of a requisite standard to enable them to escape poverty and prepare themselves for the competitive global knowledge economy.

Transformation of education was intended to promote development of a more equitable system that would produce high-quality outcomes from all of South Africa's talent. The reality is that better-resourced schools with higher-quality teachers and parents from higher social classes have been able to adjust to OBE. The gap in educational outcomes between rich and poor people persists, and is growing. Black people remain at the bottom of the skills pyramid.

There is also controversy over improvements recorded in the 2003 to 2005 matriculation results. Some accuse the Department of Education of lowering the standard of requirements for high-school graduation. Grade inflation was also said to have played a part in the 'improved results'. These concerns demand a response. Allowing young people to go through school without acquiring the requisite skills would be costly for society as a whole. It would be a cruel irony if a post-apartheid government allows itself to perpetuate the legacy of inferior education for poor black people in the name of 'equity'. Urgent equity concerns must be addressed at source – equality of opportunity, access to scientifically sound and educationally stimulating curricula, qualified and dedicated teachers who are adequately resourced and rewarded as professionals.

We need to set ourselves modest goals in policy reforms and align the scope and pace of change better with the capacity of the system to make incremental improvements. Above all we need to become less tolerant of mediocrity. Withdrawing from international competition as we have since 2005 is hardly an appropriate response. The argument that our learners are over-tested, allowing little time for intervention programmes to take root, is unconvincing in light of the lack of evidence of systematic quality-improvement schemes.

Intervention programmes such as the 102 *Dinaledi* ('stars' in Sesotho) schools instituted in 2001 have yet to show results. In April 2006 Minister of Education Naledi Pandor re-launched the programme with 490 *Dinaledi* selected schools for the promotion of science and mathematics. Unfortunately insistence on equality of treatment has constrained the education authorities from providing significantly larger additional resources to these schools to produce the improvements needed. The grudgingly allocated R80 000 top-up provided to *Dinaledi* schools is not enough to hire a single additional specialist teacher.

We seem unable to make a distinction between discrimination and differentiation in post-apartheid South Africa. Our over-sensitivity about discrimination has blinded us from focusing on differentiated approaches to promoting quality outcomes. Equal access without attention to quality is an injustice to poor people who become trapped in mediocre public services. Differentiation based on transparent criteria is essential to encourage and support those making the effort to excel. Levelling down resource provision and performance expectations is unlikely to bring about the desired change that would yield both greater equity and excellent results.

Models of intervention?
We can learn much from models being developed by educationists eager to see progress beyond the current impasse. The example of the 600 successful schools in poor areas mentioned earlier needs to be shared more widely to inspire others.

Another example is Leap School,[128] an experimental model of intervention located in the Cape Town suburb of Pinelands, servicing poor pupils from Langa and other Cape Flats townships. Leap School's experience suggests that greater attention needs to be paid to the holistic development of pupils and teachers. Leap School's commitment to excellence in performance by all participants in the teaching and learning process is reflected in the following principles:

- Academic performance and development are inextricably linked to emotional development; academic deficits cannot be remedied in social isolation.
- Family relationships are strengthened as part of Values Education, and new relationships must be created within the learning community.
- Life Orientation classes serve as a vehicle for triggering strategic life-changing interventions; real-life learning situations are used for the development of real awareness and positive change.
- Peer influence is used as a positive (albeit painful) tool for change.
- Cultural coherence is an important component in the process of adolescent development.

Leap School's code of conduct[129] forms the point of reference for self-regulation. It governs the actions and behaviour of all members of the school community, including teachers. The Life Orientation programme ensures that this code is explored fully and applied in the lives of learners.

The code's implications are that Leap School does not work with the fear of punishment to change behaviour but with the understanding of individual responsibility within a learning community. The consequences of disrespectful and damaging actions are managed within the community – learners are themselves responsible for this process. Such actions and code challenges are used as opportunities to facilitate change and develop a sense of personal accountability for learners and staff members alike.

Leap School has produced significantly improved results from the same pool of talent that township schools draw from. At the end of 2005, 93% of the 15 students who wrote matric passed, 60% received university exemption, 33% with merit and all with mathematics and science on the higher grade.[130] (In 2003 the entire Western Cape Province produced only 55 African language mother-tongue matriculants.[131])

In addition, Leap School students are encouraged to excel in the creative arts. For example, a young woman from the most desperate circumstances in Langa township won a poetry prize that took her to New York, where she received an honourable mention from the judges.

What lessons can be learnt from Leap School's approach to education that may benefit the rest of the school system? First, this school motivates young people to reach deep into their souls to set and meet high personal goals. Second, the self-regulating approach to discipline and ethical behaviour resonates with young people who tend to rebel against the authority of parents and teachers. The removal of 'the traditional punch bag' (parents and teachers) from the discipline equation forces young people to confront their own self-limiting tendencies. Self-regulation enables young people to face up to weaknesses that constrain them from realising their full potential. Peer support and feedback are actively promoted to reinforce desired behaviours.

Third, the collaborative ethos and promotion of an awareness of the social, economic and moral ethical values of society produces critical

thinkers and conceptually strong young people. Fourth, the requirement to engage with vulnerable people in their own communities promotes civic duty as part of the educational process. The school programme sets aside time for voluntary work in nearby poor communities
to assist in child-care facilities, old-age homes and homes for people with
disabilities. Field-training opportunities bring the theory behind the
code of conduct and practice together in the enactment of citizenship.

There is suggestive evidence that this experiment is working and could
be adapted to realise the goals that the government set itself in transforming the education system. Imposing Curriculum 2005 on a teacher
population that is under-qualified and ill-suited to perform according to
its requirements has failed to transform the school system appropriately.

Imagine how much more positive the outcome could have been had
there been a more intense consultative process beyond the Tripartite
Alliance (ANC, SACP and Cosatu). This would have brought in the perspectives of South Africans committed to fundamental transformation
yet able to do a reality check about the extent and pace of cultural change
the system could bear without undermining quality outcomes. Education is another arena in which local expertise with a deep knowledge of
the specific challenges we inherited from apartheid was ignored at great
cost to our country. It is still not too late to modify elements of the implementation plan to make our education system both equitable and
excellent.

What seems to stand out from all successful schools is the importance
of leadership. The principal is key in setting the vision and mission of
the school and inspiring pupils and teachers to perform accordingly.
Exemplary leadership in professional conduct, teaching preparedness,
engaging with teachers and students, and mobilising parents to support
their children are critical success factors.

South Africa could also learn from its neighbours. Zimbabwe undertook radical post-colonial transformation of its education and training
system in the 1980s. The focus of change was on making universal education accessible to all and enhancing its quality and relevance. It is remarkable how successful that transformation was and how resilient it
has been under difficult political conditions. Zimbabwean students com-

pete extremely well against South African students at all levels of education. Generally even those coming from Zimbabwe's poorest areas do better than products of some of our most privileged private schools. The continuing political turmoil in Zimbabwe risks destroying what has been an excellent education system.

The success factor in Zimbabwe's education appears to be its insistence on promoting competence in a core set of subjects that lay the foundation for further education and training. The core is taken from the Cambridge system of education and comprises mathematics, science, language development – English and indigenous – and history. Graduates of the high-school system either go the O-level route and move into technical training areas or do an extra A-level year in preparation for further academic studies. Zimbabwe has taken the best from its colonial experience with the English grammar school model and built on it for a better post-colonial human-development future.

Z.K. Matthews' words about the need to embrace what is in the national interest in an interconnected world as he saw it in the early 1940s should caution us against trying to invent an inadequate wheel while other nations are charging ahead on tried and tested models to prepare their young people for the global knowledge economy:

> The African people have demanded for their children an education which takes due account of the fact that they are living in the modern world in an environment which includes both Western and African elements linked together indissolubly. Their view has been that they will not tolerate any course which purports to prepare their children for a purely African environment when they know that such a thing no longer exists in South Africa.[132]

Matthews also rejected the view that black South Africans should not aspire to excellence because they are disadvantaged. Post-apartheid education policy makers would do well to heed this sound advice.

CHAPTER 11

The skills training
system

SOUTH AFRICA'S SKILLS SHORTAGES, IDENTIFIED AS A FATAL CON-
straint to the Accelerated and Shared Growth Initiative for South Africa
(Asgisa) launched by the government in 2006, undermine both the
public and private sectors in their drive to sustain the momentum of the
growing economy. Continued shortages reflect the legacy of our past and
the failures of post-apartheid policy interventions (see Chapter 10). In
the case of vocational and technical training too, incoherent and over-
ambitious policy choices have contributed to our inability to overcome
skills shortages.

Pre-1994, the training system was anchored by vocation-specific training colleges in areas such as teaching, nursing and agriculture services.
Most qualifications involved a three-year course coupled with practical
exposure to the profession. The training colleges were fragmented along
racial lines in accordance with the separate-development philosophy.
During the last stages of apartheid there was a feeding frenzy as more
and more colleges were built in all corners of the then homelands as part
of a growing system of political patronage.

Within industries a vibrant apprenticeship system was linked to technical colleges that trained artisans in technical skills essential to running
a modern economy. Its quality outputs were as good as any in the world,
but its racially discriminatory foundations, which excluded African workers, was a fatal flaw. Labour reforms in the 1980s did away with some of
the earlier job-reservation restrictions prohibiting Africans from being

employed in certain skills categories and excluding them from technical training. But educational and social barriers remained, effectively preventing most African workers from training under the apprenticeship system.

Transforming the inherited training system has been a major challenge. How does one tackle a discriminatory system without destroying aspects that have been tried and tested as sound? How does one create an environment for win-win outcomes between those who have traditionally benefited from exclusion and those seeking inclusion? The nature of social relationships between white blue-collar workers and unskilled black workers adds further complexities. For apprenticeship to work, a supportive partnership between trainer and trainee is needed. In our circumstances, the trainers (the 'bosses') had been conditioned to see black people as inferior. Changing attitudes is essential to success in training apprentices.

Transforming the labour market and skills-training system was further complicated by horse-trading at the negotiation table. The 'spoils of freedom' were apportioned in a manner that managed expectations from as many stakeholders as possible. Policy choices in the skills-training arena were largely driven by organised labour that has been given a disproportionate say on these matters by the Tripartite Alliance (the ANC, SACP and Cosatu). The linkages between the macro-economy (an area where the ANC used its muscle to set policy) and the micro-economy (where labour issues play a key role) were underestimated.

The impact of labour-market and skills-training-system reforms on the whole of society is such that greater say should have been given to all three parties: private sector, public sector, and organised labour. The good offices of the National Economic, Development and Labour Council (Nedlac), set up to deal with complex issues in the economy, should have been used to help both the traditional and aspirant beneficiaries of skills training to reform the apprenticeship system rather than jettison it at such a high cost to the economy. We are now overburdened by the unintended consequences of the Skills Development Act of 1998 and the Skills Development Levies Act of 1999 that have spawned an unwieldy bureaucracy.

The Sector Education and Training Authority (Seta) system

The 1999 Skills Development Levies Act sought to increase public and private sector investment in skills development by a deduction of 1% of payroll of all employers for a national skills fund.[133] Levies paid by employers to the South African Revenue Service (SARS) are put in a special fund: 80% is distributed to sector-specific Sector Education and Training Authorities (Setas) charged with overseeing the utilisation of these funds to enhance skills development, while 20% is allocated to the National Skills Fund for skills development projects that do not fall under Setas.

Setas replace and extend the work of the old industry training boards, and are accredited by the South African Qualifications Authority (Saqa). Within each sector, a Seta must develop and implement a skills development plan, be responsible for quality control, and pay out skills development grants that can be claimed by employers for having trained employees. Setas have discretionary funds, drawn from their levy income, that can be used for projects aimed at achieving sector priorities, including developing learnerships, which must be approved by the Department of Labour (DOL) before they are implemented. Learnerships are similar to apprenticeships in that both combine theoretical learning with practical workplace application, but learnerships are based on unit standards and culminate in a qualification that is registered on the National Qualifications Framework (NQF).

Many problems have plagued the changeover to a new skills training regime. One of the biggest is confusion surrounding the issue of learnerships versus apprenticeships. Some documents related to the new Further Education and Training (FET) Colleges state that learnerships have replaced apprenticeships. An online document of the Safety and Security Seta (Sasseta) states: '[L]earnerships will replace the apprenticeship system, as the DOL and Setas favour the learnership system.'[134]

In contrast, in a media briefing in February 2007, Education Minister Naledi Pandor highlighted the importance of both traditional apprenticeships and modern learnerships as connecting routes towards developing skills: 'Many small businesses which used to take in apprentices have stopped. We need to engage them as government to continue to support apprenticeship. Learnerships were never meant to replace apprenticeships.'[135]

South Africa is experiencing a severe shortage of well-qualified, competent and experienced artisans. In 2006, we produced about 5 000 artisans while research suggested that about 12 500 were needed each year for the next four years.[136] Siemens South Africa revived an apprenticeship-training programme in 2007 as part of its effort to address the shortage of skilled artisans. They see it as a long-term commitment that will produce far more artisans than they need, to the benefit of the whole country. The revival of the programme took place in alignment with AsgiSA and the Joint Initiative on Priority Skills Acquisition (Jipsa), as well as in consultation with Deputy President Phumzile Mlambo-Ngcuka and the Minister of Public Works.[137]

Such initiatives seem to hold greater hope for the success of Jipsa (intended to fast-track skills delivery in priority areas and unblock obstacles to support the AsgiSA objectives of promoting economic growth and halving poverty and unemployment by 2014) than the cumbersome, time-consuming processes involving the Setas. There are also obstacles to Jipsa's success. Different definitions of 'scarce skills' by the DOL and Home Affairs pose a major challenge. Home Affairs' list of skills that can be acquired from abroad does not provide for managers or lower-level skilled operators, effectively creating a barrier to the sourcing of lower-level artisan skills from elsewhere. This is yet another costly example of the government's failure to co-ordinate policy-making, implementation, monitoring and evaluation.

The creation of Setas in 2000 was intended to provide a supportive, coherent base for skills training. Setas were to be the primary drivers in the government's ambitious national skills development strategy. In practice, despite some successes and hard work by some committed individuals, they have spawned huge bureaucracies often headed by people with little experience in coordinating skills training on this scale. Many have proven to be unaccountable for funds under their jurisdiction. There have been numerous cases of corruption and refusals to let the Auditor General carry out audits of their books. A celebrated case involves the Transport Seta that in 2006 passed on more than R200 million of its funds to a fraudulent company, Fidentia, which has since been liquidated pending court cases against the leading players. The head of the Seta, Piet Bothma, was arrested and charged alongside the Fidentia managers in mid-2007.

Putting together unit standards of training experiences in learnerships does not necessarily constitute a coherent knowledge base for practical use. Many young people with learnership certificates find themselves unable to perform in the workplace. For instance, no unit standard can prepare one for how to help choose and serve wine for customers in a restaurant without the apprenticeship experience of watching skilled people perform.

According to government's figures, there was a significant drop in the number of apprentices trained between 1986 and 1998[138] from nearly 30 000 annually to just below 17 000. More worrying was the drop in overall sector training output from almost 290 000 in 1986 to just over 61 000 in 1998. These figures reflect a serious situation, given the rising demand for skills in our economy. The DOL's Skills Report for 2005 acknowledged widespread inefficiencies of Setas. Performance against set targets ranged from 60% by the Manufacturing Seta to 6% in the Health and Welfare Seta.

According to a recent damning report, 80% of the Setas failed to spend a total of R600 million in 2006/07. Seta representatives blamed this on the failure of their business constituencies to claim back grants for workplace skills training. For example, the Construction Seta said their unspent surplus could be attributed to the fact that most employers in the construction industry are not training their employees, leaving them with a huge amount of money collected from skills levies.[139] A review of the Setas instituted by the Labour Minister culminated in the National Industrial Policy Framework (NIPF), the crux of which was to cluster the 23 Setas around five related sectors. Roll-out of the envisaged mergers of existing Setas will take effect only in March 2010 after they have run their legal lifespan. According to the DOL, it would be 'wrong and premature to assume the Setas would be trimmed or enlarged in any manner until stakeholders have agreed through the Nedlac Seta review process'. At the ANC's recent Polokwane conference, the

ruling party endorsed the Labour Minister's vision by adopting a resolution calling for a drastic reduction of Setas to a few mega-institu-
tions.[140]

The Further Education and Training (FET) College system

While the school system and higher education received much attention
in the initial period after 1994, technical colleges were the last to be
subjected to reforms. This delay in dealing with a sector that traditionally had the responsibility of building technical knowledge and skills at
the intermediate level has also contributed to our serious skills shortages among mid-level artisans.

Under former Minister of Education Kader Asmal, the existing 152
technical/vocational colleges in South Africa were declared Further
Education and Training (FET) Colleges in September 2001, and directed to merge to form 50 multi-campus institutions which would be more
viable and effective.[141] Part of the problem of transforming old technical colleges into modern FET colleges has been that some sites in rural
areas or townships have traditionally been under-resourced and less exposed to the influence of commerce and industry, making for a very
uneven landscape of quality and relevance of training.

FET colleges are intended to give students a different option to the
theoretical and combined theoretical/practical training provided by
universities and universities of technology. They offer further education and training in a range of vocational subjects to people of all ages,
and offer FET courses in Grades 10 to 12 in schools. On completion of
General Education and Training at the end of Grade 9, learners can
choose to complete FET either in schools or in FET colleges. FET certificates are equivalent to matric and provide access to higher education.

It is still too early to say whether these colleges will meet expectations.
Their recapitalisation has taken long and the introduction of new Vocational Certificate Programmes on Levels 2, 3 and 4 of the National
Qualifications Framework to replace the old programmes only took place
in 2007. In theory, they hold the promise of a new and dynamic FET
sector that can help address skills shortages in critical areas.

In his 2007 State of the Nation address, President Mbeki alluded to an underlying problem regarding education and training: 'We do hope that our efforts to promote this area of opportunity will help send the message, especially to our young people, that artisan skills are as critical for economic growth as other levels of qualification.'[142] In a conference paper entitled 'Parity of esteem: hope or despair?' Ronel Blom of Saqa suggests that technical and vocational education has generally suffered from neglect, and that persistent incorrect assumptions about technical education being a 'lower-class' qualification or for the 'less intelligent' could hamper efforts to make the FET system succeed.[143] In 2006, 400 000 students were registered at FET colleges, while 750 000 were studying at universities.

Nursing and teacher training

Enthusiasm to transform the segregated vocation-specific colleges for nurses and teachers has created further constraints to skills development. Nursing and teacher training colleges were closed or merged with higher education in the late 1990s. The idea was to eliminate discriminatory institutions, consolidate small institutions into bigger ones to enhance efficiency, and raise the level of offerings through linkages with higher education.

There have been unintended consequences. First, moving nursing training into higher education ignored the importance of practical training, which not only imparts hands-on technical skills, but also professional conduct such as a proper bedside manner that is difficult to convey through theoretical teaching. Second, nurses trained in higher education institutions considered themselves students, not trainees. They identified with the rest of the student body rather than with their professional peers.

Third, the quality of nursing care provided by this new cohort of nurses seems to have declined. My sister, a retired professional nurse, expresses an increasing concern, shared by many in her profession, about the attitudes of some of these new nurses. Many show little empathy with patients; some are downright callous in their treatment of those in pain or facing life-threatening situations.

Finally, the number of nursing trainees has dropped significantly over the 1994-2006 period. Several factors account for this drop.

First, conditions of service have deteriorated since 1994. Until the long-awaited September 2007 increases, the take-home pay of many nurses was less than R10 000 for those with more than ten years of service. Long working hours also made it an unattractive career. Second, the prestige attached to the nursing profession has waned as young women enjoy increasingly better options elsewhere in the economy. Third, the HIV/Aids pandemic has made nursing a tougher, riskier profession. Health facilities are overburdened with sick people who are HIV positive and do not access treatment early enough. Staff shortages make for difficult working conditions. In addition, the risk of needle pricks rises with exhaustion, and could spell the difference between remaining HIV negative or becoming part of the rising tide of HIV-positive people. The increasing multi-drug resistant TB and its extreme form add to the negative image of the profession.

The opening of opportunities for international migration also contributes to our skills problems. As mentioned before, South Africa is losing significant numbers of nurses to other countries. The push factors detailed above combined with the pull factors of less burdened, professionally run health services in their countries of destination have seen more than 23 000 nurses emigrate since 1996.

Health Minister Manto Tshabalala-Msimang's first response, together with her counterparts from the rest of the African continent in the early 2000s, was inappropriate and ineffectual. Their solidarity pact not to recruit nurses from fellow African countries simply led to African nurses leaving the profession or the continent altogether. South Africa could have benefited, and can still benefit from recruiting African nurses who would prefer to relocate here during periods of instability in their own countries rather than migrate to far-off lands.

Government took too long to restructure the compensation packages of nurses, to address the gross inequity between conditions of service for experienced high-skilled theatre or intensive-care nurses earning less than half the salary of an entry-level government official with little skill and no experience. Neglect of professionals in our public service compared to bureaucrats has cost us dearly, as the 2007 public sector strike has demonstrated.

The September 2007 agreement between the government and the nursing profession is to be welcomed. It will see nurses' salaries increase by 20-88%, depending on the level of skill and experience. Entry-level nurses will earn 20% more, from R58 290 to R70 140. Professional nurses and assistant nurses will receive 24% more, from R85 362 to R106 086 for the former and R43 245 to R53 757 for the latter.[144]

The same challenges pertain to the teaching profession's conditions of service. Teacher training has also suffered from over-ambitious policy reforms. Closing down teacher training colleges, while driven by noble motives, was a mistake that the government has recognised and is rectifying. Teacher trainees need a safe space to hone their content knowledge and practical skills that is not necessarily available in the higher education institutions to which they have been entrusted. Higher education is an appropriate training level for those able to do an undergraduate degree before a teaching diploma. Most higher education institutions have weak education faculties and are hardly appropriate seats for intellectual-capital formation. The reopening of teacher training facilities is also good for desperately needed in-service training.

As with nursing, the teaching profession has lost its prestige in society, especially in poor communities where teachers are sorely needed. Factors such as poor pay, inappropriate curriculum reforms, lack of support for new ways of maintaining discipline, high levels of stress because of large, undisciplined classes, as well as high levels of HIV/Aids and alcoholism have taken their toll on teacher morale. The poor leadership of the biggest teacher union (Sadtu) has also contributed to inappropriate behaviour by teachers in classrooms. Absenteeism, alcohol and drug abuse, sexual and other forms of pupil harassment, and other examples of unprofessional behaviour are blindly defended.

Sadtu leadership's response to the inappropriate behaviour of teachers who intimidated fellow teachers (some were assaulted with whips) and pupils to support the 2007 strike exemplifies the problem. Sadtu maintained that anyone could have donned a Sadtu T-shirt and claimed to be a member, so there was nothing for which they had to apologise. In contrast, the Afrikaans teachers' union, the Suid-Afrikaanse Onderwysersunie (SAOU), was unequivocal about its displeasure at members who had participated in unprofessional behaviour. For them, the strikers had done 'irreparable harm to teachers and the profession in the eyes of parents and the community at large'.[145]

It is encouraging that the government is taking measures to address the structural problems in the teaching profession. Restructuring compensation and creating incentives for professionalism and skills development are essential in retaining thousands of hard-working teachers among the 386 000 in our schools. Creating better teaching and learning spaces, as announced by the National Minister of Education, will go a long way to providing for better performance in science and technology. Addressing the bottlenecks in implementing OBE is critical to unlocking the potential of poor pupils to learn and to close the gap between them and those in more affluent schools with better-skilled teachers. Increasing teacher bursaries – a measure reintroduced over the last two years – is vital to attracting young people into the profession.

Recently released international surveys assessing investment climate and competitiveness have identified skills shortages as the number-one problem for South Africa, which ranks 46 out of 128 countries (40th in 2006). A common theme runs through our inability to overcome the legacy of under-investment in education and training. Transformation of any system requires a built-in monitoring and evaluation system to allow for identification of unintended consequences.

In addition to corrective measures government is now taking, especially under Jipsa, we need to ensure greater coherence within the training system. It is discouraging that the DOL's own 2005 skills report indicates that cooperation between FET colleges and other partners for the purposes of workplace training and placement of qualified trainees stands at 55% with business partners and only 3% with Setas. A long, hard look at bad habits and ineffectual practices is essential.

We must have the self-confidence to confront policy choices that are not working and take bold corrective action. The sooner we jettison the dysfunctional Seta system and revert to an appropriately refined 21st-century apprenticeship system, the better – or our competitors in the global knowledge economy are likely to streak further ahead of us.

CHAPTER 12

Higher education

TRANSFORMING A DISCRIMINATORY, FRAGMENTED HIGHER-EDUCATION system with elements of excellence in a sea of mediocrity into a coordinated and uniformly excellent one has been a major challenge for post-apartheid South Africa.

In any society, higher education is the platform for the practice of high-level human and intellectual work and the training of future generations of professionals, scientists and technological experts. In the 21st-century knowledge economy, competitiveness is enhanced by the quality of a country's human and intellectual capital. Understanding the interdependence of equity and excellence, competitive societies have invested in greater access to higher education and also improved quality.

South Africa's dilemmas in transforming its higher-education system stem from perceived competition between excellence and equity. The new political elites have sometimes overemphasised equity at the expense of excellence. The entire White Paper on Education and the Education Acts that followed not once used the term 'excellence'. It is encouraging to see that in the last three years the Department of Education (DOE) and the government have become more focused on promoting excellence. The establishment of the Department of Science and Technology under a mathematician, Mosibudi Mangena, bodes well for the future.

Transformation in higher education brings together four stakeholders with distinct but overlapping roles. First, the national government as policy maker and major steering agent must ensure that the system delivers outcomes aligned to national development goals. Second, higher-education institutions with their responsibilities for teaching, learning, research and service in line with their respective missions must ensure performance on set goals. Third, students as the direct beneficiaries of higher education are both customers and long-term investors in processes to enhance outcomes. Fourth, the wider society, including the private sector, has a vested interest in quality outcomes of higher education.

Given the legacy of discrimination, few people would oppose taking corrective action to make the system more equitable. Equally logical is the imperative of promoting excellence of outcomes as measured by the quality of graduates, of research and innovation as well as service to the wider society. The difficulty arises in how to promote both goals in a system that has traditionally treated them as conflicting.

Traditionalists, especially white males, tend to be preoccupied with the need to maintain standards in higher education, professional appointments and management promotions. Suggestions of the need for change in the profiles of students and staff are met with the defence that standards cannot be lowered. The presumption is that white males embody the standard. Any new entrants would have to prove that they are worthy of inclusion in the established culture and not a threat to traditional standards.

Those calling for radical transformation also tend to have rigid views. For many activists transformation means replacing the old order with a new one, which for them amounts to replacing white male dominance with greater representation of black people. Greater access for black students and staff, greater visibility of black leadership at all levels and higher outputs of black graduates are all desirable goals. The dilemma remains how to achieve them within a reasonable time without compromising quality.

I would like to propose that excellence and equity are complementary goals – one cannot have one without the other. The exclusion of black people and women from meaningful participation in the academic enterprise has undermined the competitiveness of South Africa's higher-education system. Skills shortages combined with weak human and intellectual capital are a direct result of the apartheid system's failure to see how equity and excellence complement each other. More equitable access to opportunities offered by higher education enables society to draw from a wider pool of diverse talents. But more equitable access without creating a climate of high-quality performance would not enhance the common good. Promoting excellence is essential to the functioning of higher education. It enables societies to educate and train leaders in the public and private sectors, regenerate their knowledge production and innovation, and anticipate development challenges. It is even more critical in light of the legacy of mediocrity that permeates our education and training system.

Promoting equal access to mediocrity would be a travesty of justice. Experience worldwide points to the reality that in a situation of uneven quality of performance in an education system, those who are better off can buy themselves and their children access to higher-quality opportunities. Historical divisions between white and black institutions continue to reflect quality differences within the system.

Denial of the impact of our legacy of discriminatory education has undermined the capacity of many black people to move beyond mediocrity to meritocracy. For obvious reasons, most historically black institutions (HBIs), with notable exceptions, have been poorly led, their teaching staff poorly trained and equipped, and their students mainly drawn from poorly performing schools. How could an institution designed for mediocrity perform well without deliberate quality-improvement programmes? Such programmes cannot be instituted without overcoming denial. Quality-improvement programmes are also needed in historically white institutions (HWIs) to make them more internationally competitive.

The legacy of underperformance at HBIs has put them at a disadvantage. In the post-1994 era, black students and staff have wider choice and are voting with their feet, entering better located and resourced HWIs.

The promotion of equity and excellence in higher education involves three main domains: equal-opportunity-access programmes for staff and students; academic support for both student and staff development; and institutional change towards an inclusive culture. Transformation understood in these terms would offer a dynamic environment for vibrant scholarship in a community that celebrates diversity. In this context, affirmative action (more eloquently captured in Afrikaans as *regstellende aksie*) would correct what went wrong from past social engineering. Normalising the functioning of our institutions must involve systematic programmes to create a climate of success.

The legacy of apartheid education left gross distortions in the enrolment patterns in higher education. According to the Council on Higher Education (CHE), headcount enrolments rose from 473 000 in 1993 and 596 000 in 1999 to 737 472 in 2005, with the proportion of black students increasing from 46% in 1993 to 63% in 1997 and 66% in 2002. The 2005 figures also show that enrolment of women has risen to 53% among contact students and 57% among distance-learning students.[146]

Staff profiles in most higher-education institutions reflected glaring inequities in race and gender. In 1994 more than 90% of academic and administrative staff of most HWIs were white males. White women, who in theory had the same educational opportunities as white males, were under-represented in senior positions owing partly to biases of the male-dominated culture of these institutions. HBIs also had male dominance in senior positions.

Transformation of staff profiles of all institutions presents major dilemmas. How is one to change these profiles given the lag between education and training, and readiness for senior positions within the academy? This is a particular concern within key skills areas such as science and engineering where much longer technical and practical experience must precede appointment to senior academic positions. Either one patiently follows the traditional rules and proceeds slowly towards changing staff profiles, or one creates a fast track for under-represented academics through rapid promotions.

The slow, orderly route using the tried-and-tested process of academic progression is politically and educationally risky. The relatively rapid increases in the proportion of black students at HWIs create political pressure for change. There are also sound educational reasons for having visible black and female role models in senior academic positions if one is to promote excellence as a realisable goal for black and female students to aspire to. There are, however, risks in a too-rapid progression of black people and women that could potentially put them at levels beyond their competence. Such a misalignment could place them under undue pressure and undermine their intellectual development and future careers. Finding the right balance in the pace of change poses the biggest challenge.

From 1991-2000 the University of Cape Town (UCT), where I served as a Deputy Vice-Chancellor then Vice-Chancellor, adopted a two-pronged strategy. We actively recruited Africans in the diaspora who had left their own countries and were teaching in institutions abroad. They helped fill important positions, especially in science and engineering, and provided visible, successful role models. We also embarked on a programme of Growing Our Own Timber (GOOT), to recruit black people and women to consider an academic career. We partnered with local and overseas philanthropists and the private sector to create fast-track opportunities for masters, doctoral and postdoctoral training, and forged partnerships with universities abroad to support programmes for high-potential scholars. The positive spin-offs of GOOT are such that other institutions have adapted it for their own needs.

Changing the profile of students requires systematic affirmative action, actively recruiting talent from non-traditional feeder schools and the use of alternative admission testing to identify potential.[147] Financial aid to poor talented students is also essential. Providing academic support to close conceptual gaps arising from poor-quality schooling is critical. Such gaps are widespread, given the challenges of transformation in the school system outlined in Chapter 10.

The challenge for government

The role of the national government is to steer the system so that successful transformation of higher education addresses both its size and shape. Apartheid's social engineering of education had resulted in an inappropriately shaped system. Institutions were badly located and there was poor differentiation between them in terms of their missions matched to their strengths. Too few focused on producing high-level science and technology graduates, too many on the social sciences and humanities.

Compared to competitive countries with similar population size, the system was too small in terms of student numbers. In 1994 participation rates for white students in the 18-25 age group was close to 75%, for black students only around 5%. The system was fragmented into too many institutions lacking the critical mass needed for dynamic scholarship. It had to be radically transformed to produce the size and shape that could yield the profile of skills needed to run a modern economy and democracy.

Over much of the first decade of democracy, attempts to transform the higher-education system were undermined by its legacy. The very people responsible for transforming the system were scarred by that same legacy.

The post-1994 government's own capacity problems made it difficult for it to respond adequately to the recommendations of the National Commission on Higher Education (NCHE) Report. Part of the problem lay in the inadequacy of the report itself, which set unrealistic targets of 'massification' of higher education without taking account of a poorly performing school system. There was a lack of political will to make tough decisions to break the impasse between entrenched interests on both sides of the racial divide in higher education.

The government faced real dilemmas. How could a black government be seen to be tough on some of the black vice-chancellors who were acting irresponsibly without being accused of bashing victims of inequity? Redress became such an emotive word that to point to its abuse by those promoting personal interests was often considered politically risky. Arguments in favour of redefining redress in terms of creating an environment for the promotion of the highest quality of education for South Africa's young people were often drowned out by populism.

Equitable resource provision for the development and maintenance of institutions within a system characterised by diversity of missions and quality of outcomes became elusive as policy makers ran for cover. Advice that pointed to the strengths of the California system, in which institutional missions vary from community colleges and four-year undergraduate colleges to research universities, was brushed aside. Calls for differentiation were interpreted as calls for first-, second- and third-class citizenship within the higher-education system. This perceived class distinction was politically explosive in the context of the history of widespread discrimination against black people. It did not help that the apartheid legacy had programmed almost all HBIs for underperformance. Few, if any, would have qualified as research universities. Any suggestion of using excellence as a standard and focusing on quality issues ran into accusations of targeting HBIs for downgrading and ghettoising them into lower-level colleges.

Meritocracy was at risk of being rendered illegitimate as discriminatory in the politically charged 1990s. Differentiation of institutions by their missions and capabilities was suspect as inequitable. All institutions claimed they had the capacity for teaching, research and service at the highest levels, ascribing their failure to perform at high levels to a lack of financial resources.

An evolutionary approach that left the path open to institutions growing into roles beyond their current ones was put forward, but rejected. Either all universities were research universities or none should be. Institutions with no research or publication track records wanted to be accepted as 'universities of science and technology'.

Government's inadequate capacity to implement policy slowed progress in transforming higher education in the 1990s. Creating a system that embraced the principles recommended in the NCHE Report and enacted in the Higher Education Act of 1997 required systematic management reform. These principles were: equity and redress, quality, democratisation, development, effectiveness and efficiency, academic freedom, institutional autonomy, and public accountability. The system of higher education inherited from apartheid reflected the legacy of principles that negated almost all of these. The Ministry of Education, struggling to transform itself from the same legacy, was unable to give strategic leadership. It became a case of tilling with broken hoes.

A serious lack of sufficiently experienced staff has constrained the national DOE's capacity to steer the higher education system effectively. Between 1997 and 2006, the Higher Education branch in the DOE consisted of two professionals: the deputy director–general and one other senior professional, supported by a small team of junior professional and administrative staff. Both senior professionals were young and inexperienced. Enthusiasm was no substitute for the hardnosed skills needed to execute transformation.

If one compares the successful transformation of the Australian higher-education system in the early 1990s with South Africa's challenges, one sees how much the dice were loaded against us. Education Minister John Dawkins, who championed Australia's change process, was supported by sophisticated teams that had the benefit of international experience. Dawkins had a team of education economists compared to South Africa's zero. He had highly experienced demographers compared to our one economist, Charles Simkins. Dawkins had the backing of a government that understood the linkage between high-quality higher education and global competitiveness, and had the political will to reform the system to meet the challenges of the 21st century.

The Australian system consolidated its payroll-tax-linked student-loan scheme that permits cost sharing between individuals and society in funding higher education and remains the best performer in enabling equity of access for even the poorest students while ensuring sustainability through repayments by those earning above an agreed threshold.

Australia's higher education shed the vestiges of the Oxbridge culture and became a vibrant system steered by incentives that reward quality and relevance to its East Asian setting. Today higher education is one of Australia's fastest-growing export sectors, exploiting ICT to promote distance learning in Asia. Dawkins was part of a government ready to take tough decisions. Our government was overburdened by too many other priorities of a fragile young democracy.

Pooling resources was the only sensible option, but collaboration between the DOE and the higher-education system raised its own challenges. Respect for the role of the government department as distinct from the roles of individual institutions is key to such collaborative ventures. The government has public accountability for creating a regulatory framework within which the higher-education system must function. It must be seen to be transparent in upholding the public interest above the narrow interests of the system, let alone those of institutions within it. Framing a collaborative framework that managed the risks of conflicts of interest was difficult. Relying on experts from the higher-education system to do the analysis, present options for reform, frame implementation plans, and monitor performance against plans, put the Ministry of Education at risk of being hostage to the partisan interests of the system.

Ironically, the diversity of interests within the system helped mitigate the risk of collusion among higher-education institutions. HBIs had a vested interest in radical transformation with a focus on consigning discrimination within the system to the scrapheap. So they pushed hard for those principles of the Act focusing on equity, redress, democratisation and public accountability. HWIs were anxious to ensure protection of quality, effectiveness, efficiency, academic freedom and institutional autonomy. Many on both sides of the divide were wholly committed to all the principles; hardliners on both sides were neutralised by those who focused on the overall welfare of the system as a whole. The weak Education Department, and its Higher Education branch, were spared the additional burden of dealing with a unified block of self-interest.

The risk of the government going it alone to impose top-down reforms also concentrated the minds of higher-education players. Education Minister Bhengu's failed attempt in 1996 to impose redress measures by top-slicing the budget in favour of HBIs put the entire system on high alert. The successful challenge to the government's plan by the leadership of higher education across the historical institutional divide re-emphasised the need for collaborative, consultative approaches rather than top-down reforms. The long tradition of guarding institutional autonomy and academic freedom within historically English-speaking institutions was an asset to draw on. Higher education survived apartheid to the extent it did thanks to the efforts of a few English-language institutions such as UCT and the University of the Witwatersrand that in some important instances actively resisted encroachment of misguided government policies on the higher-education system.

Significant cultural differences within HWIs made for difficult relationships between English- and Afrikaans-medium institutions. The latter had a tradition of closer relationships to the apartheid government and were more culturally programmed to accept the post-apartheid government's top-down approaches. It was, after all, part of their political culture to follow government dictates during the apartheid period. Many were the intellectual engine rooms of much of the then government's policies. But English-language HWIs' need to mobilise public support in defence of academic freedom and institutional autonomy in the latter stages of the apartheid era forced them into alliances that promoted greater public accountability. Top-down government approaches by the apartheid system were successfully challenged in the courts and backed by public support.[148] Reframing relationships between the government and higher education became an important part of the challenge of transition to democracy.

Challenges facing the higher-education system and institutions
In grappling with dilemmas of transformation, the higher-education system also has to contend with stubborn apartheid ghosts that continue to frustrate progress. In the early stage of transformation historical divisions played themselves out at the system-wide level as well as in relationships between institutions. The South African University Vice-Chancellors' Association (Sauvca), formed in 1995, continued to reflect the divides between English- and Afrikaans-medium universities on one hand, and those between HBIs and HWIs on the other.

Most HBIs were located in so-called homelands, characterised by poverty, unemployment, poor morale and corrupt petty politicians who sought to benefit from the system. There was no private sector with which to partner. Innovation was limited by poor research and postgraduate capabilities. They were trapped in a cycle of failure.

While the University of Fort Hare had seen better days as the intellectual home of Oliver Tambo, Govan Mbeki, Nelson Mandela and their contemporaries, it was not immune to the post-1994 exodus of some of the best staff and students. As the only relatively viable institution in a sea of poverty, it was under immense pressure to provide employment for the local population after the demise of the homeland system. (In the 1990s, Fort Hare was said to have employed three tractor drivers for every tractor owned by the university.) The moral pressure to keep support jobs for poor people had to be weighed against the imperatives of good fiscal management to meet its primary mandate of providing sustainable education.

Denial of the nature and extent of these structural problems by many of the leaders of HBIs led to resistance to change. Instead of acknowledging the reality of the legacy of apartheid, they sought to defend the track record of their institutions against mounting evidence of the urgent need for change. Much energy went into making the case for financial redress, as if more money was the solution to critical structural problems.

Some staff and students feared that acknowledging the poor performance of HBIs could see them blamed as black people 'who cannot manage'. This fear is not to be underestimated in a racist society that still has strong undertones suggesting black inferiority. Never mind that it was white people who designed, established and ran these poorly performing institutions, black people now found themselves defending them as if they were their own creations. None of the NP supporters over the years under apartheid has been willing to own up to the mistake in conceiving of HBIs. They have now become a black problem – another 'black man's burden', to use Basil Davidson's phrase.[149]

Resistance to fundamental change had much to do with the perceived risk to jobs and status for many inside the system. Many vice-chancellors and other executives in higher education have very comfortable jobs compared to their peers in the public and private sectors. In an environment of high unemployment, being a vice-chancellor with a compensation package of R700 000 to R1 million annually is not insignificant. Many institutional councils, to whom vice-chancellors report, have in their ranks people with little experience of institutional governance and performance management systems. There is also a gap in the 1997 Higher Education Act that leaves the national minister with no mechanism to demand and enforce performance against plans set out by institutions. Good governance and fiduciary responsibilities are seriously inadequate in many institutions.

In the 1990s many leaders of HBIs found themselves with their backs to the wall as student enrolments fell below sustainable levels – a result of greater choices for black students and the mushrooming of distance-learning programmes offered by entrepreneurial (largely Afrikaans) institutions. Survival became their focus. They wanted government to bail them out from massive debt. HWIs favoured in the old system were in a better position – their urban locations, superior facilities and higher levels of human and intellectual resources made them more competitive.

The sense of unfairness with regard to how history has unfolded leads to confusion in political discourse on transformation. For example, when I became vice-chancellor of UCT in 1996, some former activist colleagues accused me 'selling out' the cause of freedom. In their view, it was inconceivable that I would promote the interests of an institution that would not have admitted me as a medical student in the 1960s because of my racial classification.

Black people's hesitation to seize opportunities to take charge of the institutions that excluded them in the past attests to deep-seated unresolved issues around transformation. The same people who have difficulties accepting HWIs see no contradiction in taking over the reins of government and occupying the very seats used by the former oppressors to rule over an oppressed people. The symbolism of taking over government's levers of power is unambiguous; making institutions work in the new dispensation is more difficult to handle.

The absurdity of the continuing 'them' and 'us' in post-apartheid South Africa brings to mind economist Amartya Sen's observations on identity and 'choiceless singularity', which refers to the tendency to ascribe a single identity to individuals to the exclusion of all other possible identities:

> The descriptive weakness of choiceless singularity has the effect of momentously impoverishing the power and reach of our social and political reasoning. The illusion of destiny exacts a remarkably high price.[150]

This 'choiceless singularity' leads to the temptation to embrace HBIs, overtly created by the apartheid system to prevent black people from aspiring to greener pastures not meant for them. It is the impoverishment of our social and political reasoning that created 'the illusion of destiny' that makes us prisoners of history instead of agents of its making.

If we allow ourselves the space to use our power of reasoning, we would conclude that all South African institutions, whether historically black or white, are tainted by apartheid to a greater or lesser extent. They all need to be transformed. My choice of UCT as a staging post was strategic. I saw an opportunity to leverage the institution's pre-eminence in the higher-education system to effect greater impact nationally.

Overcoming the elitist, exclusionary nature of white-dominated higher education was an essential part of transformation. UCT suffered from credibility problems as a result of this legacy. My challenge was to nurture the public's trust in the institution's ability to transform itself, a tall order, but not impossible, given the strong foundations laid by my predecessor, Stuart Saunders.

Enhancing access and academic support

Facing up to the need to complement access with academic support elicited mixed reactions. Many black students regarded academic support programmes as equivalent to ghettos to which they were consigned within HWIs. The reality of the gaps in their conceptual framework and development was hard to swallow. Early versions of such programmes were inadequate, and their white proponents were consumed by guilt about instituting programmes for black students. It was difficult not to have one side labelling the other as racist or over-sensitive and uninformed.

Many students who refused academic support obtained mediocre degrees that added to the challenge of getting desired jobs as black graduates in a world in which racial prejudice is still rife. Their poor qualifications played into the racist myth of black inferiority. Some students with poor foundations dropped out without any accredited qualification after six or seven years at university, with little prospect of earning enough to repay their loans. Institutions also face the challenge of unrecoverable student debt.

A 2000-2004 study by Ian Scott, a UCT academic specialising in academic-support programmes, found that even after four years of study only about a third (36% of university and 26% of technikon students) had graduated.[151] Many of those who drop out literally drop out of the opportunities post-apartheid society has to offer.

The success of UCT's Engineering faculty in transforming itself from a predominately white male preserve up to the 1980s to the largest producer of black engineers in South Africa demonstrates the value of well-designed academic-support programmes. The pioneer of Academic Support in Engineering Training (ASPECT) was the late Prof. John Martin. As dean from 1983-1996 he implemented the kind of programmes he had seen working at Brown University, USA. UCT moved from producing zero African engineers up to the 1980s to producing 47% of all African engineering graduates by 2004, according to the Engineering Council of South Africa. If one uses the inclusive term 'black', UCT produced 37% (886) of all black engineering graduates (2 414) between 1999 and 2004.

After a long period of confusion, academic support has become an accepted feature of higher education in South Africa. The earlier resistance by black students reflected tensions between acknowledging the legacy of poor education and the fear of being labelled as intellectually inferior. Academic-support programmes were seen as humiliating to black students who in most cases came into higher education as star performers from their schools.

The case of a PhD student in the Science faculty in the early 1990s comes to mind. She had obtained a distinction in her masters' programme at a sister university before enrolling at UCT. The assessment administered to all doctoral students revealed significant gaps, and she was asked to do a foundation year before enrolling for her doctoral studies. The student had accepted this reluctantly until she heard from fellow black students that this was a fate reserved only for black students to 'put them in their place'. She was referred to me after failed counselling by her advisers and supervisors. I shared my own story with her. I had to start mathematics in Grade 11 since Bantu Education had offered me only arithmetic up to Grade 10. The fact that I was top of my class countrywide at the end of Grade 10 did not take away the reality of the gaps in my knowledge base. I told her that I requested support for mathematics from the principal, which enabled me to graduate from high school with a first-class pass including higher-grade mathematics. I urged her to reconsider her objections to the proposed academic support. She cried, but in the end relented. She completed her doctoral studies and has become a trailblazer as a black woman in mathematics.

The gap between the experiences of predominantly black students and largely white academic staff constrained open conversation about fears and aspirations. Black students needed reassurance that their hard-won achievements against huge obstacles to gain entrance at university were not discounted. Predominantly white staff members struggled to find a language to communicate the reality of skills gaps in these high achievers to ensure greater future success. Anger and frustration often boiled over. The charge that HWIs were racist and did not want to see black people succeed became conventional wisdom amongst activist students and some staff. Many white professors felt embarrassed about being labelled racists. Some rolled over and gave in to students' demands to be allowed to follow the normal curriculum even when the risk of failure was high.

Changing the institutional culture

It is to be expected that institutions founded by white males for white males would have very strong male cultures. Academic institutions worldwide reflect an ethos flowing from the dominant roles that men have played as students, teachers and researchers. In South Africa's case, our sociopolitical history has left a deep imprint on the higher-education landscape. Racism, sexism and authoritarianism are deeply embedded in the cultures of many institutions. Changing these cultures requires systematic processes to minimise the risks of driving undesirable elements underground.

HWIs were initially blind to the need for change in their institutional cultures to enhance access and create a climate for quality performance by all regardless of race, gender and class. They were in denial about the extent of the change needed to make them truly South African institutions that performed on a par with their peers worldwide. South Africa's isolation during the apartheid years had made HWIs complacent about their competitiveness. A benchmarking study done in the late 1990s showed that only UCT and Stellenbosch came anywhere near being competitive.

There are persistent fears on the part of white people of losing what they have taken for granted for so long. For some HWIs and their staff, it was hard to recognise that traditional white English liberal approaches to higher education were unsuitable for post-apartheid South Africa.

Afrikaans-speaking institutions were sometimes more preoccupied with yesterday's Anglo-Boer language disputes than with being part of the solution to South Africa's massive skills crisis. There was little acknowledgement that as institutions closest to the power structure of the NP that systematised apartheid, they had a moral responsibility to help redress the legacy of the past.

At UCT, my predecessor Stuart Saunders had the foresight to institute a systematic study of the institutional culture, culminating in the 1992 Equal Opportunity Employment Policy together with anti-racist and anti-sexual-harassment policies that paved the way for cultural transformation. For the first time white male professors who may have been accustomed to sexually harassing women without any expectation of being held to account found themselves at risk.

Black male students who fell foul of the anti-sexual-harassment policy resented my championing of these policies. UCT's traditional culture tolerated sexual harassment as a part of life in university residences. This transcended racial and class barriers at the university, reflecting the male chauvinist culture in the wider society. As an educational institution UCT had a responsibility to help young students to develop into responsible men. Sexual harassment had to be tackled head-on to create a positive climate for women and men to learn and work together creatively.

Black male students felt particularly vulnerable to the anti-harassment policies. While many white students had apartments and private homes where they could do as they pleased and hide their behaviour, many black students could not afford privacy and acted out their harassment of black female students in the public domain of residences. Offenders maintained that their behaviour was in line with African culture. I pointed out that ghetto culture that tolerated harassment of women could not be equated with African culture and that culture had to change to meet new challenges.

An essential aspect of education in a society with a human-rights constitution is challenging the notion that there are special features of African culture that permit abuse of women and children. In discussions with students, I pointed out that oppressed people in different cultures and geographic settings tend to take out their fury on the least powerful in their midst – anger turned against the self. Abusing women and others less powerful than oneself cannot be defined as an African cultural trait.

Inwardly directed anger is a phenomenon observed across the globe. Industrialising Europe, impoverished Ireland, and poor communities in Latin America are but a few examples. Changing the frame of reference of what being a man or a woman entailed was an essential part of the transformation of social relationships. Eliminating abuse was not only good for the abused but also for the human dignity of the abusers, who are often brutalised by their own brutality.

Student leaders questioned my motives: 'Why are you so focused on challenging sexual harassment, undermining black students and their culture? Why are you allowing yourself to be used as an instrument of feminists and white people in belittling black students?' Suggestions that the policies I helped introduce were targeted at black males could not be further from reality. But it clearly represented one of the biggest issues black male students felt strongly about.

Women students welcomed the changes that freed them from intimidation and harassment they had endured in the name of black solidarity. Reporting rape and harassment had up to then been regarded as disloyalty to fellow black students, given that it puts the career of the offender at risk. This logic puts the onus on the victim of abuse to protect the abuser.

Discontinuing noisy parties in Jameson Hall in 1996 made me more unpopular. These get-togethers often resulted in damage to property and injury to students related to alcohol abuse and intrusion by outsiders. The argument that students needed outlets for relaxation and fun was far outweighed by the negative spin-off. Putting our institution at risk in the name of entertainment for a few students made no sense.

Students were encouraged to have smaller parties in their residences. Personal development of students also helped them choose behaviour appropriate to their future roles in society as responsible citizens. It was pleasing to see the change in tone on the campus.

A young woman professional I met mid-2007 spoke to me about the impact of the anti-sexual-harassment intervention on women at UCT:

> We were the envy of fellow students from other universities where sexual harassment was rampant and the risk of rape was a reality in a woman student's life . . . We could wear whatever we liked without risking punishment from male students who regarded miniskirts and hot pants as 'invitations to be raped'. You created space for us to be ourselves.

Challenges of student politics

Activist student politics worldwide can be traced back to the radicalisation of politics in the 1960s. South African students were also influenced by international student radicalism to ask tough questions of their society. The National Union of South African Students (Nusas) and South African Student's Organisation (Saso) became major foci of anti-apartheid activism. Students remained crucial role players in the affairs of our nation until the last stages of the struggle for freedom.

During the transition to democracy in the early 1990s, student organisations tended to align themselves to the major liberation-movement formations. The South African Students Congress (Sasco) placed itself in the ANC tradition. The Pan African Students Organisation (Paso) was affiliated to the PAC. The Azanian Students Congress (Azasco) aligned itself to the Azanian People's Organisation (Azapo).

These ideologies generated energy and tensions within student politics. The shared anti-apartheid focus allowed for collaboration. After 1994 student politics became more belligerent towards university establishments and their leadership. Higher-education leadership was seen as reactionary and too slow in embracing transformation. University Transformation Forums (UTFs) were called for and demands were made to have them function like the national negotiation forum, the Convention for a Democratic South Africa (Codesa) at the World Trade Centre near Pretoria.

Radical transformation of UCT became a hot issue for student leadership in the run-up to the political settlement. Emboldened by the new national political landscape, they made far-reaching demands, disregarding the fact that they were short-term leaders of a transient student community within institutions that by their nature must have a long-term focus. They denounced white male domination of the leadership and the lack of adequate participation of students in decision-making. They demanded greater transparency in how decisions were made with regard to policy, staff appointments and allocation of resources, and a transformation forum in which students, staff, the university council and the executive would thrash out how to reshape the institution.

UCT student leaders demanded that the institution be more responsive to the aspirations of many young people for whom the institution remained an ivory tower on the hill. They pointed to the poor representation of township students, especially Africans, in the student body in which the majority were middle- and upper-class Capetonians, and to the weak links between the UCT and under-performing schools in the poor areas.

Student leaders also complained about UCT's institutional culture that continued to reflect its Anglo-Saxon roots. They complained about the exclusion of mainly black students on academic and financial grounds, pointing out that these students were victims of apartheid education and poverty and should not be denied the chance to prepare for a better future. The University Transformation Forum (UTF) established many working groups to address issues of governance, academic and financial exclusions. The process was participatory as a deliberate strategy of building trust.

Stuart Saunders was exemplary among the leaders of higher education in the early 1990s. He took a personal interest in transformation and attended the UTF workshops. Students respected him because he cared deeply about their welfare and that of the institution. Saunders had been one of the first leaders of higher education to find loopholes in the apartheid legislation to open access to UCT's residences to black students and to raise funds to provide financial support to poor talented students.[152]

The development of a new mission statement was initiated early in 1995 by a working group under the joint leadership of Don Qwelane, a law student and a member of Paso, and Chris Brink, a mathematics professor of Afrikaner descent. A more unlikely pair one could not have imagined. But they were the embodiment of South Africa. Don was a wiry man in his mid-twenties who came from Kimberley in the Northern Cape Province. He spoke English with a strong accent, rolling his r's. Chris had grown up in a Calvinistic cultural milieu that largely supported apartheid but he was one of a new generation of Afrikaners at ease with themselves as citizens of post-apartheid South Africa and committed to making it prosperous. He has a mild manner and a dry sense of humour.

As convener of the working group, I acted as facilitator while they led the drafting of the mission statement. The students were sceptical about the commitment of staff members to genuine participation by the students in a manner that would be 'empowering'. It was rewarding to watch that scepticism give way to mutual respect. I could see the student participants, especially Don, grow in self-confidence and trust. Inclusiveness contributed to a mission statement we could all be proud of.

The governance working group tackled the vexed question of participatory decision-making. What should be the role of the university council, given its statutory fiduciary and policy-making responsibilities? How does one let students participate in decision-making on long-term issues, given their status as a transient population? How much participation by students is desirable in matters of academic judgment in which students have vested interests?

Equally important was vigilance against populism. Sister institutions that gave in to populist demands by students found themselves in serious trouble. Students cannot be allowed to participate in decisions where conflicts of interests are so glaring as to make a mockery of the integrity of higher-education institutions. For example, dealing with appeals against academic exclusions is one thing; allowing students to pass judgment on the quality of the examination scripts of their peers is another.

UCT kept a firm stance about maintaining boundaries between appropriate and inappropriate participation in decision-making domains. The leadership view was that universities have the extraordinary responsibility to think beyond the needs of present generations. It was a tough line to maintain against the pressure for radical change.

The same line had to be drawn regarding student participation in selecting a new vice-chancellor to succeed Stuart Saunders, who was to retire in 1996. Student leaders and trade-union representatives wanted open interviews and an equal say alongside the university council on the final decision. The council and the senate wanted to prevent it from becoming a public 'beauty contest'.

A compromise was reached. The selection process would be conducted under the guidance of the UTF to ensure the process was participatory and transparent. The university council would retain the statutory responsibility of making the final appointment. There would be a public presentation of candidates to give the university community the opportunity to listen to the visions of each and to raise questions.

My attempts to avoid putting my name forward for the position of vice-chancellor failed. I came under pressure from many people, including President Nelson Mandela. Being a reluctant candidate allowed me the freedom to turn the public undressing by student leaders into a healing process.

Black male students verbally attacked me on that public platform, using me as a scapegoat for all their anger and frustrations at UCT. They did not trust me as a champion of transformation. To them, my reputation of being tough on poor performance and irresponsible behaviour indicated my lack of commitment to the interests of black people. I tried to answer without humiliating them.

I was accused of using promises to promote transformation at UCT as my ticket to get onto the 'gravy train'.[153] They assumed I was set to earn a huge salary as vice-chancellor. I told them there was no station yet at UCT for me to catch the 'gravy train'. Laughter brought some relief.

Fortunately my successor, Njabulo Ndebele, did not have to go through the same ordeal at his selection. Enthusiasm for the public hearings of the old-style selection processes has waned. There are now more dignified public presentations by short-listed candidates, followed by questions to gain clarity on important issues.

From administration towards management

There is much debate within the academy about managerialism in higher education. Many analysts view it as a negative development that undermines the collegiate culture.

The idea of 'first among equals' is at the heart of the Anglo-Saxon collegiate model of university leadership, which evolved from the Oxbridge complex of universities that had in turn evolved from the monastic culture that founded Oxford and Cambridge. It is a culture-specific model that assumes homogeneity and a shared value system, and customs that have been handed down from generation to generation.

At its heart is a centralised administration headed by a bureaucracy, at the head of which is a registrar, the custodian of all laws, regulations and procedures governing the academy. This system has over the years been modified in countries like the USA, Canada and Australia.

South African higher education could hardly escape fundamental change in its approach to managing institutions. First, the assumption of a smoothly running collegiate undermined by 'managerialism' was not based on objective analysis. HWIs were not homogenous in their approaches to administration and management. There were differences between Afrikaans- and English-language institutions that reflected philosophical orientations regarding the place of academia in society, including its responsiveness to social imperatives.

Many senates and councils took the view, based on their experiences with the apartheid system, that any proposal from government had to be viewed with suspicion lest it lead to control of the system by political ideologues. Many HBIs welcomed government involvement as an essential mechanism to effect redress of inequities of the apartheid past. Some Afrikaans-language institutions kept their heads low, avoiding any confrontation with government even on matters that were blatantly based on misguided policy options. The dilemmas of democratising senates and councils stem from the increased role of students, workers, and representatives of civil society who might not necessarily have the requisite understanding of how higher-education institutions ought to function to meet the needs of individuals and society.

In this section we look at some of the key areas of change, how institutions, UCT in particular, responded to the challenges, and how the higher-education system has been reshaped.

Leadership challenges in the post-1994 era were decidedly different from the past. Each institution had to re-examine its mission and map its own vision to enhance its performance in increasing access to both students and staff from previously excluded sectors of society, quality teaching and learning, research and innovation, and service to society, especially to neighbouring communities.

This included decentralising power and portfolios that had traditionally resided in the registrar's office, leading to the establishment of an executive team working with and reporting to the vice-chancellor, including the first-ever executive directors of finance, communications and development working together with deputy vice-chancellors and the registrar. It was not easy for the registrar to relinquish power and focus on proper administrative duties.

A participatory process of formulating a new mission statement and a new vision was followed. UCT's vision was 'To be a world-class African university' and its mission to promote equity and excellence in teaching, learning and the conduct of research.

Streamlining of our academic faculties led by the deputy vice-chancellor, Dan Ncayiyana, established a model for the entire higher-education system. Out of ten disparate faculties driven by traditional rivalries emerged six coherent faculties, including The Centre for Higher Education (a new entity focusing on promoting academic development to support quality teaching and learning).

The debate about the vision statement reflected the deep-seated differences within the institution. Apartheid ghosts reared their heads once more. My response to questions regarding our aspiration to world-class scholarship focused on three key issues. In the first instance, our mission statement had already committed us to taking excellence as a benchmark for all we do, and the vision had to be in alignment with our mission. How could one know that one was excellent except by comparing oneself with appropriate benchmarks?

Second, the competitive pressures facing South Africa in the global knowledge economy demanded world-class scholarship. The role of premier institutions such as UCT was to be a torchbearer for society. Mediocrity was simply not tolerated in the competitive global environment. Moreover, UCT had already demonstrated its capability to engage in world-class scholarship. The world's first successful heart transplant was performed at UCT's Groote Schuur Hospital in 1967 by Chris Barnard, a UCT alumnus. In 1996 UCT was home to 22 of South Africa's 48 A-rated scientists.

We also needed to re-emphasise that transformation of higher education would make sense only if it promoted excellence and equity. UCT's experience over the first five years of transformation (1993-1997) demonstrated that by paying attention to issues of equity, we could draw in a larger pool of talent that enhanced our performance in the quality of teaching, learning and research in our areas of expertise.

Mediocrity is unaffordable to poor people. People with adequate resources can afford second chances; poor people might only have one. Many poor black students came to UCT because they aspire to high-quality academic engagement. They cannot afford to repeat courses and risk losing scholarships. Tolerance of mediocrity would betray their aspirations. Black people did not fight against apartheid only to settle for mediocrity.

The third imperative was geographic. We had much to gain from turning our location on the African continent into an opportunity for excellence. The enormity of the challenges Africa faces calls for innovation. Research focusing on local socio-economic and bio-technological challenges can contribute to global knowledge in ways world-class institutions elsewhere could not. For example, South African chemical engineers created innovative approaches to the process of converting coal into oil because of oil embargoes during the apartheid era. The disease burden in our society also provides a rich clinical base for innovative health science research and treatment approaches. South African medical scientists have been at the forefront of research into the special challenges of Africa.

The use of the term 'African' in the proposed vision statement evoked much emotion. For indigenous people who had been dispossessed by the colonial experience, the term 'African' symbolised a reaffirmation of their belonging. Why would they share this hard-won re-identification with the very people who had dispossessed them? I reminded them that excluding white people from the African heritage was not what the new South Africa should be about. We had to be bigger than our former oppressors. An inclusive vision would be critical to success.

The inclusion of the term 'African' in the vision deliberately refocused UCT on the continent. UCT needed to reflect its African cultural heritage while acknowledging European influences in its foundations. The term also challenged South Africans who tended to view themselves as European first to come to terms with their Africanness.

The participatory development process of the strategic planning framework forced open many questions. What principles would govern our approach to management? How would we handle collaboration within the competitive higher-education environment? What change-management approaches would we adopt?

The adoption of a Strategic Framework Paper in July 1997 marked a major departure from UCT's traditional planning approaches. Past practice was that the vice-chancellor, supported by the advice of the registrar and deputy vice-chancellors, would propose priorities for the institution. This was a year-on-year agenda-setting approach.

The resource base of the university rested on the government subsidy and research support from the national research council (now the National Research Foundation) and the Medical Research Council, generated by internationally recognised researchers. My predecessor had supplemented these inadequate financial resources with aggressive fundraising, but there was never enough. Choices had to be made. What was missing was a transparently agreed way of setting priorities to enable those not supported to understand the decision-making logic.

A new energy surged through the institution in 1997-1998. Heads of units rose to the challenge of positioning their units within the new strategic framework. The devolution of goal setting and resource allocation to suit set priorities at the faculty and departmental levels created much excitement. Students also felt excited about being brought into substantive strategic management processes.

Executive deans who were both scholars and managers became an essential part of the newly configured system of strategic management. The tradition had been for faculties to elect one of their peers to become the dean of the faculty. This system worked well in the Science and Engineering faculties where the best leaders were chosen to become deans. The deans were senior, productive teachers and researchers who modelled excellence in their fields.

But other faculties tended to select academics for whom teaching and research was no longer a priority or who had little prospect of rising to the top of their fields as scholars. The Health Sciences faculty stood out in this regard.

Weak deans were functional to the traditional model of leadership and power dynamics at the UCT Medical School. The heads of Medicine, Surgery, Paediatrics, and Obstetrics and Gynaecology wielded enormous power. Once appointed, they were permanent heads until retirement. There was little accountability to those below them, given their authoritarian leadership model. A weak dean was essential for maximum autonomy by these powerful heads.

Much of the power of the heads of department was symbolic. The power to appoint heads of departments in one's division was most important. There were no transparent appointment processes. White women who were just as well qualified as white males were routinely passed over for promotion. Appointments to senior positions tended to reflect the profiles of heads of departments. White males remained dominant.

Research funding is a critical resource in academia. Endowed funds within the faculty were controlled by the heads of divisions. In addition, there was a significant flow of clinical-research money from the pharmaceutical industry for clinical trials. The pharmaceutical industry benefits from the low costs of high-quality clinical trials in South Africa. The average cost of clinical trials in the USA has risen to nearly 60% of total development.[154] South Africa's weaker currency and a less demanding regulatory environment within university hospitals make it a favoured site for clinical trials.

The University of the Free State has developed a framework that benefits all parties. By 1999 it derived R30 million per year from clinical-trial funding, using it to develop the academic infrastructure. The medical

school is the major beneficiary. In addition, the formal relationship between the university and the pharmaceutical industry ensures stability
that has opened up ongoing opportunities for trials involving healthy
volunteer students.

By contrast, academics at UCT utilised the university's infrastructure for commissioned research, including clinical trials, without much
consideration about the cost of maintaining it. Funds paid to them were
put into research accounts over which there was minimum accountability. Even more disconcerting were payments in kind that funded trips
and other personal costs, with little transparency. (Ian Sims, chair of
the university from 1993 to 1997, used to point to the irony of finding
himself, head of BP South Africa, in the company of UCT medical professors who were first-class platinum frequent flyers.) A strong dean
would be a threat to these empires that depended on this patronage. But
change had to come.

This change signalled a new orientation, away from a medical focus
dominated by medical professors, towards a more holistic approach that
gave pride of place to all the professions that contributed to better health
care. But even more important was the need for the Health Sciences faculty to face up to the reality that the incumbent dean would not meet
the new standard of scholar and manager.

Medical schools are often the most difficult parts of a university to
manage. They have a sense of superiority and as professional schools
they have many points of accountability, including the provincial government that funds teaching hospitals.

Respectful of this delicacy, I met with senior faculty members to seek
their advice about how to manage the transition with the least disruption.
They agreed that the incumbent dean's skills set did not match what
was required in the new environment, but would not agree on how to
manage the transition. I decided to deal directly with the incumbent
dean, who finally agreed to a settlement, after which I took the matter
to the wider faculty assembly.

Helen Zille's advice as director of communications was critical to the
success of the Medical School Faculty Board meeting. Addressing a
packed Anatomy lecture hall, with staff and students well represented,

I announced that the dean had agreed to step down in the interests of the institution and praised his decision to create space for new leadership to help manage the change process.

The audience raised questions about the new strategic thrust of the university and the risks in the new environment. They were anxious about the declining budgets of teaching hospitals, as the new government understandably shifted resources to primary health care for underserved communities. The Western Cape was particularly hard hit by the shift in government policy to rebalance allocation of resources between primary and tertiary care as well as from better-off provinces to poorer ones. I explained that the only way we could survive and still provide high-quality teaching and research would be by being more strategic in our approach to managing diminishing resources.

Appointing executive deans and encouraging their active role in strategic management created a positive atmosphere for those committed to the promotion of excellence and equity. The deans, in turn, appointed strong heads of departments with better incentives to help strengthen the teaching and research platform and contribute to much-needed curriculum reforms. The gloom and fear that came with uncertainty gave way to optimism.

Our academic programmes also had to be reformed. Professor Wieland Gevers, senior deputy vice-chancellor at the time, left an invaluable legacy by leading the process of a total rearrangement of UCT's academic programmes. This was a painful, unpopular and long process that saw UCT jettison the antiquated, non-structured course approach that shortchanged many students. In the social sciences and humanities, the incoherence of the course offering was such that students could leave with a collection of credits but no lucid knowledge base that could guide future development of their careers. The science and technology area also produced graduates painfully ignorant about general matters of society and ethics.

The revolution that accompanied the restructuring of teaching and learning created coherent programmes that are as good as any in the world. UCT's partnerships with international institutions that send their students to us for semester courses have been enhanced as a result of the clarity of our offerings. For example, the Politics, Philosophy and Economics programme has proven popular with students from liberal-arts undergraduate programmes in the USA. So too is our Media Studies programme that has opened both an academic and a practical job-oriented career stream. Many sister institutions have adopted these programmes to enhance their academic offerings.

Transformation of the higher-education system remains work in progress today. We have seen consolidation from 36 to 23 institutions. Greater articulation between universities and universities of technology (previously technikons) has set the stage for students to move from one into the other with greater ease and appropriate accreditation. It remains to be seen whether this objective is being achieved. There is a risk of 'mission creep' between the university and the technology side, with serious consequences for our vulnerable technology training capacity.

Thirteen years into the transformation process, there is greater clarity about the importance of both equity and excellence. Populists who demanded equity at the expense of excellence are no longer able to hold the system to ransom. It is now generally accepted that the focus should be on the performance of the system as a whole through supporting both strong and weak institutions on clearly agreed mission-specific objectives and outcomes. For example, more targeted support is being given to the development of centres of excellence at those institutions with demonstrated capacity to contribute to our technology and knowledge base.

Well-performing institutions are being supported to focus on more inclusive access and support programmes to enlarge the talent pool and promote diversity in science and technology and other critical skills areas. Weaker institutions are receiving targeted support for developing clearer missions, strengthening management and leadership, and enhancing academic performance of both students and staff. Provision of academic-support programmes to redress the foundation-skills gaps flowing from the legacy of inferior education has now been accepted as part of mainstream support for higher education. Government financing of these programmes is now part of the resource base of the system, although debates on the adequacy of the resource allocation continue.

The government's National Student Financial Aid Scheme (NSFAS),[155] a means-test-based assistance programme initiated in 1991 by the Independent Development Trust (IDT) and now run fully by government, grew to about R1,7 billion in 2005, covering about 30% (120 000 in 2005) of the total student population of 737 472. In 2005, 90% of the recipients were African, 7% Coloured, and 2,5% either of Indian origin or white. Women comprised 53% of those assisted. It is one of the most successful redress programmes that enable poor students to access higher education. But the low cut-off point of R100 000 excludes a significant proportion of working-class and lower-middle-class students whose family incomes exceed this. This figure is not only low in absolute terms given the cost of living, but families with more than one student to finance would find it very difficult to afford higher education.

The merger of Sauvca with the Committee of Technikon Principals (CTP) to form Higher Education South Africa (Hesa) signals the commitment of all institutions of higher education to work together. Greater collaboration enhances economies of scale and cross-pollination. The unfinished agenda is performance enhancement to promote higher-level outcomes in both quality and quantity to meet our urgent scarce-skills needs.

According to the Department of Education's 2006 report, in 2005 the higher-education system produced a total of 120 000 graduates with formal qualifications, of whom 33 551 were from science and technology fields; just over 28 000 from business and management; about 29 000 from education and just above 29 000 from the rest of the humanities and social sciences.[156]

Only a few institutions make significant contributions to skills outputs at the highest levels. Of just over 120 000 graduates in 2005, just under 8 000 had masters degrees and 1 171 qualified with doctoral degrees. The institutions making the greatest contributions at these high levels are the University of Pretoria, UCT, Stellenbosch University and the University of the Witwatersrand.

Demand for skills continues to outstrip supply in the South African economy. Engineering skills shortages are particularly acute. According to the Engineering Council of South Africa's 2005 Report,[157] the slow trickle into the profession is failing to address the problem. Between 2004 and 2006 only a total of 5 290 professional engineers of all categories registered, of whom 52% are black.

One would have thought the concept of unemployed graduates an oxymoron, but it is a reality created by the widespread practice of focusing on equitable access without sufficient attention to excellence. Estimates suggest that there are at least 63 000 such young people who cannot find jobs in the scarce-skills climate of our growing economy.[158] Almost all of them are black. Their education and training has not equipped them with essential cognitive, conceptual, communication and analytic skills. Many also lack the social skills to present themselves well in interviews. This phenomenon of unemployed graduates who are largely black reinforces the worst stereotypes and prejudices in our still racist society. Higher education has failed them.

South Africans must hold all higher-education institutions that benefit from the public purse to a higher standard to ensure that this travesty does not continue. Equity and equal access to mediocrity is an injustice that undermines the future of our nation. All young people deserve the opportunity to develop their talents to the fullest. We have the resources to invest in promoting both excellence and equity, but do we have the political will? History will judge unkindly if we fail to rise to this challenge.

CHAPTER 13

Haunted space:
HIV/Aids

THE HIV/AIDS PANDEMIC COULD NOT HAVE COME AT A WORSE TIME for our fledgling democracy. It bore all the hallmarks of a spoiler of the hard-won freedom. How could our young democracy manage the risks this pandemic posed to reconstruction and development, given its strong sexual undertones, and given that we are uncomfortable talking about sex? How could we manage the risks it presented without reinforcing the stereotypes about black people and their sexual mores?

The HIV/Aids pandemic has confounded the global community, challenging health-care professionals and policy makers to revisit their basic assumptions about health and disease.

First, HIV/Aids is not just a health issue but a development challenge. It poses socio-economic and political challenges by its very nature and its attack on populations over long periods. Second, HIV/Aids is deeply personal in its mode of transmission. It raises questions that societies worldwide are reticent about: sexuality, sexual orientation, sexual mores, personal and cultural practices. Third, HIV/Aids threatens the entire health-care system in affected countries. It overburdens it throughout the active stage of the disease, and undermines the capacity of the system by attacking its human resource base – nurses, doctors and other care-givers. Finally, HIV/Aids undermines the social-capital base of affected countries. Deaths of the economically active people leave families and communities without livelihoods, and essential knowledge, culture and wisdom is lost to Aids orphans left to fend for themselves.

The National Party (NP) government had known about the HIV/Aids threat since the early 1980s but failed to act. The first entry point was the predominantly white male gay community. Given the socio-economic status of this community, they learnt quickly from the available scientific knowledge to take preventive action and gained access to anti-retroviral treatment. This branch of the pandemic was nipped in the bud and many survivors are leading productive lives, but the agony of confronting the affliction takes its toll on affected individuals.

The second entry point, and by far the most significant, was the migrant-labour system – the flow of thousands of men into South Africa from surrounding countries where the pandemic had already taken root. Their emotional needs were neglected by captains of industry who continued Lord Milner's approach of extracting the benefits of their labour unencumbered by their families and loved ones. Some became opportunistic homosexuals to meet their sexual needs. Migrant men's vulnerability also increased as the sex trade flourished in the sprawling informal settlements that sprang up on the edges of labour compounds in the 1980s.

In *A Bed Called Home*, I analysed the impact of the living conditions of migrants whose dignity was under assault on a daily basis.[159] The effect of limited physical space on the psychological well-being of black people during the apartheid era was devastating. Restricting people to inhuman living conditions limits their ability to construct a positive self-image and to conceive of themselves as agents of their own destiny. Self-respect and respectful relationships cannot thrive.

The chickens of the migrant-labour system have come home to roost with a vengeance in the HIV/Aids pandemic. As South African and other migrants from initially non-affected countries such as Lesotho, Swaziland and Botswana became infected, these migrants in turn became the carriers of HIV to the rural periphery that traditionally serviced the needs of the urban areas in most countries. By the late 1980s the heterosexual variant of the pandemic had taken root in South Africa and neighbouring countries. Still the then government did not act decisively. Nor did the mining industry intervene in any meaningful way.

High levels of illiteracy and lack of basic knowledge about human biology fuelled the spread of the heterosexual variant of HIV/Aids. Breadwinners returning home after nine months away on the mines turned into bearers of the deadly disease. Their wives and partners and unborn children became victims. The high prevalence of TB among people with compromised immunity also increased the vulnerability of rural communities to virulent drug-resistant TB.

There was a view during the apartheid era among some conservative establishment white people that HIV/Aids might be a blessing in disguise. Given its mode of spreading as a sexually transmitted disease, and its focus on black people, they believed it could solve the demographic problem they faced as a white minority. The feared *swart gevaar* (black peril) would be dealt a blow. Whatever the apartheid government did at the time was too little, too late. They provided some educational programmes and advised people to use condoms.

The apartheid government also lacked the legitimacy to tackle a disease with such sexual overtones. There had already been controversy about the promotion of family planning in the 1980s. It was seen as a strategy by the white minority government to reduce the growth rate of the black population for political motives. Promoting the use of condoms met with stiff resistance from a suspicious population. By the early 1990s the estimated HIV/Aids prevalence rate was more than 2% of the total population.

Much harder for the post-apartheid government to concede is the third wave of the HIV/Aids pandemic. Many returning exiles who had spent their youth in high-risk environments in affected southern African countries such as Zambia, Tanzania and Zimbabwe carried the virus back with them. The late Chris Hani led a discussion within the ANC in Maputu, Mozambique, before their re-entry into South Africa in the early 1990s. He urged the ANC to take appropriate precautions to address the risks of HIV/Aids by creating a culture of openness, acceptance and support to prevent further infections. The proposed programme also emphasised promotion of good health through responsible sexual practices. Hani's untimely death from an assassin's bullet in April 1993 robbed South Africa of a champion of reason in managing the risks of the pandemic.

The tragedy of returning heroes turning into unwitting Trojan horses for this deadly virus is too painful a reality to admit. It took a while for the new government to acknowledge the problem of HIV/Aids. Even President Mandela failed to use his stature and moral authority to overcome the fear of reinforcing stereotypes about black people's sexuality in our society. Neither the ANC nor the Government of National Unity used its considerable moral authority to overcome the power of conservative customs that discouraged talking about sex. Breaking this silence is a vital part of effective prevention. The first post-apartheid government missed an important opportunity to tackle the scourge of HIV/Aids at a time when it could have been contained.

Whatever attempts were made by the then Minister of Health, Nkosazana Dlamini-Zuma, made matters worse. Her intolerance for different viewpoints alienated civil-society groups that were keen to work with government to tackle this threat to our democracy. She also made a series of errors of judgment. She backed an expensive R14 million anti-HIV/Aids play that was a doubtful tool for public-health education, and the process used to select the service provider violated rules of good governance set up by her own government. The play was later abandoned as an educational tool without any benefit to the public. Attempts by the Parliamentary Portfolio Committee on Health chaired by Manto Tshabalala-Msimang to hold Minister Dlamini-Zuma accountable for breaching procurement rules were scuttled by ANC heavyweights. They came to Dlamini-Zuma's defence in a manner that undermined the capacity of the legislature to hold the executive branch accountable.

Minister Dlamini-Zuma was never held to account for this violation of procurement rules. The then director-general of Health, Olive Sishana, refused to be made the scapegoat, insisting that her advice to follow the rules had been ignored. She resigned and went to Geneva to work for the World Health Organisation for a number of years. She has since returned to South Africa and is making a significant contribution as a specialist in public-health policy at the Human Sciences Research Council (HSRC).

Minister Dlamini-Zuma also clashed with well-respected experts at the head of the national Medicines Control Council (MCC), who refused to break with protocols on clinical trials to allow the testing of Virodene, a chemical mixture its inventors presented as an anti-retroviral agent.

Peter Folb, then head of the MCC and the head of UCT's Pharmacology department, had worked well with Minister Dlamini-Zuma at the ANC's health desk before 1994. He failed to convince her to follow sound scientific advice on protocols governing clinical trials in the interests of the larger long-term public good. She authorised clinical trials of Virodene – a product that turned out to be an industrial solvent. In the end, Peter Folb and his colleagues resigned under pressure from government, which appointed new members of the MCC more willing to comply with its wishes. This is yet another example of the failure of the new political elite to heed the advice of experts at great cost to ordinary citizens.

It is ironic that Minister Dlamini-Zuma's successor as Minister of Health after the 1999 election, Manto Tshabalala-Msimang, had tried to make her accountable for her actions. She too faltered after a promising start. Soon after her appointment to the cabinet, she visited Uganda to learn at first hand from their successes and failures in dealing with HIV/Aids.

Uganda, much poorer than South Africa, has turned a national disaster of HIV prevalence rates near 20% in the 1980s into an opportunity. Consistent political leadership by President Yoweri Museveni was essential to success. The emphasis on changing sexual behaviour that was contained in all government-supported HIV/Aids programmes was a core strategy in the prevention of infections. Raising the age of first sexual encounter, abstaining from extra- and pre-marital sex, and a requirement to have HIV tests before marriage all helped reshape societal attitudes. Uganda also encouraged a comprehensive care programme that included anti-retroviral treatment early in the 1990s. Smart partnerships with NGOs and private citizens supported those affected to access anti-retroviral treatment because Uganda did not have the resources to provide the drugs. Prevalence rates dropped from 18% in the 1980s to less than 8% by 2003. Uganda's public-private-partnership approach is also a model of effective national mobilisation of the government, the private sector, non-governmental organisations and faith-based organisations in the fight against HIV/Aids.

Tshabalala-Msimang came back bullish about South Africa's chances of doing better than Uganda in halting the pandemic. She was determined to draw on South Africa's bigger resource base – a proficient science and technology platform, stronger health sector, and an active civil society – to tackle it. But President Mbeki's questioning of the very foundations of the science that underpinned global approaches to prevention and treatment stopped her in her tracks. Mbeki's viewpoints were shaped by dissident scientists' views he encountered on the internet. He honed in on the view that Aids was a disease of poverty, and questioned the link between Aids and the sexually transmitted HIV.

The president associated himself strongly with dissident views in his public statements, challenging what he saw as racist motives behind the link between sex and HIV transmission. For example, in a speech at Fort Hare University on 12 October 2001, he said:

> And thus does it happen that others who consider themselves to be our leaders[160] take to the streets carrying their placards to demand that because we are germ carriers, and human beings of a lower order that cannot subject its passions to reason, we must perforce adopt strange opinions to save a depraved and diseased people from perishing from a self-inflicted disease. . . . Convinced that we are but natural born promiscuous carriers of germs unique in the world, they proclaim that our continent is doomed to an inevitable mortal end because of our unconquerable devotion to the sin of lust.

President Mbeki's statement was tragic on several counts. First, the choice of audience could not have been more unfortunate. University students are the prime vulnerable age group ranging from 15-35 years. Many institutions at the time were launching intense educational programmes to help young people come to grips with the reality of their vulnerability to this deadly disease. The message that the association of HIV/Aids with sexual intercourse played into the racist stereotype of black people being promiscuous undermined the work of those trying to promote change in sexual conduct as part of preventive action.

Second, the statement undermined the government's own objectives of promoting the development of skills to drive socio-economic growth.

Challenging the association between sexual conduct and the risk of contracting HIV/Aids put South Africa's future human-resource base at risk. What would be the point of investing in enhancing access to higher education for young people who would be at risk of dying within a decade of graduating?

Third, the choice of a university as a forum to make a statement challenging the scientific validity of the causality of a disease with such deadly outcomes was unfortunate. Universities are appropriate places to raise critical questions about matters affecting science and society. But challenging accepted scientific facts in a context offering little opportunity to air alternative viewpoints left the audience with only the president's view to reflect on. He would also have been aware of the weight his audience would attach to his words as a respected leader of our country.

Finally, there was strong symbolism in the choice of Fort Hare – treated with reverence as the historical fountain of knowledge for many African leaders – as the venue for the statement.

The impact on the rest of society was no less significant. The labelling of the science behind HIV/Aids causality as racist silenced many scientists and health professionals. In the delicate politics of transition from apartheid, who would challenge the president and risk being associated with racist notions? Moreover, the scientific community was predominantly white, and white scientists felt particularly vulnerable to being misunderstood.

The existence of pockets of excellent science is not enough to empower ordinary South Africans to engage in critical debates on matters requiring a basic understanding of science. Excluding the majority of the population from the practice of science over the many decades of apartheid education has proven to be very costly for the country.

White people, who represent the majority of scientifically literate citizens, have been muted in their public comment on the government's policy position. Many fear being accused of racism for criticising a majority black government. Many scientifically literate black people kept quiet for fear of being labelled disloyal. The private sector remained silent partly because of its complicity in creating inhuman conditions in labour compounds that fuelled the pandemic among migrant workers and their families. Others feared offending the president and putting their businesses at risk.

Many prominent scientists and health professionals joined discussions held at the instigation of the president that included dissident scientists. The hope was that open debate would lead to a consensus based on the available evidence nationally and internationally. Time and resources were devoted to convening meetings between South African and other international scientists, including dissidents, to thrash out debates that had been settled in the early 1990s. The president's spokesperson at that time, Parks Mankahlana, became increasingly confrontational in fielding questions about Mbeki's position on HIV/Aids, saying those who insisted that HIV causes Aids 'can go to hell'. Ironically, Mankahlana died in his thirties under circumstances that are only too suggestive of a link to the same disease.

William Makgoba, then president of the government-funded Medical Research Council (MRC), also fell out with President Mbeki over these dissident views. Makgoba, a molecular scientist, could not associate himself with Mbeki's views, nor would he allow them to undermine the credibility of mortality statistics that the MRC produced. Government challenged a 2001 MRC report on the trends in mortality rates that pointed to an alarming increase in deaths attributable to Aids. Its release was delayed, and a witch-hunt instituted to trace the source of leaks of the report to the media. Makgoba resigned in 2002, becoming vice-chancellor of the University of Natal.

Hard as it is to understand President Mbeki's position, an appreciation of the power of stigma in a racist society helps to make sense of why he would be so adamant about alternative explanations for the HIV/Aids pandemic. Here we see stubborn ghosts of our past strutting about with a vengeance, making choices difficult. How could President Mbeki have challenged the stereotype about black people's sexual promiscuity without falling prey to costly denial about the causality of such a deadly disease? Was there a way of learning from the approach of President Museveni of Uganda who must also have been acutely aware of this stereotype, but chose to transcend it?

Museveni refused to be defined by racists. He did not allow their stereotypes about black people's promiscuity to undermine his ability to make appropriate decisions to enable his country to fight a deadly enemy.

He confronted cultural sexual practices that fuelled the pandemic: polygamy, multiple sexual partners, and inheritance of widows by members of the extended families. He used plain language. He required that every cabinet minister address this issue before dealing with any other matter of state policy at all public functions. He enlisted the support of religious leaders who became important public-health educators and imposed moral standards that saw a significant decline in pre-marital sex and other risky behaviours. It worked. Uganda has reaped the benefit of this leadership intervention, as can be seen by the steep decline in its HIV/Aids prevalence rates.

President Mbeki is not unique in making pronouncements about technical matters best left to experts. President George Bush infamously asserted in the early years of his presidency that the science about climate change was not yet clear when experts had enough evidence to suggest otherwise. The tendency of political leaders to assume roles that are beyond their level of competence is even more problematic in developing countries where poorly educated citizens are more susceptible to believing whatever leaders say.

Political authority and the exercise of state power is strengthened, not weakened, by the support of technical experts providing a foundation for evidence-based policy making, implementation, monitoring and evaluation. Wise political leaders exploit the skills base within the wider society to commission analyses that lay firmer foundations for policy making. Evidence-based policy making and implementation is the hallmark of successful scientifically proficient societies. South Africa has the depth of scientific and technological skills to help government establish informed policy positions to tackle the HIV/Aids pandemic.

President Mbeki's ascription of greater weight to the role of poverty in Aids causality and the questioning of the link with HIV also carried emotive undertones. Certainly apartheid actively impoverished black people and made them susceptible to infectious diseases, but to focus on poverty as a causal factor is problematic in the face of scientific evidence. Recent history provides us with cases of people who could not be described as poor who succumbed to the disease – President Kenneth Kaunda's son, children of President Mandela and Nkosi Mangosothu Buthelezi.

Nicoli Nattrass, a UCT economist, examined the links between vulnerability to HIV/Aids and poverty.[161] She used survey data and demographic studies to demonstrate various levels of linkages between poverty and HIV/Aids. Poor people are more likely than not to be uneducated. Poor uneducated women were found to lack the basic knowledge about how HIV is transmitted. They had difficulty understanding how condoms and safe-sex practices could minimise infections. Poor people, especially women and girls, are also likely to be less able to exercise choices of safe sexual practices because of their dependence on men for support. Men who refuse to use condoms simply insist on their right to have sex the way they like it.

Nattrass also describes the 'sexual economy' that operates between men and women on a continuum of a scale of benefits ranging from basic-needs provision to luxury goods in exchange for sexual favours. Younger women (15-25 years) are particularly vulnerable to 'sugar daddies', usually married older men, who provide for their material needs in return for sex. Nattrass's study also shows that access to employment, which is linked to higher levels of education and skills, correlates with lower levels of HIV infections. In both South Africa and Swaziland people with higher levels of education and skills, who are likely to be employed, have lower levels of HIV infections than poor uneducated, unemployed or unskilled labourers. Poverty is linked to hunger and malnutrition that further compromise the body's immune response. Poverty makes people vulnerable to HIV/Aids, it does not cause Aids.

Even more unfortunate was President Mbeki's argument against the provision of anti-retroviral treatment. He argued that even if HIV caused Aids, South Africa could not afford to provide anti-retroviral treatment to all those needing it, starting with prevention of mother-to-child transmission. It is often forgotten that it was the South African government that successfully challenged the international pharmaceutical industry's insistence on its intellectual property rights in the face of the international HIV/Aids crisis. Our government's courage in taking on the big pharmaceutical giants and the US government that backed them eventually forced a settlement, negotiated with the help of the then head of the World Health Organisation, Gro Bruntlandt. There is a cruel irony in our government winning the battle for affordable anti-retroviral treatment that has brought so much benefit to poor countries, yet losing the war on HIV/Aids at home.

Studies by both public and private researchers show that South Africa cannot afford *not* to afford comprehensive HIV/Aids prevention, care and treatment for all its citizens. Brazil, a country at a comparable level of development, has demonstrated that comprehensive care and treatment lessen opportunity and direct costs to society over time. For example, a study estimated that between 1997 and 2001 Brazil's health sector saved $1,2 billion in opportunity costs by providing free anti-retroviral drugs. In addition, saving the lives of citizens ensured that they continue to be productive.[162]

Nattrass and her colleagues estimated the additional cost of providing comprehensive treatment including anti-retroviral drugs to the South African health-care budget at no more than R20 to R40 billion per year in 2003. Given that the total health budget of R33 billion at that time was already bearing the burden of opportunistic infections from HIV-positive people, the additional cost was affordable. An estimated 60-70% of hospital admissions during the period 2000–2003 were linked to HIV/Aids-related infections. Factoring in the opportunity costs of skills losses and the risks to the investment climate, providing treatment became even more affordable. The alternative was unsustainable development of our democracy.

Companies such as Anglo American, BP, Unilever and others were convinced of the benefits of anti-retroviral treatment by economic analyses and in 2002 started providing comprehensive treatment and care to their workers. They accepted that the costs of not providing treatment were higher than those of providing it, especially if one factors in absenteeism, additional medical costs, lower productivity and the cost of replacing trained and experienced workers. Moreover, extensive studies show that anti-retroviral treatment lowers the viral load and makes those infected less infectious, dampening the pandemic's ferocity.

UNAIDS' 2006 figures estimate that at least 11% of South Africa's population is infected by HIV/Aids. At least 5,5 million people are infected in a total population of just over 47 million[163] – the largest recorded number of infected citizens of a single country. The overwhelming majority are black people in their prime. A nation losing so many people in the 15-35 age group is a nation at risk. Every day during 2007 an estimated 1 000 South Africans died of Aids, an increase from 600 per day in 2006. This is the equivalent of nearly three jumbo jets[164] crashing daily in a single country. A single crash once over a period of many years would be treated as an emergency and be fully investigated.

Many studies estimate that the opportunity costs of the pandemic are equivalent to lost economic growth of 1-1,5% GDP per year. A 2003 study by the World Bank[165] suggests that the methodology used to obtain these figures underestimates the long-term costs. Every day young men and women are buried, many of them nurses, teachers and other skilled personnel. KwaZulu-Natal, which has the largest provincial education system at 2,7 million learners and 75 000 educators in nearly 6 000 schools, is the province hardest hit, with an HIV/Aids prevalence rate of approximately 35% among women in ante-natal care. The death rate among teachers in a sample of 100 schools rose from 406 in 1997 to 607 in 2001.[166] The inherited thin human-capital base is eroding even further.

Growing numbers of Aids orphans, estimated at more than a million in 2006, are weakening the already strained social fabric as children become heads of impoverished households. Children growing up without parental guidance and emotional security are at risk. Many drop out of school and become vulnerable to exploitation that may further fuel the pandemic. Life expectancy dropped from 65 years in 1998 to less than 50 years in 2006[167] – almost back to the level at the beginning of the 20th century.

To make matters worse, South Africa has witnessed a horrific epidemic of sexual assaults on young girls, including babies, by men believing the myth that sex with a virgin cleanses one of HIV. Although statistics on sexual offences are unreliable, given the high level of under-reporting, available evidence shows that sexual violence against children, including raping of infants, has increased by 400%. The South African Institute of Race Relations estimates that 40% of rapes in South Africa are committed against children, with an estimated 62 children raped or targeted for rape each day. Unisa estimated that one million women and children are raped in South Africa every year.[168] While estimates vary, the main issue is that sexual violence has reached epidemic proportions at the very time that the risks of HIV/Aids are high. This level of sexual violence further undermines the trust relationships in poor communities.

Entrenched sexism in our society adds fuel to the HIV/Aids fire. All South African cultures – black and white – have strong sexist roots. Male dominance is still a fact of life at all levels. But it is among the lowest socio-economic classes that the impact of sexism is most felt. The lack of control many women have over their bodies makes preventive measures difficult. Men, as fathers, husbands and brothers, control women's bodies at various points in their life cycles. This powerlessness makes women vulnerable in many traditional societies. It is not surprising that 58% of those living with HIV/Aids in Africa are women.

Women's bodies are once more forced to carry the burdens of sexist societies. HIV/Aids violates women's bodies and defiles their life-giving force. Nurturing mother's milk has become poisonous to their babies. Not much work has been done and published on the psychological impact of HIV/Aids on child-bearing women, but we would do well to factor psychological support into the comprehensive care of people living with HIV/Aids.

South Africa's strong civil society, armed with all these analyses, took up the challenge of forcing the government to protect the socio-economic rights of those living with HIV/Aids that are enshrined in our constitution. The Treatment Action Campaign (TAC) took the government to the Pretoria High Court in 2001 on the basis that failure to provide comprehensive care and treatment to people living with HIV/Aids constitutes violation of their socio-economic rights. They won. Government then appealed to the Constitutional Court on the grounds that the High Court could not order the government to perform in such a specific manner without usurping the power of the executive branch to make policy decisions.

The Constitutional Court case was withdrawn before it could be heard. One can only assume that the government was persuaded that it should avoid the embarrassment of fighting such a case. The withdrawal of its appeal showed great wisdom. It was also symbolically powerful for our democracy that the executive branch was seen to be respecting the judgments of the judicial branch. The outcome of this case set the scene for the government to perform as directed by the High Court. In August 2003, government finally announced it would roll out a comprehensive anti-HIV/Aids programme by the end of that year. It did so at the end of November 2003 – almost ten years too late, but better late than never.

The outcome was a victory for citizenship as stewardship. The TAC under the leadership of a person living with HIV/Aids, Zackie Achmat, took the risk of challenging the government consistently on this issue. Despite government's failure to perform, the TAC kept up street demonstrations and mobilised labour and faith-based organisations in a civil-disobedience campaign to press their demands. Nelson Mandela's support to the spirit of the civil-society campaign (he was careful not to be associated with civil disobedience) added to the weight of opinion that forced government's change of policy.

Quiet diplomacy by Nelson Mandela within the ANC had failed. Mandela went as far as to acknowledge publicly that it was his failure as president of the first post-apartheid government that had set the stage for the growing pandemic, thus hoping to pave the way for his successor to become less defensive. But that, too, failed. President Mbeki's statement in September 2003 at a United Nations (UN) meeting in New York that he did not know anyone with HIV/Aids, nor anyone who had died of the disease, is inexplicable. A country that is losing 1 000 people a day from HIV/Aids-related causes needs an explanation from its president. Even if he had no personal relationships with those affected, one would expect our leader to seek to publicly show his empathy for those affected.

Much has been accomplished since the roll-out of anti-retroviral treatment to all who need it. Minister of Health Tshabalala-Msimang's ambivalence has not stopped the momentum. Her deputy minister (1999-2007), Nozizwe Madlala-Routledge, forged a strong bond with NGOs to make the roll-out a success before her dismissal in August 2007. Nelson Mandela's human touch in the first roll-out stands in sharp contrast to the continuing ambivalence of his successor. Mandela made a special trip in December 2003 to Lusikisiki village in the Eastern Cape to hand over treatment to the first person to receive it, a young woman clearly touched by Mandela's presence.

But Minister Tshabalala-Msimang's inconsistent attitude towards comprehensive prevention, treatment and care of HIV/Aids has led to a slower roll-out of the programme across the country. Provinces such as the Western Cape with the capacity to establish and maintain strong programmes are doing well, whereas poorer provinces such as Limpopo and the Eastern Cape lag behind. The mixed messages from the Minister of Health about the role of nutrition in the fight against HIV/Aids create confusion. The established role of nutrition in the care of sick people as a complement to essential anti-retroviral drugs cannot replace the life-giving impact of these drugs in keeping the viral load down and permitting HIV-positive people to lead normal, productive lives.

Revitalisation of the National HIV/Aids Council under the deputy president following South Africa's embarrassment by Minister Tshabalala-Msimang's performance at the Toronto World HIV/Aids Conference in 2006 is giving fresh hope to poor people. The minister chose to focus the South African exhibition at the World Aids Conference on her controversial alternative remedies: garlic, beetroot and African potatoes. Anti-retroviral drugs were hastily added as the embarrassment of those hosting the exhibition mounted in the face of the shock expressed by delegates. It is puzzling why our government has permitted this incoherent policy response to such a major threat to our socio-economic well-being for so long.

Serious consideration must be given to managing HIV/Aids like any other public-health threat. A concerted effort to reduce new infections requires consistent messages directed at all sexually active people to change behaviour. Every health post should routinely counsel and test all who come for consultations to ensure that no one is left behind. Botswana has already instituted this routine in its management of the HIV/Aids epidemic and early signals are of success.[169] Treating HIV/Aids as any other public health challenge will have to be accompanied by public commitments by all leaders political, religious and private sector to stand by those affected and fight stigmatisation. The alternative is a downward spiral in our already high mortality rate and a further reduction in life expectancy.

More than any other challenge we face as a new democracy, HIV/Aids demonstrates the danger of allowing ourselves to be defined by racist stereotypes. We must free our psyches from racist myths and confront this pandemic. We have the financial, scientific and technological resources and the civil-society resolve to mount a concerted effort to defeat this enemy in our midst. What is needed is consistent leadership.

PART FIVE

Black Economic
Empowerment

CHAPTER 14

Ends and means

CENTURIES OF WHITE DOMINATION AND THE INEQUITABLE DISTRI-
bution of socio-economic benefits have left our new democracy in an
untenable situation. Political power without economic power is unsustainable. At the time of transition to democracy, South Africa was in the
unenviable position of being one of the most unequal societies in the
world, alongside Brazil, with a Gini coefficient of over 0.60. Inequality
needed to be tackled urgently to promote social stability.

The gap between the affluent and poor sectors of the population is
large and growing. It does not help to formulate the inequality debate in
terms of the 'first' and 'second' economy. There is only one economy,
which marginalises the majority of South Africans who are the poorest,
least educated and least skilled, while rewarding those with sought-after
skills and those connected to people with power and influence. This
fundamental economic reality is central to formulating appropriate responses to the growing inequality in our society.

Well-intentioned attempts by Deputy President Phumzile Mlambo-
Ngcuka to address 'problems of the second economy' are unlikely to
yield lasting solutions. One cannot deal with one side of a problem of
power relationships and hope to produce sustainable equitable outcomes.
Take the example of male dominance. Inequalities between men and
women cannot be eliminated by focusing on the issue as a women's problem. It is a problem of power relationships between men and women that
requires comprehensive strategies. In the same way, structural economic

inequalities must be dealt with in a comprehensive way to root out the effects of centuries of inequities.

Wealth accumulation in South Africa was accomplished largely on the backs of black people. In addition to the dispossession of land – a basis of capital formation – black people were systematically kept poor, denied education and training, and ownership of property. A post-apartheid South Africa in which only white people are wealthy is unsustainable. Democratising wealth creation and distribution is crucial. Black Economic Empowerment (BEE) is an economic and political necessity.

The private sector took long to acknowledge the imperatives of BEE. The Mineral Charter drawn up in 2002 by the then Minister of Mineral and Energy Affairs, Phumzile Mlambo-Ngcuka, was a wake-up call to the private sector, signalling government's impatience with their lack of action to democratise economic participation. In 2002, during my tenure as Managing Director at the World Bank, private-sector lobbyists contacted me frantically, hoping that the World Bank would put pressure on the South African government to stop pushing ahead with BEE – a curious response by the private sector given its earlier experience of dealing with economic empowerment of Afrikaners after 1948.

In the 1950s, Anglo American Corporation and its peers recognised the need to economically empower Afrikaners who had become the dominant political force. Gencor (now BHP-Billiton) is a success of that early economic empowerment. Afrikaners, like black people today, had political power after winning the 1948 elections, but lagged behind their English-speaking white compatriots in economic power.

Established English-speaking business people took steps to empower Afrikaners, facilitating their access to economic resources and encouraging them to play an active role in wealth creation. This was considered essential to social stability.

Among Afrikaners themselves, strides had already been made before 1948 in taking up the challenges of entrepreneurship through self-help movements such as the Reddingsdaadbond ('our act of rescue') and the Helpmekaar ('help one another') study fund. Prominent Afrikaner institutions and companies such as Volkskas, Sanlam, Rembrandt and what later became Naspers were already in existence and benefited from the more supportive socio-economic and political environment for Afrikaners after 1948.

Critics of the earlier forms of BEE during the early 1990s questioned the wisdom of the focus on transfer of assets from white companies to a few black men. Many were offended by the lack of attention to the plight of the majority of black people who continued to live with high levels of unemployment and despair.

Moeletsi Mbeki, businessman, political commentator and President Thabo Mbeki's brother, has been a consistent critic of the brand of BEE focusing on asset transfer, charging that it adds little wealth-creation value to the economy. He is particularly critical of the corrupting influence of a policy that makes a few black people feel entitled to wealth they have not earned through hard work. He is equally scathing of the manner in which preferential procurement has spawned front companies. 'Fronting' involves the use of black people's names for a consideration without their having any real say in the enterprise. It is another form of corruption that has spread like a cancer. Moeletsi Mbeki questions its long-term impact on our society. How are young people to understand the value of hard work and the importance of professionalism in wealth creation, given their exposure to inappropriate role models?

The 2006 Ramaphosa Report on Black Economic Empowerment addressed many criticisms against BEE as practised in the 1990s, proposing a more broad-based approach. In addition, the government sought to tackle bottlenecks in access to funds for new entrants into the productive sector. The National Empowerment Fund (NEF) promotes access to credit to buy stakes in going concerns or establish new enterprises. The Development Bank of Southern Africa (DBSA) and Industrial Development Corporation (IDC) tend to focus on larger deals, while the NEF focuses on small and medium enterprises.

BEE has evolved into a sophisticated policy instrument as reflected in the Broad Based Black Economic Empowerment (BBBEE) Codes of Good Practice published by the Department of Trade and Industry (DTI) in 2006. The DTI is also responsible for administration and regulation of the implementation of this policy, and monitoring and evaluating its impact. The scorecard by which entities are measured to see if they comply with the Codes looks for the potential to transform the economy into one that is more equitable, faster growing and sustainable:

- Ownership of 51% or more by black people – 20%
- Black management control – 10%
- Employment equity – 10%
- Preferential procurement from black-owned enterprises – 20%
- Skills development – 20%
- Enterprise development – 10%
- A residual category – 10%.

Incentives for private-sector companies to contribute to BBBEE have been carefully calibrated to induce appropriate behaviour. For example, Level One contributors, who achieve a 100% score, are rewarded with lucrative opportunities of preferential procurement by government. Those attaining a score of less than 30% are designated as non-contributors, and stand to lose from being marginalised by both government and their own peers whose records would be blemished by dealing with them. By law, public entities would not be allowed to procure goods and services from such non-contributors to BBBEE.

To establish how BBBEE has performed thus far, I shall focus on a few key performance areas: ownership of the productive capacity, employment equity, and preferential procurement.

Ownership of productive capacity

A review by Business Map, sponsored by Standard Bank,[170] concludes that significant progress has been made in broadening the ownership base of our economy from almost zero to 6% black ownership of the Johannesburg Securities Exchange's (JSE) R5 trillion market capital in 2006. If undisclosed BEE deals are included in the calculation of ownership, the ownership figure increases to 10% of the JSE. Many BEE deals involving non-listed entities would add considerably to the estimated R400 billion plus of equity in black hands.

Much criticism is still directed at the nature of beneficiaries of BEE equity deals, who tend to be the same people or consortia who are politically well connected. Even though progress has been made in going beyond the 'usual suspects' of the earlier period (such as Tokyo Sexwale, Patrice Motsepe, Cyril Ramaphosa, Saki Macozoma), there is still too high a concentration of deals in the hands of people who have benefited before. This is partly due to the perceived benefits of doing deals with people with clout in government circles, who can position their partners appropriately for government contracts or business opportunities that government facilitates. The facilitation role of BEE partners opens the door to corruption and nepotism. Moeletsi Mbeki's concerns remain valid. Reliance on relationships in business dealings rather than on open, transparent, competitive bidding carries high risks of corruption.

The 'win' imperatives of the policy – a broad base and active participation by beneficiaries – pose challenges. Too broad a base of economic participation in business deals increases the risk of including people with inadequate skills who can add neither economic nor transformative value. Widening the base too much opens the way for fronting. Poor people with less sophistication in business become convenient vehicles for fronting, making it possible for companies that are not ready for fundamental change to claim broad-based ownership. Such claims, if untested, would protect companies from the inconvenience of having to deal with black people with management capacity who might ask uncomfortable questions about broader transformation within the enterprise.

The use of 'race-based' criteria to identify beneficiaries creates serious dilemmas for BEE. The major objection to 'race-based' empowerment is that the population registration categories of the apartheid era are used. The inequity we are wrestling with, however, results from the use of this same policy instrument. How can we use the same categories to frame policies to transform our socio-economic relationships? Many critics argue that we should rather use socio-economic measures to enable those at the bottom of the ladder to access opportunities regardless of their racial category. This is a plausible approach, except that many of its protagonists lack the credibility to make the argument, being direct beneficiaries of the 'whites only' affirmative action of the previous era.

Their opponents ask why 'race-based' affirmative action cannot work for black people now, if it has worked for whites during the apartheid era.

In addition, the approach of focusing only on socio-economic status misses an important point. 'Race politics' have left a deep imprint on our society, making 'race' matter much longer than many South Africans would like. There is a symbolic and substantive imperative in black economic empowerment. 'Whites only' ownership of the economy is not sustainable in a democracy with a majority of black citizens. The same applies to continuing white dominance of senior management and professional ranks.

Employment equity

Aspects of the 1998 Employment Equity Act (EE Act) were discussed in Chapter 4. In view of the widespread misunderstanding of its intentions and the confusion that sometimes exists between the concepts of employment equity, affirmative action and BEE, it is worth repeating that this Act seeks to promote greater equity in access to employment opportunities for all South African citizens. It recognises that inequity is unjust and has opportunity costs for the society as a whole. South Africa's poor competitiveness is traceable to inequities that deliberately promoted under-investment in skills development in the majority population. No country can compete effectively in the global knowledge economy without correcting such inequities.

The goal is not to replace white people with black people or men with women. Success should be measured by greater participation by all South Africans in growing our economy and sharing the benefits of growth equitably. The importance of this goal has eluded many in decision-making roles in both the public and private sectors. South Africa has lost invaluable skills because many white South Africans felt rejected in their own country and left to seek greener pastures. This is a strategic error on our part, and reflects our lack of understanding of the interconnectedness of the global economy and the high mobility of skilled people who are sought-after everywhere in the world. The narrow interpretation of employment equity that excludes rather than includes raises the greatest criticism and emotions in the transformation debates in our society, for understandable reasons. No one likes to feel that one's talents as a citizen have no place in the economic life of one's society.

This narrow interpretation stems from misunderstanding and ignorance, and abuse of power. Equating employment equity and affirmative action is a confusion of ends and means. Employment equity is a public good from the point of view of both justice and enlightened self-interest. Affirmative action is the *means* we employ to achieve our goal of employment equity, and has a number of components:

- The base from which one recruits staff must be broadened to ensure that previously excluded sectors of the population are included.
- Recruitment and interviewing procedures must be reviewed for biases against those who are under-represented.
- It is critical to review appointment criteria. A distinction must be made between essential skills to do the job and skills that help the candidate fit into the 'traditional club'. This is not about appointing unqualified people, but redefining qualification criteria to reduce biases.
- Auditing the institutional culture for biases reflecting the past is essential.
- Establishing support networks to ensure the success of new recruits is not a luxury, but an essential retention strategy. This might entail mentoring and coaching.
- Investing in skills development is at the heart of best practice. Such investments strengthen the pipeline of employable skills.

Seen in this light, it is difficult to understand calls for a moratorium on affirmative action. Even more disturbing is that these calls are not just coming from those feeling threatened by the risks of poor implementation of employment equity, but from senior government officials. This shows a need for the government itself to get greater clarity about the ends and means of employment equity and the role of affirmative action in it. What needs to be abolished is the abuse of employment equity and affirmative action to settle political scores and allocate political patronage. Replacing competent white people with unqualified and incompetent black people is unjust to both parties, and exceedingly costly for society. Such practices are at the heart of poor service delivery in the public sector.

Threats by the Commission on Employment Equity to remove white women from the list of designated groups of intended beneficiaries are disconcerting. The argument is that white women have been disproportionate beneficiaries of employment equity. An examination of the current profiles of participation in our economy, especially on the employment front, indicates continuing white male dominance. According to the 2006-2007 Report of the Commission on Employment Equity, black people, who constitute 88% of the Economically Active Population (EAP), occupied only 23% of top management positions in the private sector companies reviewed, of which black females constituted just less than 7%. White people, constituting just less than 13% of EAP, occupied 75% of top management positions, of which white women occupied just less than 15%.

These figures show that white people at top management levels are eight and a half times their EAP numbers, whereas black people are a quarter of their EAP numbers. The situation is similar at senior management levels, with slightly smaller gross levels of under-representation of black people at 27%, of whom 8% are female, and 71% white people, of whom 19% are female.[171]

The Chair of the Commission on Employment Equity, Jimmy Manyi, who is also the Chair of the Black Management Forum, cites these numbers in calling for a 'sunset clause' for white women. Using demographic profiles to set targets that match opportunities in the economy to sectors of the population, this is seen as an essential tool to rebalance the distortions of the past that persist to date.

There are risks to this approach. First, the goal of transformation is to create a non-racial, non-sexist, more equitable, prosperous society. Transformation is not about social engineering apartheid style, but enabling everyone – black, white, male, female – to contribute to growing the cake of prosperity to be shared by all.

Second, there are risks in underestimating the legacy of exclusion from education and training. Skills shortages are a reality. The impact of apartheid's legacy cannot be wished away. We must fight against those continuing to put obstacles in the way of women and black people that prevent their talents being utilised.

Third, white women have traditionally been discriminated against despite their formal access to the same education and training opportunities as white men. Look at their under-representation relative to males and ask why they are not at least 50% of the 75% of top management that is white, instead of only 15%. Black women should be at least 51% of the 23% instead of only 7%. The progress white women have made should be celebrated as a demonstration of the effectiveness of removing barriers to the development of talent, but progress is nowhere near what it would have been had sexism not been such an embedded part of our culture.

We should focus on how to make more progress, given that both black and white women lag behind in visible leadership positions in the private sector. Sexism undermines women in both the public and private sectors. The more women – black and white – succeed in senior positions, the more positive role models young people – male and female – will have.

There might be a more sinister interpretation behind this discomfort with the progress of white women in the economy. Why are they singled out as disproportionate beneficiaries in an economy dominated disproportionately by male beneficiaries, black and white? Why is the Commission on Employment Equity not targeting black men who are benefiting ahead of black women, who are the largest demographic group in the country? There is an undertone of male chauvinism in calls to slow the gains white women are making.

There seems to be an assumption that by not appointing white women, more black men and women would be appointed. This indicates a lack of understanding of the relationship between skills and employment. The greater the number of skilled people in the economy, the more jobs they are likely to help create. For instance, for every one job in the tooling industry 25 additional jobs are created,[172] while four jobs are created for every one job in the software industry.[173] Empowering skilled white women together with all those previously excluded from opportunities is more likely to generate greater economic growth.

Fourth, a focus on 'redress' of past wrongs without a holistic view of desired goals risks making the whole empowerment process a compensatory mechanism for past wrongs, not a mechanism for creating an equal-opportunity climate for all. A compensatory model holds the danger of rewarding people with senior positions without an adequate performance framework that demands that they demonstrate the value they contribute. Redress applied in this manner also reflects vain attempts to strip white women of their inalienable rights to use their education and training to advance themselves.

Finally, career choices do not necessarily follow demographic profiles. They are a product of complex processes including exposure to various career options. Given our legacy, more black people aim to establish their own enterprises than ever before. The idea of working for someone else may not be as appealing as it may be for white people, especially women with a pent-up appetite to demonstrate their professional competence. An abnormal development pattern cannot be normalised in one generation.

Many white male critics of employment equity also like to cry wolf about being excluded from economic opportunities. Current profiles of participation in our economy, especially in employment, indicate continuing white male dominance. The 2006-2007 Report of the Commission on Employment Equity presents a picture that is at variance with some of the media reports of white people being pushed out of key positions in the workplace.[174] White male dominance at the top and senior management positions persists and is a logical outcome of our economic history. The challenge is to transform this profile in a manner that repositions us for greater productivity, sustainable growth and socio-economic equity. Affirmative action – *regstellende aksie,* to put right what is clearly wrong – is critical to addressing this imbalance.

Many private-sector institutions have not even begun to confront the alienation that might result from inappropriate institutional cultures. Some have focused on décor to include more African motifs and 'Proudly South African' slogans, but a big gap remains in actual management practices.

But even if all negative practices were eliminated, our socio-economic history has not nurtured enough black people and women to fill senior positions. Our education and training system cannot yet produce the pipeline of graduates able to compete for top and senior management positions. This puts pressure on institutions to create opportunities for those already qualified, but lacking experience to match the traditional norms. Investment in strengthening the pipeline is essential. The emphasis in the BBBEE Codes on skills development reflects its importance.

Some aspects of affirmative action create ethical dilemmas, especially where people compete for finite opportunities. Take the question of admission to highly desired institutions with limited places. These are real dilemmas that entities such as UCT's Medical School have had to contend with since the end of apartheid. How does one justify admitting a black student with an 'A pass' ahead of a white student with an 'A+ pass'?

First, a black student from a poor background with an A pass is a super performer compared to a white student with an equivalent outcome. Poor black families cannot provide the support that many white students take for granted. Moreover, schools serving the poor areas where black people live are often inadequately resourced. An A outcome under such conditions should be regarded as equivalent to an A+ outcome.

Second, even if the black student does not come from a disadvantaged background, he or she can help to constitute a class that reflects the diversity of South Africa's people. Such a class can better prepare young people – black and white – for the realities of their society. In addition, such a student would most likely act as a positive role model for other aspirant black students and help swell the ranks of professionals. Closing the gap between white and black professional participation rates in our society is in the public interest and needs to be pursued vigorously over many decades. Every opportunity should be used to enlarge the pool of black professionals.

These arguments are cold comfort to individuals who are passed over. In the USA inequalities persist after many decades of Civil Rights legislation. In a highly publicised case of a disgruntled aspirant Michigan University Law School student who was passed over in favour of a lesser-qualified black student, the US Supreme Court found that there was a 'compelling interest in racial diversity'. Justice Sandra O'Connor was unequivocal:

> Today, we hold that the Law School has a compelling interest in attaining a diverse student body . . . The Equal Protection Clause (of the US Constitution) does not prohibit the Law School's narrowly tailored use of race in admissions decisions to further a compelling interest in obtaining the educational benefits that flow from a diverse student body.[175]

In the South African situation where black people are in the majority, the compelling social or public interest is even stronger. It is not desirable to have white students dominating classes in higher-education institutions. Young South Africans need to learn together so that they can live and work together.

The same applies to three other elements of affirmative action that David Benatar refers to.[176] First, 'the tie-breaker affirmative action' in which two equally qualified candidates compete for a position. Benatar gives the black candidate the job because such an appointment advances the transformation process without any cost to productivity. The added value of a positive role model in society is immeasurable.

The second form of affirmative action Benatar refers to is 'strong-preference affirmative action', where a less qualified black candidate is appointed ahead of a more qualified white candidate. The additional value a less qualified person may bring might more than make up for the technical-competence difference between the two. Such value may include complementary attributes that make for a stronger team and language skills that are absent or poorly represented, and reach into market segments that offer big opportunities. Such a candidate would also need to be willing to work hard and to learn to close the technical gaps.

However, certain critical professions cannot tolerate any compromises in technical requirements and should not practise this form of affirmative action – e.g. specialist medical/surgical professions, pilots, engineers, and key management areas in technical fields including financial markets. The responsible approach here would be to appoint the best qualified candidate, but offer the less qualified person the opportunity to grow into greater strength through understudying the other and preparing to compete for future opportunities.

The third policy dilemma is what Benatar refers to as 'set-asides', known as quotas in the USA. There are two types – numeric and strategic. Numeric 'set-asides' are pursued with a goal of matching employment profiles with demographic ones. There are elements of this approach across the country, including in the Western Cape where the issue has reached absurd levels in the public health sector. It is no longer good enough to have black medical specialists, they must be subdivided into African, Coloured and Indian.

This is absurd. To assume that specialist medical professionals would match so-called demographic realities of the post-1994 population is to ignore the impact of historical distortions on skills profiles. How many Africans living in the Western Cape were trained in our medical schools in the pre-1994 period and have progressed to the point of being specialists? What about the more lucrative opportunities African graduates see in careers in the private sector? Set-asides in areas of scarce skills are inappropriate and have huge social costs. We should aim to attract every medical specialist – black or white – to revitalise our health services.

Numeric set-asides based on population registration categories may also fuel divisiveness. There seems to be a growing tendency to establish degrees of disadvantage as a basis for allocation of patronage. The Western Cape political scene is reeling from conflicts fed by the hierarchy of categories of disadvantage. The 'ethnic entrepreneurship' that Neville Alexander[177] warns about is already evident. Those involved have lost sight of the purpose of redress and affirmative action.

In contrast, strategic set-asides have 'compelling social value', to quote Judge O'Connor again. Take the example of Reserve Bank governor Tito Mboweni. The governor of the Reserve Bank or Central Bank is a political appointee in any country, given the strategic role the institution plays in setting and monitoring the impact of monetary policy. In view of our history and the symbolic importance of the governor's position, the appointee had to be a black person.

Mboweni admits how little he knew about central banking when he was appointed. The government ensured that the retiring governor, Chris Stals, stayed long enough for Mboweni to get exposure to essential central-banking skills. He developed close relationships with Alan

Greenspan in the US Federal Reserve and Ed George, then governor of the Bank of England. It is generally accepted that Mboweni turned out to be one of the best Reserve Bank governors this country has ever had. His visionary leadership and engagement with higher-education institutions are inspiring young people to see value in careers in banking.

I agree with Benatar that appointing unqualified people to positions beyond their competence in the name of affirmative action is indefensible. Such appointments are a travesty of justice for the individual, who cannot perform. It is unfair to recipients of services who are subjected to poor-quality services. Such appointees tend to become aggressive and abusive under pressure, further undermining the public interest by abusing the poorest people. Such appointments undermine the productivity and sustainability of long-term economic growth.

The public sector has far too many examples of the more negative approaches to affirmative action employment. Inadequate state capacity is largely responsible for, and in turn due to, these practices, creating a downward spiral in performance. Balancing political imperatives with performance requirements should have been a greater focus of the post-1994 government.

Appointing incompetent people in the name of affirmative action does a disservice to poor black people who depend on public services for basic needs. Poor public services are particularly disabling in essential service areas such as health and education, records of births, deaths and identity by Home Affairs, and basic water and sanitation. There is a crisis of performance in these areas. Municipalities serving poor people are dysfunctional, with little accountability by local authorities meant to represent residents. These bad appointment practices give a bad name to all black people in a racist society that still tends to associate black people with incompetence. The only beneficiaries of bad appointments are the incompetent people who earn disproportionately large salaries for simply occupying those positions.

Preferential procurement

Preferential procurement, another key aspect of BBBEE, creates incentives for economic players to support transformation by ensuring that those previously excluded from the benefits of supplying goods and services are brought into the marketplace. As the main procurement agent, the government has a major role in promoting this objective. The private sector would not want to risk losing lucrative public contracts.

The practice has produced mixed results. On the positive side, private sector attitudes to small and medium enterprises (SME), many of which are run by black people, have changed. Entry-level and SME players are increasingly included in mutually beneficial partnerships that provide them with invaluable business opportunities and the development of technical skills. For traditional businesses, BEE credentials and business development opportunities are enhanced in those sectors of the community where they would have had no entry point, while new entrants benefit from participation in established businesses providing cash flow and technical experience.

An example is the sustainable model of a supply chain of SMEs that Anglo American Corporation has developed under the umbrella of AngloZimele.[178] The central principle is to provide budding entrepreneurs with start-up capital to supply essential services to the mining giant. From modest beginnings in the 1990s with capital of about R20 million, there are now thriving businesses worth R2 billion. This has created a win-win scenario. Anglo American gets the outsourced services that make for greater efficiencies, credits for enterprise development and other BEE points in terms of the Codes of Good Practice. The participating entrepreneurs gain access to other opportunities beyond just supplying Anglo. They are truly empowered business people.

Where preferential procurement has gone wrong, however, it is generally as a result of its misuse for rent-seeking purposes by public officials and political party operatives. The worst form of this occurs where public tenders are allocated in irregular ways to benefit the friends and families of decision-makers. This misuse of public office takes many forms, including set-asides that are unlikely to stand the test of legality in the courts. Local authorities seem to have the biggest problems in this regard, partly due to the knock-on effect of weak management and leadership that results from improper appointments in the name of employment equity and affirmative action. Appointing incompetent and technically unskilled people opens the way to irregular practices out of both ignorance and greed.

The case of the Cape Town City Council under ANC mayor Nomaindia Mfeketo comes to mind. The municipal council lost most of the skilled personnel essential to running a modern city: engineers, town planners, surveyors, financial managers. Over five years, the mayor assembled an all-black team of executive directors, called *Inkwenkwezi* (stars). Few had experience of local government, let alone governing a city of over three million people. With such a poor base of technical skills and experience, how could they do better? Neglect of the city infrastructure, inefficient services and non-transparent procurement processes have undermined the public interest.

The most serious impact of inappropriate appointments on poor people is in housing. Poor people who cannot afford second chances find themselves in settlements such as the N2 Gateway project with substandard flats constructed by inexperienced builders. Cape Town's long wet winters create humidity that must be planned for in construction. No qualified builder would have failed to ensure adequate ventilation and damp protection in the foundations and walls. There seem to have been lapses in the regulatory process too. Where were the building inspectors to ensure proper standards were met? It remains to be seen how the contract was allocated and how government will rectify these and other major defects. The showcase that the national Minister of Housing, Lindiwe Sisulu, launched so proudly may become an embarrassment to all.

Also worrying is the apparent tolerance of tender irregularities across the country at national, provincial and local levels. Irregular tenders have become an inherent part of the political patronage system, which comes at great cost to the public purse. The opportunity costs of not providing services because of failure to perform by inappropriately selected BEE companies are disproportionately borne by the poorest sectors of our society. They have to go without houses because BEE contractors have taken the money and disappeared. Their children attend schools under trees because constructors have gone missing before completing jobs for which they have been paid.

The flaunting of ill-gotten gains by BEE beneficiaries adds salt to the wounds of those left marginalised. Expensive cars, ostentatious houses and partying out of all proportion to the previous lifestyles of the nouveaux riches have become commonplace. In my home town, Polokwane, this has reached absurd proportions in a suburb named Tender Park, filled with new mansions. I am told that as soon as one wins a tender, one becomes eligible for all sorts of services: purchasing a car, expensive trips, commissioning the building of one's residence, etc. Polokwane is not alone in this.

The chain of beneficiaries feeding off irregular preferential procurement practices is long and complex. Not only are there kickbacks to decision makers who award contracts, but also to friends and families in their networks. In some cases, decision makers become part of the consortia that win contracts. But suppliers of goods and services – both black and white – such as car dealers, architects or constructors also benefit from the proceeds of crime by accepting payments from ill-gotten funds linked to this practice. The entitlement culture that Moeletsi Mbeki and others have warned against has become part of our social life.

There is mounting anger and frustration among poor people in the face of this incompetence. People in Khutsong Township, those living in what used to be single-sex hostels, N2 Gateway residents in Cape Town and many more are up in arms. We can expect more social instability unless something is done to halt the slide into cynicism and despair by poor people who feel cheated.

Who are the winners and losers?

Even critics of BEE have to concede that overall, policy intervention by the government to promote the broadening of participation in the economy by those previously excluded has been a great success. The most important gain is unprecedented robust growth over the last decade.

This economic growth is likely to be sustained as a result of its widespread nature involving primary commodities, infrastructure development and the supporting goods and services industries. Consumer demand has grown and continues to grow for all manner of goods and services spurred on by the growth in employment. Employment equity has spawned a new class of consumer, the so-called 'black diamonds',[179] who are first-generation beneficiaries of freedom of choice in education and training, and unlimited career opportunities.

Other sectors of the economy have become winners in this booming, broader-based wealth creation. The property sector, both private and public, is witnessing sustained and unprecedented growth. Gauteng is seeing the convergence of Pretoria and Johannesburg as more and more suburbs are established to cope with ever-increasing demand for homes. In 2007, we even ran out of cement to meet the growing demands of the booming building industry.

In a cruel twist of irony, the government's own incoherent policy-making is likely to undermine this economic growth. Failure to invest in infrastructure threatens sustainability. The current shortage of power is the most recent example. The management and governance of Eskom in the post-apartheid era embodies most of the dilemmas of transformation we are facing as a nation.

First, there seems to be persistent ambivalence towards state-owned enterprises. Despite the professed intention to privatise them with corporatisation as first step, not much progress has been made to bring the private sector into power generation. The government remains the sole shareholder of Eskom.

Then, the post-apartheid government has sought to use state-owned enterprises like Eskom as instruments for black economic empowerment, much like its apartheid predecessors did to empower Afrikaners. The laudable goal of visible black leadership and management may have trumped effectiveness and efficiency. The loss of skills from Eskom, where the workforce was halved from 66 000 to the current 30 000, has contributed to poor maintenance and weak management of crises. According to the trade union Solidarity, training programmes (presumably apprenticeships) have been shut down at Eskom.[180] This is a classic case of undermining the public interest through the pursuit of short-term political interests of narrow black economic empowerment. Inadequate expertise and experience compounded the supply challenges Eskom is facing. The whole economy is put at risk by the pursuit of party-political objectives that undermine the common good.

Third, the government's failure to heed expert advice about the need for expanding generating capacity as far back as 1998 and again in 2004 reflects the ambivalence towards the role of expert knowledge in the governance process. Political leaders have the mandate to make policies and to implement them, but they do not necessarily have the expertise to underpin complex policy choices. Effective political leaders leverage expertise to lay sound foundations for policy making and implementation. Where this approach has been followed we have seen much success. For example in macro-economic policy that has laid the foundation for our economic growth. The failure to respond swiftly and effectively to the challenges of HIV/Aids and power generation is the cost of political leaders second-guessing experts.

Fourth, Eskom's problems also reflect inadequate accountability in our public service. The complex relationship between Eskom's management and the government, its sole shareholder, must have a constraining impact on management's ability to challenge government policy even if such policies pose risks to the common good. Management that perceives that its interests are best served by submitting to political mandates rather than sound judgements promoting effectiveness and efficiency is unlikely to fulfil the impartial role of protecting the public interest. One can only hope that the repeated apologies by the President and his cabinet ministers mark the beginning of a culture of greater accountability by the government to the people it is meant to serve.

A final observation about the Eskom debacle is the failure of 'big business' to raise the alarm over all these years. President Mbeki has been meeting regularly with 'big business'. How could such a major risk to our economic growth have been kept secret for so long? Why was the public kept in the dark until the lights literally went out? One hopes that 'big business' is not falling into cosy business-government relationships such as experienced during apartheid to the detriment of the public interest.

We need to extract lessons from the failures of Eskom. Government should resist the temptation of being a referee and a player in areas of the economy where it does not have comparative strengths. Government needs to respect expert advice to enrich its policy making and implementation role. Black economic empowerment that promotes a few people beyond their level of competence and discards the cumulative expertise and experience in the wider society is suicidal. The poorest people in whose name the government governs are the greatest losers in this case: loss of jobs, inconvenience to consumers at every level and risks to health and lives as essential services are put at risk.

Notwithstanding the above criticisms, BEE has undoubtedly benefited the entire economy. The financial sector is the biggest winner of all. The unusual nature of the structures of BEE deals that brings together investors without capital on the one hand, and traditional capitalists on the other, creates unlimited high-value engagements for the banking sector. They benefit all the way up the value chain as advisers for a fee, financiers at attractive rates, and investors with equity kickers.[181] The growing economy has also stimulated unprecedented consumer credit demand that has swelled bank profits.

There are also winners among specific population sectors. The 'first-movers' have benefited from early successes, but some have burned their fingers with badly-structured deals and over-priced assets. A celebrated case is the JCI deal with Mzi Khumalo and his partners. Those early lessons left much wiser players in the market, including Khumalo. First-movers in the BEE space have been able to cash in their investments to gain more liquid assets for further investments.

Those who are politically well connected made their money early and continue to make more – an inevitable outcome of the nature of earlier versions of BEE that benefited mainly former ANC political figures who entered the private sector as pioneer empowerment players. The 'usual suspects' became sought-after partners by the private sector. It was a win-win-win scenario for the government, the private sector and the individuals involved.

Women have been late entrants into BEE. The male-dominated nature of the private sector has made their entry difficult. Most captains of industry have no real experience of dealing with women as business partners and feel more comfortable with other men. Black men, who share this lack of experience of women partners, have fallen comfortably into the male-club culture.

Women have yet to be given adequate opportunities to demonstrate the particular value they can add. Sexism in institutional cultures, both public and private, remains intact. There are signs of progress, however, as women become more aggressive in forming consortia that have managed to negotiate significant deals, for example, Peotona, with former ambassador to the UK Cheryl Carolus and her partners.

White women have clearly been significant beneficiaries of the broadening of the base of economic participation. Those who entered the entrepreneurial space have greater access to opportunities and capital through their networks within relatively wealthy white families. Their education and skills, an essential success factor, are a decided advantage beyond employment equity gains. It remains to be seen whether the greater participation of white women in the private sector will have a transformative impact on its institutional culture.

Although the broadening of the base of participation and the BBBEE Codes have opened opportunities for a wider segment of the population, access to affordable capital is still a constraint. This is an area that promises to add the greatest momentum to the thrust of broadening economic participation that should include new entrants, especially women and rural people.

The losers in the BEE space are those at the margins of the growing economy. The weaknesses in the state's capacity add to their burden. Abuses of preferential procurement hurt poor people more than any other sector of the economy. Tolerance of persistent blatant irregularities is leading to despair among those left stranded without services.

Land reform, agricultural development and other opportunities for enhancing rural livelihoods have lagged behind. Land-reform bottlenecks perpetuate apartheid geography. The government, as the largest land-owner,[182] seems unable to leverage the release of land for integrated development to benefit poor people in both urban and rural areas. Why should poor black people continue to be confined to living on the outskirts of cities while the government owns tracts of land that used to serve as buffers between black and white residential areas within cities?

Requiring that in all property development projects, a certain proportion of land should be set aside for public use under the government's authority offers additional opportunities. What plans does government have to transform the apartheid landscape, and what is the time frame for integrated housing development?

Rural development is neglected. Land restitution has failed to deliver on its early promise. It is estimated that up to 2003 only 36 686 claims benefiting 83 661 households had been settled out of a total of 79 000 valid claims. (My own family was fortunate – the land at the foot of the Soutpansberg that had belonged to the Seakamela clan including Kranspoort Mission where I grew up, was restored to them.) Where settlements have been reached, beneficiaries have often been unable to utilise the land productively as they lack the strategic and operational capacity.

There is an opportunity for the government to mobilise the goodwill that still resides in many white farming communities who have the skills and experience to help build capacity of the local authority and communities. The Land Bank should finance such agricultural efforts with communities willing to invest 'sweat equity'. The question is whether the Land Bank has the capacity to discharge its mandate as it did in the era of supporting poor white farming communities.

The Land Bank has been criticised recently for poor debt management, financial irregularities and a dismal rate of returns on loans. In October 2007 the government injected a further R700 million into the institution on condition that it change its strategy. According to media reports, a forensic audit has revealed that senior Land Bank board members mismanaged R1 billion in Land Bank funds.[183] What is to be done to ensure that poor people are not again going to bear the cost of power games for the benefit of a few politically well-connected black people?

The success of BEE has spawned interesting adaptations across sub-Saharan Africa. It has provided a much-needed instrument to enhance the indigenisation of private-sector activity and wealth creation in African economies. Africa's comparative advantage in the global economy is its human capital (young growing populations) and natural resources. Greater participation in wealth creation by indigenous populations holds great promise for the continent's sustainable-growth prospects.

The government should be proud of its achievements in BEE as a novel, home-grown policy. Still, the unintended consequences of BEE must be monitored and corrected to ensure that the greatest good accrues to the largest number. We must heed Moeletsi Mbeki's warning about the risks attached to the corrupting influence of BEE. Enrichment that is not earned through entrepreneurship and hard work breeds entitlement. Entitlement breeds insatiable greed that can consume our society.

But an even greater cancer is embedded in this policy. The investment of 'racial categories' of apartheid-era population classification with economic value creates vested interests in the continuing divisions in our society. It is only natural that for as long as there is a benefit from being labelled 'historically disadvantaged' one would want to retain the label and cash in on its largesse. There is, however, a risk in projecting black people, especially African people, as perpetual victims in need of redress. The victim status projected on black people risks undermining their assumption of the rights and responsibilities of citizenship.

BBBEE is meant to give those previously excluded from economic opportunity a leg up to enable them to participate in wealth creation. It is not meant as a reward for being black, a woman, or disabled, entitled to benefits without adding any value. BBBEE is about broadening the base of participation in growing the economy to enlarge the economic cake that can be shared more equitably. We dare not confuse ends and means.

PART SIX

Leadership
challenges

CHAPTER 15

Neighbourhood challenges

SOUTH AFRICA'S TRANSITION TO DEMOCRACY HAS ALSO BEEN SHAPED by the dynamics of neighbourhood influences. Neighbourhoods matter to households and communities as well as to countries. The natural human tendency to be competitive drives us to rise to or above the standards set by our neighbourhood. Peer pressure within neighbourhoods also enforces certain standards. Neighbours act in self-interest in protecting their property's value from threats posed by lowered standards of care and behaviour. Neighbourhoods might use both negative and positive reinforcement to achieve their goals.

As mentioned in Chapter 1, transitions to democracy are tough, even if one has a supportive big brother. Former East Germans are still not on par with their siblings from the former West Germany in terms of many social indicators. There were also teething problems in other Eastern European countries and countries of the former Soviet Union that had to make major socio-economic adjustments. According to a 2002 World Bank study,[184] there has been impressive progress in just one decade in most of these countries.

South Africa, too, has done remarkably well in its transition to democratic rule and greater social justice. It did not have much international or neighbourhood support beyond the symbolic. In addition, South Africa had set the trend in signalling a new approach to Africa's self-image and the continent's repositioning of itself for more sustainable development. This is President Mbeki's proud legacy. But there is controversy within our society about the extent to which we should be our neighbours' keeper and the costs of doing so.

The African Renaissance

The famous 'I am an African' speech delivered on 8 May 1996 by the then deputy president, now President Thabo Mbeki, marked a turning point for the new South Africa and its role in Africa.[185] The symbolism of the occasion – an address to the parliament of the new South Africa following the adoption of the new national constitution – weighed heavily. This was a celebratory moment and the final step in our journey to becoming a free society governed by a human-rights framework.

Mbeki linked his definition of himself as an African with the histories of the diverse cultures that made up the new South African nation.

> I am born of a people who are heroes and heroines . . . Patient because history is on their side, these masses do not despair because today the weather is bad. Nor do they turn triumphalist when, tomorrow, the sun shines . . . Whatever the circumstances they have lived through and because of that experience, they are determined to define for themselves who they are and who they think they should be.
>
> We are assembled here today to mark their victory in acquiring and exercising their right to formulate their own definition of what it means to be African.
>
> The constitution whose adoption we celebrate constitutes an unequivocal statement that we refuse to accept that our Africanness shall be defined by our race, colour, gender or historical origins.
>
> It is a firm assertion made by ourselves that South Africa belongs to all who live in it, black and white.
>
> It gives concrete expression to the sentiment we share as Africans, and will defend to the death, that the people shall govern.[186]

Mbeki was acutely aware that this moment might not have been possible without the generosity of fellow African countries that bore the brunt of the total onslaught of the apartheid government against supporters of the liberation movement. Mbeki affirmed the interconnectedness between South Africans and the rest of the continent. He placed the achievement of South Africa's adoption of its constitution within the context of his notion of the African Renaissance:

> This thing that we have done today, in this small corner of a great continent that has contributed so decisively to the evolution of humanity, says that Africa reaffirms that she is continuing her rise from the ashes.
>
> Whatever the setbacks of the moment, nothing can stop us now! Whatever the difficulties, Africa shall be at peace! However improbable it may sound to the sceptics, Africa will prosper! [187]

Mbeki was also signalling the readiness of the younger generation of African leaders to win respect for the continent in a globalising world.

Mbeki has over the years elaborated on the concept of the African Renaissance. In addition to drawing inspiration and self-confidence from the historical achievements and creativity of African societies over the centuries, practical action was needed to liberate Africa from the conditions that hampered its progress:

> The call for Africa's renewal, for an African Renaissance, is a call to rebellion. We must rebel against the tyrants and the dictators, those who seek to corrupt our societies and steal the wealth that belongs to the people. We must rebel against the ordinary criminals who murder, rape and rob, and conduct war against poverty, ignorance and the backwardness of the children of Africa . . . to be a true African is to be a rebel in the cause of the African Renaissance, whose success in the new century and millennium is one of the great historic challenges of our time.[188]

To give concrete expression to the ideals of the African Renaissance, Mbeki has worked with leaders such as Olusegun Obasanjo of Nigeria, Abdelaziz Bouteflika of Algeria and Abdoulaye Wade of Senegal to implement a practical development programme under the New Partnership for Africa's development (Nepad). Nepad is a strategic framework with four main objectives: eradicating poverty; promoting sustainable development for African countries individually and collectively; enhancing the integration of Africa into the global economy; and accelerating empowerment of women.

Africa's success in attaining these objectives would rest on the ability to tackle the numerous constraints to its development. Conditions for sustainable development were to be created by ensuring peace and security, democracy and good political, economic and corporate governance at all levels, regional cooperation and integration, and capacity building.

This call to action was met with scepticism both at home and abroad. In South Africa, the dominant view was that our own challenges – to make the transition to democracy a success and tackle socio-economic disparities – should take priority over any focus on the rest of the continent. Others viewed the idea of an African Renaissance as a pipedream, given the history of failure on the continent. They doubted the capacity of African leaders to overcome short-term personal-power interests and focus on the larger continent.

Abroad, the level of scepticism amounted to derision. When I arrived at the World Bank in May 2000 to take up the position as the first African Managing Director in the 50 years of the institution's existence, I was greeted by an issue of *The Economist* that reflected the widespread cynicism about Africa's chances for success under the headline: 'Hopeless Africa?'[189] The analysis, based on traditional economist sources and data, documented countless failures in Africa, making a strong case for the world to write it off as a doomed continent incapable of helping itself or responding appropriately to others who wished to assist it.

Unlike those abroad, home critics of the African Renaissance ignored fundamental realities of neighbourhood politics. First, South Africa could not divorce itself from the Afro-pessimism that engulfed the continent and discouraged foreign investment. It had to make peace with being part of Africa, not an outpost of Europe attached to the tip of an Africa with which it had little in common.

Second, one cannot choose one's neighbours in the world of politics and international affairs. One must engage in responsible actions to improve the neighbourhood one finds oneself in.

Third, South Africa cannot lift itself out of the economic doldrums that have plagued it over the decades without paying attention to intra-regional linkages, particularly given our economic history that linked our mining and other sectors to neighbouring countries through labour and investment relationships.

The fourth reality home critics ignored is that Africa's development challenges are in part due to the irrational colonial boundaries that fragmented the continent into 53 states, with 48 countries in the sub-Saharan region, of which 15 are landlocked. Many of Africa's national entities are not sustainable on their own either culturally or economically. Africa is unlikely to be competitive against other emerging markets with large populations that offer economies of scale on many fronts. Intra-Africa cooperation holds immeasurable benefits for South Africa and the continent. The estimated 800 million population of sub-Saharan Africa represents a sizeable market for goods and services if greater collaboration could be forged across colonial boundaries. Such a large consumer market would support increased investments in manufacturing and service industries across the region.

Africa also has the advantage of a growing population that can be turned into a dynamic human-capital base through investments in high-quality education and training. South African institutions stand to benefit from collaboration on this front too. For example, UCT has benefited over decades from being the institution of choice for Zimbabwean students, many of whom rise to positions of leadership in student politics and development. They form an important core of a growing network of Africa's future leaders. Research and teaching collaborations are also blossoming across the continent, giving Africa the opportunity to have a meaningful role in knowledge creation and adaptation for its own use as well as in contributing to global knowledge.

Finally, South Africa has been partly responsible for some of the failures in our neighbourhood. Destabilisation was pursued by the apartheid state in Mozambique, Angola, Zimbabwe and Zambia in the vain hope of stopping the wind of change that brought democracy southwards. 'Fighting terrorism' also took the form of destabilising transitions to democracy in our neighbouring countries in the hope of delaying democracy at home.

International critics have also had to rethink their view that Africa should be left to its own devices because it represents too great a burden for the international community. The terrorist attacks on Wall Street in New York and in Washington DC on 11 September 2001 demonstrated that the interconnectedness of the globalising world does not permit anyone the luxury of living as 'an island entire of itself'.[190] Problems in far-off regions such as Afghanistan came knocking at the door of the world's premier capital market in the most brutal fashion. There is a growing momentum behind campaigns for sharing the benefits of globalisation and ensuring that 'failed states' receive support before they become international disasters.

How has Nepad performed?

Nepad has recorded some important successes. First, it put Africa on the map in a more positive light. Second, Nepad became an advocate for acknowledging progress in areas where achievements are visible while urging more effort in respect of those where problems persist. The growing acknowledgement of Nepad as a development platform by the Group of 8 most industrialised countries (G8) is an example of success.

The third success has been in institution building. The African Union (AU) has replaced the moribund Organisation of African Unity (OAU). In 2001, Nepad was adopted as Africa's principal agenda for development within the institutional framework of the AU.[191] The AU has in turn spawned the Pan-African Parliament that sits in Midrand, near Pretoria. Ms Gertrude Mongella, Speaker of the Pan-African Parliament, is one of the visible woman leaders who are emerging in this new political climate. An African Human Rights Commission has also been set up, although its effectiveness has yet to be demonstrated.

Fourth, Nepad's African Peer Review Mechanism (APRM) is another innovation to enhance good governance through neighbourly peer pressure and support. Members are eminent persons with political experience, including former presidents. The APRM is designed to help set standards of performance by governments in relation to the Nepad principles.

By mid-2007, 26 countries had volunteered for APRM by signing a Memorandum of Understanding, and another had requested accession. At that stage Ghana, Rwanda, Kenya, South Africa and Algeria had largely completed the review process, while Benin's process was supposed to be finished at the beginning of 2008. The review was also in progress in seven other countries.[192]

Although the APRM is a slow process that raises questions about its effectiveness as a tool for improving governance practices, South Africa's report released at the end of 2007 gives an indication of the value countries can derive from an assessment of their strengths and weaknesses. The report identified 18 best practices worth emulating in other countries, including innovations such as our BEE charters and the Mzansi bank account. Among our strengths were our progressive constitution, strong economy, and a political environment that is conducive to debate. The report also highlighted challenges to be addressed in a programme of action: racism, xenophobia, under-representation of women in the private sector, and high levels of gender-based violence.[193]

The most important success achieved by Nepad has been in setting the strategic framework for engagement with international partners. The World Bank Africa Regional Strategy is now mapped to a 2000 study led by South African-born Alan Gelb, then regional Chief Economist, as a collaborative project between the World Bank, the African Development Bank and the Economic Commission on Africa: *Can Africa Claim The 21st century?* This study sought to provide the intellectual underpinnings for the implementation strategy to meet the Nepad objectives. The development approaches of many development partners have been framed with a view to supporting Africa's own priorities as set out by Nepad and adapted by individual countries. There has also been greater movement towards funding regional projects especially in infrastructure development.

African leaders have become a regular part of the international leadership efforts on the edges of the Group of 8. Africa has been able to press its claims for debt relief, increased donor support and international trade with greater or lesser success on some of the issues, especially trade liberalisation. The booming global resources markets driven by China's insatiable appetite to fuel its economy have also made Africa a desirable destination for long-term investors. According to the 2007 Africa Competitiveness Report, in 2006 Africa's GDP grew by 5,5% and that of sub-Saharan Africa by 5,7%.[194] These figures were expected to increase to 6,2% and 6,8% respectively in 2007, boosting confidence in the region's economic prospects.

African leaders have reason to be proud of their positive record in tackling conflicts. To a greater or lesser extent, Rwanda, Burundi, the Democratic Republic of the Congo, Cote d'Ivoire, Sierra Leone and Liberia have seen peace descend on their troubled lands, paving the way for sustainable development. Africa has become a trusted partner with the UN in peacekeeping missions across the continent. South Africa has played a key role in dispute resolution and participated in peacekeeping.

With regard to infrastructure development, various regional collaborations are under way. For example, the Maputu Corridor with road and rail connections between South Africa and Mozambique is improving access to markets and exports. Submarine fibre-optic cables along Africa's west and east coast will enhance connectivity and cater for bandwidth demand.

A Pan-African Infrastructure Fund was launched in July 2006, with the initial target of raising US$1 billion under the guidance of the Public Investment Commission (PIC) of South Africa. Its purpose is to mobilise African pension funds for Africa's own development. African countries have over the years invested their public pension funds with foreign companies, essentially using African money to fund developed economies. It is estimated that the backlog of infrastructure development in Africa is about US$120 billion.

Zimbabwe has emerged as a persistent challenge to Nepad principles and peer review over the last decade. As it has descended deeper into despotic rule and economic implosion, it is threatening to take the region with it. President Mbeki's policy of quiet diplomacy has yet to bear fruit at the start of 2008, as Robert Mugabe continues to defy world opinion.

Civil liberties have eroded, the economy is in free fall, and HIV/Aids is being fuelled by hunger and destitution. Refugees are pouring into South Africa and Botswana.

Tackling HIV/Aids is high on the agenda, given that Africa has 62% of the world's young people in the 15-24 age group –the most vulnerable people. Twenty-five million people have died from the pandemic so far, with a further 25 million infected.[195] Performance in curbing the spread of this pandemic remains mixed, with prevalence rates of 20% or more in Botswana, Swaziland, Zambia, Zimbabwe, Malawi, Lesotho and Namibia. South Africa's HIV/Aids pandemic, with the largest number of people infected in a single country (5,5 million or 11% of the population), is likely to get worse from the spillover effects of the cross-border migration of desperate people.

The South African Migration Project, an NGO based in Pretoria, estimated in 2004 that nine to ten million people from the rest of Africa cross legally and illegally into South Africa every year, escalating by about four million entrants per year.[196] As the receiving country for political and economic refugees, South Africa faces increasing challenges.

Democracy and good governance

Democracy and good governance remain Africa's Achilles heel. In Chapter 3, I referred briefly to Nigerian novelist Chinua Achebe who put his finger on the fundamental problem of Africa's failure to establish democratic governance in his novel *Anthills of the Savannah*, as quoted by historian Basil Davidson:

> The prime reason . . . can't be massive corruption though its scale and pervasiveness are truly intolerable; it isn't the subservience to foreign manipulation, degrading as it is; it isn't even this second-class hand-me-down capitalism, ludicrous and doomed. All such miseries of malice and incompetence or greed could be blamed for 'the prime failure of government'. But they were not the cause; they were the effects. The cause was to be found elsewhere. It lay in 'the failure of our rulers to re-establish vital inner links with the poor and dispossessed of this country.[197]

In committing themselves to ensuring democracy and good governance on the continent, Africa's leaders may not have paid sufficient attention to Achebe's diagnosis of the roots of its governance problems. Unless the failure of our leaders *to re-establish vital inner links with the poor and dispossessed people* of all our countries is recognised and tackled, Africa will remain plagued by governance problems. Our defensiveness in dealing with our failures constrain our ability to learn from other parts of the world that wrestle with similar challenges.

As mentioned in Chapter 3, Davidson suggests African leaders could learn from the experience of anti-imperial struggles in Poland and Romania before World War II, where returning exiles failed to re-establish any meaningful links with the people without whom the nationalist struggle could not have been won.

The sad reality is that post-colonial Africa does not seem to have learnt from such examples. 'Exile leadership' in some cases includes those of us who did not leave our shores but became exiled from vital links with the poorest and least educated among us. The elites of post-liberation struggles across Africa have had as their point of reference their own political comrades, not the least among their fellow citizens. The numbing of any form of empathy with poor people has taken many forms – Mobutu of Zaire's extravagant banquets while his people starved, Malawi's Kamuzu Banda's extravagant furnishings in his residences in poverty-stricken Malawi.

Kofi Annan's injunction at the July 2007 Nelson Mandela Lecture is a timely reminder of the dangers of continued tolerance of the abandonment of poor people's dreams and the trampling of their human rights:

> Africans must guard against a pernicious, self-destructive form of racism – that unites citizens to rise and expel tyrannical rulers who are white, but excuse tyrannical rulers who are black.

How else can we explain the stony silence of Africa's leaders in the face of gross violations citizens' rights in Zimbabwe? Much as quiet diplomacy has its place, it is incomprehensible that not one African leader would speak in support of the Zimbabwean people's right to dignity and security. How can one explain the silence of Africa's leaders when women are forced to abandon their babies while being flogged by security force members? Would they have kept quiet if Mugabe were white and saying, as he does, that those assaulted by security forces deserve what they get?

African leaders have yet to show they are on the side of poor people rather than on the side of their fellow leaders and comrades-in-arms. Many remain distant and act as 'rulers' rather than servants of their people. Nepad's APRM could profitably organise a series of discussions to promote awareness of this 'pernicious and self-destructive racism' that makes us defend black leaders even where they are violating the rights of ordinary people. Africa's attempts to consolidate democracy and promote good governance are unlikely to succeed until we confront this cancer.

Capacity constraints

The biggest constraint to progress is the capacity to plan, implement, monitor and evaluate programmes. State-capacity constraints that are holding back African countries, including South Africa, are reflected in the AU and its new institutions, including Nepad. Much of this weakness stems from technical gaps in most government machineries. The overemphasis on political appointments at the expense of technical expertise continues to be costly.

Most post-colonial African governments have deliberately marginalised the intellectual elites in their countries. This is partly due to the nature of transitions to democracy that resulted from liberation wars fought by those who sacrificed their careers to secure freedom for their countries. The post-colonial government machinery has been used to reward former comrades-in-arms, leaving little room for those who were outside the active service ranks but have the requisite expertise to contribute to an efficient civil service.

The insecurity of the new political elites tends to make them suspicious of any advice from well-meaning citizens beyond their inner circle. Independence of thought and analysis is often seen as a threat to cohesion and loyalty within the dominant party-political system led by former liberation leaders. An appreciation of the value of loyal citizens who are not necessarily members of political parties tied to liberation movements has yet to evolve. Opposition parties are often seen as the enemy rather than a partner in a multiparty democratic system.

Africa's development partners have tended to undermine indigenous expertise in their assistance programmes. For example, until 2001 the World Bank discouraged the use of African experts in its economic and sector analyses of countries in the region and the development of appropriate development-policy options and advice. World Bank officials and their donor-country consultants would descend on a country, do their analysis, write a country report and recommend development-policy advice to a particular country without any reference to local expertise. When I enquired about the logic of this, I was told it prevented biases that local African experts might introduce as interested parties.

Fortunately for the World Bank and Africa, Calisto Madavu, a Zimbabwean and Vice-President for Africa at the bank until his retirement in 2005, took up the challenge of putting African experts to the test. The quality of economic and sector work done with and by African experts not only met but in many cases exceeded the standards, according to independent reviewers of the World Bank's development work – a logical outcome of using local knowledge to enhance global knowledge.

To add insult to injury, developed countries that are also donors insist on their own citizens being included in the list of consultants used as experts in these studies and in implementation of projects. This practice of 'tied-aid' guarantees foreign nationals training and experience in developing countries while African experts are marginalised. In cases where local people are utilised, it is often as research assistants with little input into the framing of the questions asked. Consultants from developing countries are employed under contracts that include their compensation as well as overheads for their institutions; African experts are often treated as casuals, thereby encouraging moonlighting among academics. Moonlighting is costly to the performance of those academics involved, and undermines institution building in African universities that forego the overhead charge that could boost their revenues streams.

Not surprisingly, Africa has suffered a crippling brain drain over the last few decades. According to the International Organisation for Migration (IOM), Africa has lost one third of its human capital and is continuing to lose skilled personnel at an increasing rate since 1990.[198] An estimated 20 000 doctors, university lecturers, engineers, and other skilled professionals are leaving the continent every year. There are currently an estimated 300 000 highly qualified Africans in the diaspora, 30 000 of whom have doctorates in their fields. Africa as a whole has about 20 000 or 3,6% of the world's scientists, with a resultant diminishing share of scientific output.

Health and education have suffered most. The impact of the brain drain on the continent with regard to doctors and nurses is immeasurable, given the growing disease burden from high levels of HIV/Aids, TB and malaria.[199]

Africa is essentially funding the education of its brightest talents who then leave to service the needs of developed countries. For example, in Kenya it costs US$ 40 000 to train a doctor and US$10 000-15 000 for an undergraduate at university for four years. Although remittances by migrants are estimated at US$45 billion a year, this cannot compensate for the loss of intellectual, human and social capital to a continent that needs its brightest to join in tackling the challenges of development. The loss of so many teachers, nurses and doctors undermines a country's capacity to educate its population and keep it healthy. It also robs a country of leadership skills critical to good governance and sustainable development.

African governments have yet to appreciate the importance of knowledge and skills as a comparative advantage in today's global economy. Nor do many of them recognise the risks of losing their intellectual-capital base to more competitive economies in an interconnected world in which skilled people can sell their skills to the highest bidder. African governments must address the under-utilisation of professionals, discrimination in appointments on political grounds, poor working conditions, and the declining quality of education.

At the same time that Africa is haemorrhaging skills, it is spending US$4 billion per year (35% of development aid to the continent) to employ 100 000 experts from Western countries to provide technical assistance. Many are citizens of the countries providing aid tied to the use of their experts and procurement of their products – a process of round-tripping aid for the benefit of the donor.

Tied-aid not only burdens Africa with the opportunity costs of the financial benefit of the US$4 billion per year which is recycled back to donor countries, but denies it the opportunity to train and retain Africans to be experts in the development of their own countries. Africa continues to pay the price for this practice, which persists notwithstanding the commitments by donors to untie aid. The quality of aid is as important as the quantity of aid. Both must be enhanced to support sustainable development.

Regional collaboration and trade: how well does it work?

Agreement to establish a Pan-African Economic Community pre-dates Nepad. In 1991 the Abuja Treaty was adopted, setting the timetable for meeting this goal by 2025. Existing regional economic communities were to be the foundation. The gains from intra-African trade are potentially life-changing for the continent. The Commission for Africa[200] estimated that in 2002 intra-regional trade in Africa as a share of GDP was only 5,3% compared to that for East Asia at 26,5% and Europe and Central Asia at 15,3%. The stagnation of Africa's contribution to world trade between 1948 and 2003 is largely due to Africa's weak capacity to trade (owing to infrastructure and regulatory barriers) and international trade barriers within and outside the continent. Improving intra-regional trade holds great benefit for Africa's ability to trade itself out of poverty and promote the prosperity of its people.

But the road to intra-regional trade is a difficult one. The proliferation of regional communities and protocols has complicated coordination. There are currently seven main regional trade formations[201] and geographically limited subsets of the larger groups. To add to the complexity, many countries have multiple memberships in these regional entities, potentially over-extending officials.

Some success has been achieved in harmonising trade policies and lowering tariffs. For example, the Southern African Development Community (SADC) and the Common Market for Eastern and Southern

Africa (Comesa) have agreed to a common external tariff structure and coordinated negotiations with the European Union, while the Economic Community of West African States (Ecowas) and West African Economic and Monetary Union (Waemu) have agreed to plans for a monetary union.[202] Comesa's Free Trade Area (FTA) launched in 2000 aims to integrate their economies by strengthening investment and trade links. This brought tangible benefits to members in the form of a 15% increase in trade from 2002 to 2003. The competitiveness of goods within the region was also enhanced, boosting exports in terms of the USA's Africa Growth and Opportunity (Agoa) programme from US$457 million in 2002 to US$880 million in 2003.[203]

Africa must also deal with non-tariff trade barriers that hamper its competitiveness –cumbersome customs procedures, excessive bureaucracy, poor governance and corruption, lack of transparent regulatory frameworks, lack of automated systems, and low levels of human capacity. These require active policy reforms and commitment from government to implement and monitor reforms. Gains from such reforms can make a significant contribution to prosperity.[204]

Individual African countries that have taken steps to address these non-tariff trade barriers are benefiting. Mozambique's efforts since 1996 have seen 130 corrupt officials charged, increased training for staff and general support for efficiency leading to 62% of goods cleared through customs within 24 hours and customs revenue increased by 38%. The Trans-Kalahari Corridor between South Africa and Botswana has led to a reduction in border processing time from 45 to 10-20 minutes. Lesotho is reaping the benefits of improved revenue services at the border, with increased collection from US$700 000 to US$2, 9 million per month.

Despite these gains, challenges remain. Nepad's own limited capacity is hampering its effectiveness. Likewise, the desired regional integration is undermined by the weak human and technical capacity of most institutions. The tendency of African governments to make political rather than merit-based appointments has burdened regional institutions with inappropriate staff. Integrating regional trade institutions and reducing overlaps would harness the limited human capital more efficiently. But dealing with the vested interests of the bureaucrats who are blocking change requires a stronger political will than most African governments have shown so far.

At the World Economic Forum in Cape Town in June 2007, President Mbeki expressed his frustration about the lack of capacity of African states to take advantage of the opportunities of intra-African regional trade. He described the situation as so dire that even contracting with the private sector to address technical gaps in the public sector is not enough. The benefits of public-private partnerships cannot be harnessed if the public sector is too weak to negotiate mutually beneficial contractual relationships. This is a critical success factor in infrastructure and bulk public-services provision where Africa is weakest.

African governments must work together to recruit and retain skills currently residing outside the continent. Such programmes should be coordinated and harmonised conditions of service devised to ensure that the best and brightest return with the experience and technical know-how to support Africa's development. Recruitment and retention programmes would have to involve a radical departure from political appointments that disregard technical skills. Non-transparent procedures would have to be replaced by merit-based, open-competition systems; corruption and nepotism would have to be rooted out.

Another area where quick gains can be achieved is drawing on Africa's unique strength – the substantial role women play in the economy. Women in business tend to integrate their family responsibilities and the demands of the enterprise in family-owned and run businesses.[205] The synergies between fulfilled and productive women can only have a positive impact on the quality of family life and investment in the education and health of their children. Africa's human-capital base can be enhanced by empowering women and removing barriers to their entry into the private sector.

Agriculture and food security

Africa is the only continent that cannot feed itself. Over the last 15 years, it has gone backwards in trying to reduce poverty and hunger. The HIV/Aids pandemic has worsened the plight of poor people who are losing their food growers and nurturers. The increased vulnerability of women in the prime of their lives in the age group 15-35 years is taking its toll on the ability of African families to maintain the health and well-being of their children. Conflicts and the targeting of women and children for sexual and other abuse in civil wars such as in the Sudan also contribute to deepening poverty and hunger.

No continent has ever achieved sustainable development without being able to feed itself. Asia and Latin America benefited from the green revolutions of the 1960s-1980s. Partnerships between the Rockefeller Foundation and international development agencies such as the World Bank worked to establish networks of research institutes to develop seed varieties that would be more productive, and resistant to droughts and pests. Today Asia and Latin America feed themselves and export surpluses. Africa was by-passed by this first green-revolution wave.

In 2006 the Rockefeller Foundation launched another effort, the Alliance for the Green Revolution in Africa (Agra) in partnership with the Gates Foundation. It was re-launched at the World Economic Forum (WEF) in Cape Town with the announcement of Kofi Annan, former UN secretary-general, as chairperson. Agra will focus on the development of seed varieties, increased access to fertilisers, water management, access to markets, and general technical and business support for African farmers, female and male, to enhance productivity.

Food security for Africa would eliminate hunger, reduce vulnerability to diseases and provide a source of sustainable revenues from the export of surpluses. Much has been written about the benefits of liberalising global agricultural trade for developing countries, and fairer trade is a Nepad objective. Welfare benefits from removing trade barriers are estimated at US$19, 8 billion.[206] But benefits from agricultural trade is less than what could be harvested from a focus on enhancing productivity in agriculture and promoting inter-African trade in agricultural goods estimated at US$50 billion per year.

There is reason for optimism that this time the green revolution will take off in Africa. First, this is an Africa-initiated[207] and led effort. Kofi Annan has lent his leadership stature to the project, and many senior programme officers are Africans. Second, Agra has adopted a coordinated approach to revitalising Africa's agricultural sector by integrating various interventions. Access to world markets is only part of the strategy instead of the main focus. The programme is being rolled out in five pilot countries to ensure that learning from mistakes will inform the scaling-up in the rest of the continent.

South Africa as leader

South Africa – the largest economy in Africa, at nominal GDP of US$261,7 billion in 2006, representing a quarter of its GDP – is the engine of growth for the continent and its spearhead in global integration. South Africa leads the continent in industrial output (40% of the total) and mineral products (45%), and generates over 50% of the electricity. Thanks to the Gear programme, the country is in a better position to assume its role as the engine of growth for the benefit of the entire continent. South African private-sector entities have also woken up to the opportunities of the improving neighbourhood in the sub-region, investing aggressively in Africa. Sectors most likely to benefit are financial and banking, mining, infrastructure and general services.

The size of South Africa's economy relative to the youthfulness of its democracy has plunged it into a leadership role beyond its experience and capacity. This role has been thrust upon the country by respected African leaders such as the late President Julius Nyerere of Tanzania and strongly endorsed by the US Clinton administration and its Bush successor. However, expectations have not always been matched by resource support from the international community. The country is bearing a disproportionate burden in peace-building and peacekeeping processes across the continent. Had South Africa found itself in a more stable and more prosperous region, it might not have had to punch above its weight. The risks of over-extension are real.

Being the strongest economy in a continent has its drawbacks. South Africa became a magnet for HIV-infected migrant workers in search of employment in the mining industry in the 1980s, igniting the second of the three waves of HIV/Aids infections. South Africa also faces the challenge of coping with economic and political refugees flowing into its territory.

As a result of persistent weaknesses in Home Affairs, our country risks being labelled a violator of the human rights of the many refugees whom we are failing to protect in terms of our obligations under United Nations treaties. We seem to be in denial about the extent of the refugee challenge, exacerbated by the Zimbabwean economic collapse, with an estimated daily influx of 3 000 to 6 000 people from across the Limpopo. The idea that poor communities in a poor province such as Limpopo can simply integrate refugees into their residential areas, as Minister of Home Affairs Nosiviwe Maphisa-Nqakula suggested, shows a lack of understanding. South Africa is a signatory of the Human Rights Conventions that oblige us to give refuge to those who flee oppression and repression. Zimbabweans fall into that category.

Xenophobia is a major threat to our responsibilities as a good neighbour and a country with a human-rights constitution. There are major weaknesses in our procedures of treating migrants. The Lindela Detention Centre in the Gauteng Province is unsatisfactory, and corrupt officials are adding to the burdens of detainees. In provinces such as the Western Cape Somali refugees have been targeted by communities, with up to 20 murders reported in 2006. Media reports suggest that Somalis' success in running small trading stores more competitively than locals has made them targets. Our law-enforcement system is failing to protect them.

South Africa's leadership role on the continent is controversial. There is ambivalence among African leaders about the risks of being dominated – particularly acute in the post-Mandela period. Mandela's successor faces challenges as he tries to assert his leadership in a continent not accustomed to strategic alliances and coordinated foreign-policy approaches. Besides, the recent history of South Africa as a bully-boy of southern Africa in the 1970s and 1980s, both in support of its own agenda and as an ally of the USA in the Cold War, has left bitter memories in neighbouring countries.

The intervention by our army in Lesotho in 1998 to quell civil conflict precipitated by election disputes demonstrated some of the risks South Africa faces. Although the intervention was sanctioned by others in the region, the South African army was too inexperienced to handle a complex civil dispute and keep the peace with minimal use of force. The outcome was unsatisfactory, leaving the Basotho feeling betrayed by a neighbour led by people to whom it had given sanctuary not long before.

South Africa's leadership role is also weakened by inadequate knowledge of the complexities of the continent. Apartheid successfully isolated South Africans from their continental roots, and neither formal education nor the media helped to educate them about their continent. Many South Africans who lived in exile in Africa succumbed to the superiority complex that comes from being citizens (albeit second-class ones) of a more industrialised country. They missed many opportunities to learn from fellow African countries.

South Africa can only be an effective leader to the extent to which it is prepared to listen to its neighbours and learn from them. African intellectuals in Africa and the diaspora are an untapped resource for forging a different future for the region. President Mbeki is acutely aware of the role of the intelligentsia in tackling development challenges. In the 2001 Nepad policy document he was quoted as saying: 'Our own intelligentsia faces a challenge, perhaps, to overcome the class limitations . . . and ensure that it does not become an obstacle to the further development of our own revolution.' We need to overcome 'class limitations' not only for the intelligentsia, but also for political elites, whose links to ordinary citizens are tenuous.

A related question is whether the intelligentsia have been taken seriously by President Mbeki and his fellow political leaders. There is yet to be a demonstrable political culture of drawing on the best brains in Africa – both at home and in the diaspora – to address Africa's challenges. The tendency of national presidents to cast themselves as 'scholar-leaders' or 'philosopher-kings' makes it difficult for them to utilise expertise available in their own countries. The political authority of being head of state is too often confused with the authority of experts to speak on matters related to their specialist fields.

Successful countries draw on their brightest to inform public policy. Successive US governments have relied on the National Academies of Sciences and Engineering for advice to inform policy options. Issues ranging from national security to education to environmental challenges and climate change are put to panels of scientists for analysis, leading to recommendations to policy makers. With some exceptions, the USA largely promotes the values of science and reaps the benefit of its investments in science and technology. Africa can learn from this approach.

African leaders are yet to embrace intellectuals as partners in development. There is much mistrust of independent thinkers, with constructive criticism often seen as 'betrayal of the revolution'.

President Mbeki's over-anxious attempts to prove Afro-pessimists wrong may have unintended consequences. There is a risk of being defined by one's detractors rather than remaining focused on set goals. Centralising control to minimise risks in this environment may burden the president too much. Some of his bold statements on the African Renaissance are aimed at shifting the frame of reference by which the world judges Africa from expectations of failure to realising Africa's potential for success.

Although the Nepad initiative has injected a greater sense of purpose in African leaders, major challenges remain.

In the first instance, Mbeki's political base, the ANC, has yet to complete the transition from a liberation movement to a political party within a competitive democratic political system. The ANC remains a 'broad church', with its alliance with Cosatu and the SACP becoming increasingly dysfunctional. Why do the SACP and Cosatu remain within the alliance, given this fundamental difference on socio-economic policy? One can only surmise that the relationship remains functional to all parties at some level. For the ANC, the alliance assures it a large majority in parliament, just above two thirds of seats. In return, the ANC offers its alliance partners an avenue for participation in government. In addition to the satisfaction of wielding power and influence, the material benefits of such participation are significant, given that South African cabinet ministers and MPs are among the best paid in the world.[208]

Much is also made of Mbeki's 'dancing to the tune of global capital'. The sad reality is that critics holding this view live in a world that no longer exists. South Africa cannot insulate itself from the competitive global economy. Certainly this global economy is ruthless and unfair.

The issue of agricultural subsidies is egregious. Subsidies to rich farmers at the cost of US$1 billion per day keep poor farmers in countries such as Burkina Faso and Niger poor by closing cotton or rice markets to them. Europe, the USA and Japan are the key offenders in this regard.

Less industrialised countries led by middle-income countries such as Brazil, India, China and South Africa are learning to challenge this hegemony of the North, as demonstrated in Cancun, Mexico, in September 2003. But opting out of the global trade arena is not an option. South Africa's own successful 2001 Pretoria Supreme Court challenge of attempts by multinational pharmaceutical companies to hang on to their patent rights in the face of the national HIV/Aids pandemic is proof that one can influence even the mightiest players in the global economy through strategic interventions. South Africa has much to learn from countries in Latin America and Asia in this regard.

The charge that the South African government changed its economic policy in response to the prescriptions of the World Bank and the IMF reflects the real concerns many members of the tripartite alliance have about the Bretton Woods sister organisations. The infamous Washington Consensus of the 1990s that promoted unbridled privatisation and the overbearing influence of the USA has tainted them severely. Many countries have been left in difficulties by the rigid promotion of privatisation of state-owned enterprises and opening up of weak economies to competition without much attention to regulatory frameworks. For instance, the privatisation of Mozambique's cashew-nut industry in the 1990s was not a great success. It substituted state ownership with a monopoly by 'middlemen', leaving peasant farmers no better off.

But to impute that every bit of advice the post-1994 South African government received from the World Bank and IMF was detrimental is to underestimate the ability of the new political elites to discriminate between good and bad advice. These two institutions, for better or worse, represent a pool of global knowledge that countries tap into for their own benefit. China has managed to benefit from World Bank and IMF advice, selectively using advice in line with its development needs, without succumbing to their dictates. India too has recently shown a willingness to learn from others.

Are there lessons from these two countries for South Africa? The reality is that South Africa's ambivalence towards the Bretton Woods institutions has come at a cost. As one of the founding members of these institutions, the country could have derived much more benefit that it has. Gear in itself is not a problem. Instead, it is the lack of capacity to deliver and to honour socio-economic commitments that is perpetuating poverty and increasing inequality. This lack of capacity is an unavoidable part of the legacy of apartheid. But failure to own up to the problem is delaying action to address it. Denial remains one of the biggest challenges post-apartheid South Africa faces. Why not accept advice from others, evaluate it with the help of local experts, and then apply it in a manner that suits our local conditions?

The global climate is no longer conducive to socialist experiments based on burying one's head in the sand in the face of the harsh realities of the global economy. History has also not been kind to such experiments. One does not have to abandon social-democratic values to function in the global market economy, as Scandinavian countries continue to demonstrate. Finland made its transition from a poor paper-and-pulp industrial base in the 1960s to being the home of Nokia and a leader in the knowledge-based economy. They took advice from the World Bank and IMF, modified it to suit local conditions, and invested in science and technology education for all their people. They also actively promoted public-private linkages to stimulate innovation and turn research outcomes into products and services.

According to a World Bank study,[209] the elements that enabled Finland to move from relative poverty in the 1970s to becoming a world-class competitor are: increased research and development; major structural changes in the economic and social structures and specialisation in high technology; evolution from a resource-driven to a knowledge-driven economy; industrial renewal benefiting from liberalisation of trade and lifting restrictions on capital flows; and a policy shift from macro- to microeconomic reforms.

South Africa stands to profit from taking advice from the World Bank, given its global knowledge and experience. It can draw on lessons from other countries in the South such as Brazil, Bangladesh and Indonesia about how community-driven development enhances effectiveness and empowers poor people. It might also learn from Chile, Brazil and Mexico how investments in science and technology enhance development and prosperity.

The question remains: would South Africa have done better if it had been in a different neighbourhood with a less loaded legacy? Or could a different neighbourhood with tougher established standards of behaviour have moulded the style of leadership of South Africa's new democracy differently?

The Commission for Africa and its establishment of an Investment Climate Facility to support African countries in their efforts to improve their competitiveness as a destination for investments and also as a business partner, point to the benefits of continental partnerships. President Mbeki and his fellow leaders have to be credited with the successful conclusion of debt-relief discussions that have seen Africa benefit from the US$40 billion written off by the World Bank.

The centrepiece of Mbeki's legacy is likely to be his visionary leadership in forging African unity and repositioning the continent in the interconnected globalising world. His fierce attacks on Afro-pessimism have changed the tone of discussions on and with Africa. He has shifted the frame of reference from Africa the failed continent to Africa the continent of infinite possibilities and investment opportunities. Mbeki has made it possible for more people to say proudly: 'I am an African!'

Transformative leadership

LEADERSHIP IN THE TRANSFORMATION PROCESS MUST ITSELF BE TRANS-formative; it must embody the vision, values and principles of the society we aspire to become.

South Africa's transformation requires an understanding of the deep structure of the legacy of apartheid and an even more profound understanding of the foundations of our envisaged society. Transformative leadership is essential to laying the ghosts of our legacy to rest, thus freeing the future to unfold. Too often transformation has come to be seen as a numbers game of replacing white people with black people, a way of compensating previously disadvantaged people rather than creating opportunities for all citizens to contribute.

The compensatory approach to transformation poses the greatest risk to our democracy and to sustainable development. Understandably, those who were involved in the liberation struggle have expectations of participating in the exercise of power through state organs. But simply occupying positions of power and influence without adding value undermines our objectives as a society. Transformative leadership is not just about having black people, women or other previously disadvantaged people in leadership positions. It is about credible, visionary leadership that expands the boundaries of possibilities for all citizens, enabling them to contribute their talents, experience and skills to create a successful, prosperous democracy.

Transformative leadership is largely about shifting the frame of reference from old ways to new approaches. As I argued in Part II, we must deal with stubborn ghosts that still haunt us and undermine the attainment of our envisaged self. To transform a racist, sexist and authoritarian culture into one that is aligned to the ideals of our national constitution entails a radical cultural shift.

An example from the private sector that approximates the complexities we face is that of a merger between major entities with radically different cultures and serious levels of mistrust between the parties. Developing a shared vision is an important starting point. We have done a great job in developing such a shared vision in our constitution. Agreeing on who makes the decisions and takes charge of developing and implementing policies reflecting the new shared vision was also handled well. The Government of National Unity including the ANC, the NP and the IFP saw us through the delicate stage of the transition between 1994 and 1997/9. A group CEO at the helm of a big merged entity must have vision, charisma, and the courage to make difficult decisions. We were fortunate to have such a CEO in the person of President Nelson Mandela.

Mandela is the quintessential transformative leader. He led from the front and changed the course of history. His charisma, his genuine love for people and his real interest in them are among the attributes that made him a visionary and credible leader at the delicate stage of our transition. Success in transformative leadership entails taking people to places they may not have known existed or to places they would otherwise not have wanted to go. For people to follow a leader, they need confidence in him or her that goes beyond cold logic. Mandela became the rainmaker in our change management process.

Transformative leadership in the post-Mandela era had to give practical effect to the feel-good factor that President Mandela represented. We now need to live and work as citizens of a democracy willing to explore the challenges of our new identity as a democratic state inhabited by people with a diversity of identities, yet sharing a common national identity as South Africans. We need leadership that will take us beyond aspirations towards a lived experience of our democracy. Such a process of transformation towards our envisaged self as a nation must include a number of critical elements.

First, we must ensure that the resource base on which our democracy stands is firm. President Mbeki made a seminal contribution by promoting modernisation and greater competitiveness of our economy during the last years of his tenure as deputy president under Mandela. He showed decisiveness in breaking with past orthodoxies of 'centralised control of the commanding heights of the economy'. He established a new frame of reference for economic and monetary policy. He took risks, knowing that the ANC's alliance partners were likely to be unhappy. History is likely to judge him kindly for turning a weak economy into one that has been growing at unprecedented levels for more than a decade.

Second, we need to follow through with coherent and coordinated policies to make our commitments come alive in the lives of all citizens. We have done well in developing creative, complex policies, but implementation has been patchy. Part of the challenge of effective implementation is that the cultural change towards teamwork, rather than viewing other citizens as competitors, has not yet happened. We must confront the competitive approach to power that is an entrenched part of authoritarian systems. Within government, intra- and interdepartmental rivalries detract from the coherence of policies and their implementation. Cooperative government at different levels is also undermined by failure to work in a coherent and coordinated manner. Within professional ranks in both the public and private sector, the same tendencies hamper team effectiveness and productivity. Transformative leadership is essential to lifting the gaze of those mired in competing for power at the expense of the common good. That may entail letting go those unwilling or unable to contribute to the greater coherence, co-ordination, efficiency and effectiveness of government services. It is astounding that in the midst of so much mismanagement and inefficiency so few public servants have been held to account and opportunities created for those committed to public service to take over. Transformative leadership must mobilise effective management of public resources to achieve set national goals.

Divisions that are part of our legacy also rear their ugly heads. Black/white, men/women, rich/poor are all South Africans who must learn to work together. Transformative leadership is needed to lead a change in culture, replacing destructive competition with greater collaborative approaches. Both *ubuntu* and the human-rights tenets of our democracy are platforms on which to build a society that recognises the benefits of mutually empowering relationships. International evidence is strong that egalitarian societies are better able to build sustainable prosperity.[210]

Third, we need transformative leadership to address the binding constraints in our development efforts. The skills constraints that undermine implementation of our laudable policies, especially in the public sector, need creative approaches that only transformative leadership can provide. Deputy President Phumzile Mlambo-Ngcuka is playing a critical role in helping us to harness our human and intellectual resources better. We need to also harness the talents of white citizens better instead of losing them to our global competitors. Their skills represent investments that our country made in them.

Fourth, transformative leadership must help us develop the capacity to learn from both success and failure. We are still too sensitive to criticism. Successful people are those who make and admit mistakes rather than fear to confront failure. We need to acknowledge where we have fallen short. For example, there is widespread praise for the courage and technical expertise that has brought us unprecedented economic growth. We have made history: no country, according to expert analysts quoted in Chapter 1,[211] has ever managed to make the fundamental economic transformation we have achieved after a transition to democracy.

Yet our leaders are oversensitive to criticism in areas where we have not done so well, for example, in the social sectors – education and health. Given our investment in health of R62,7 billion (10-11% of government expenditure)[212] in 2006, we must confront the declining key health indicators, such as the increase in infant and maternal mortality.

Denial of the extent and impact of HIV/Aids over much of the first decade is part of the problem, but lacklustre implementation of comprehensive HIV/Aids care has undermined the gains we could have made even as late starters. At the heart of our underperformance is the culture of our National Health Department of second-guessing scientific evidence. This tendency has been costly for our society. Transformative leadership is critical to moving us away from oversensitivity towards enhancing the performance of our health system.

There is an emerging trend of blaming the poor performance of the public health sector on the private sector. Much of this mud-slinging is based on examining the symptoms of the problem, not its root causes. There is 'dramatic inequality in the health sector', as reported by the Health Systems Trust.[213] For instance, 60% of health expenditure is attributed to the private health-care sector and 73% of medical practitioners are in the private sector, as are 41% of nurses. This dramatic inequality is directly attributable to the failure of the public sector to maintain what had been its leadership role in the health sector.

Misguided shifting of resources away from tertiary and quaternary services and from teaching facilities has forced professional expertise out of the public sector. The most dramatic statement of lack of confidence in the public sector comes from no less a person than Health Minister Tshabalala-Msimang, who has on occasion chosen private facilities for her own medical care. If it is 'not just or ethical for the per capita expenditure in the private sector to be seven to eight times that of the public sector', the minister should put her money where her mouth is and use only public facilities. Legislating for people to use the public sector is another misguided approach. People will spend their money where they derive value. Leadership is urgently needed to revamp the failing health-care system and forge public-private partnerships.

Fifth, we must remobilise ordinary citizens to participate actively in transformation. The starry-eyed approach of the new 1994 government, presuming that it could deliver goods and services to poor people as spelt out in the RDP, must give way to acknowledgment that development cannot be done 'to' people. People have to become agents of their own development. The intention to 'deliver' houses, jobs, health care and schooling 'for all' is understandable, but nowhere in the world has poverty been eradicated through hand-outs. Government has a responsibility to create an enabling environment for citizens to contribute to their own development.

The active demobilisation of civil society post-1994 as the ANC asserted their hegemony as liberator and inheritor of the levers of power has been costly. South Africa's liberation was not simply the result of a war of liberation. Our freedom was won on the streets and on factory floors, as well as in all sectors of civil society. The yearning for freedom and the energy it generated was channelled into no less than 55 000 non-governmental organisations (NGOs), among other areas, at the dawn of freedom. These independent energy sources were regarded by some as a threat to the new government's desire for control. Foreign governments that had supported these NGOs understandably shifted their resources to government as part of forging bilateral political relationships, without much thought for the bottlenecks that might result. Over the years, significant donor funding has had to be returned to donors unspent while NGOs with the capacity to spend it have been left to die.

Whatever the ideological flaws of the apartheid regime, their civil servants had a passion to serve 'their people'. Doing well was married to doing good for the 'volk'. There are no recorded cases of welfare payments destined for poor white families being siphoned off by officials earning huge salaries at that time. Nor are there records of the pervasive defrauding of poor Afrikaners by the public officials serving them in the registration of births, deaths and marriages.[214]

The quality of service black public officials render to 'their people' often leaves much to be desired. There are thousands of public servants who make me proud to be a citizen of our country. But a significant proportion do not seem to understand that they are there to serve the public as their employer. Unlike the Afrikaner civil servants, our civil servants are the servants of all the people – black and white. They must observe the precepts of our constitution of equality before the law. The responsibility and challenges are greater. They must service current needs, and backlogs left by their predecessors in the apartheid government. A major constraint to addressing backlogs is inadequate capacity and skills. Transformative leadership is needed to hold the feet of public servants to the fire.

As a resident of Cape Town's suburban areas, I am protected from much of what poor people across our country have to endure to access public services. However, people close to me complain about the cancer of discourteous, callous, fraudulent and irresponsible behaviour of many public servants. My close connections with my rural base in Limpopo Province, my Eastern Cape networks and my ongoing involvement with ordinary people across the social spectrum mean that I regularly hear these stories.

Much of my time is spent helping poor people tackle obstacles placed in their way by public officials which prevent them from accessing their entitlements. It is disheartening to see young black people scream at old people, ignore those in pain, cheat those most vulnerable of the little they have. Equally shameful are cases such as that mentioned earlier of more than 40 000 public servants[215] who defrauded the social grant system for their own benefit. Public servants like these tarnish the image of the entire public service and undermine our democracy. They should be rooted out of the public service.

I would like to suggest that the major difference between the Afrikaner civil servants and some public servants today lies in the existence or not of what novelist Chinua Achebe in *Anthills of the Savannah* called 'vital linkages' with the poor people whom one serves. Unfortunately many liberation-movement leaders on our continent have had to de-link themselves from their own people in order to fight for freedom – either through exile or through alienation from their families and communities.

In addition, the humiliations of poverty and deprivation, coupled with the inferiority complex of being black and poor, added to the desire to distance oneself from one's people. Success becomes measured by how different one is from those wretched souls. 'Making it' becomes associated with leaving the village, the township, even the language of one's community. Add to this the insecurity of not being properly skilled or experienced. It comes as no surprise that such people may lash out at those who awaken in them the 'stereotype threat' – that they are expected to fail because they are black. Poor people's problems are by their nature complex. They might threaten the false comfort zones that many such public servants have woven around themselves.

I know of no liberation movement that has developed successful programmes to address these deep psycho-social dissonances. Rwanda might come closest. President Kagame seems to have been acutely aware of confronting the legacy of genocide in a manner that would help both victims and perpetrators establish a new understanding of what it means to be Rwandese. Appointments to public service are accompanied by careful matching of skills with tasks, with a culture of learning and training at its heart.

The Cabinet leads by example in including both Tutsis and Hutus, but also non-party appointments for the skills they bring. Gender equality is entrenched because it is a requirement of their constitution, but is also recognised as essential to sustaining the peace won in no small measure through the active participation of women across the murderous divide. It is not surprising that Rwanda has the largest proportion of women in parliament (48,8% in the lower house and 34,6% in the upper house).[216]

We have underestimated the importance of restoring vital linkages between ordinary citizens and those at all levels of the public service. We have become complacent about the growing divide between those who are doing well in the public and private sectors, and the large sectors of the population still experiencing grinding poverty. David Hamburg, President Emeritus of the Carnegie Corporation of New York, made a profound observation in his address to the Carnegie-sponsored Poverty Conference in 1984:

> Poverty is partly a matter of income and partly a matter of human dignity. It is one thing to have a very low income but to be treated with respect by your compatriots; it is quite another matter to have a very low income and to be harshly deprecated by more powerful compatriots. Let us speak of human impoverishment: low income and harsh disrespect . . . to speak of impoverishment in this sense is to speak of human degradation so profound as to undermine any reasonable and decent human standard.[217]

Hamburg's comments were made in 1984. The disrespect he was referring to was being visited on poor black people by racist apartheid public officials. How much greater must the pain be of those who find themselves poor and disrespected by their fellow black compatriots?

How have we done?

How far are we from the reaching the goal of our envisaged self? What are the gaps between our aspirations and our reality? We need to examine our performance in terms of the key indicators set out in our vision for our society: democratic practice, non-racism, non-sexism, and greater equity.

Democracy

We can proudly proclaim that, in institutional terms, democracy has taken hold in our society. We are a multiparty constitutional democracy with strong foundations in our parliamentary, executive and judicial branches. We have made strides in developing the policy frameworks to translate commitment into practical programmes to make democracy come alive. We have ensured that 'the people shall govern' through regular and orderly elections at local, provincial and national levels. Our Independent Electoral Commission (IEC) is a lauded model and a trusted partner to lend support in difficult transitions in other African countries.

We have also been blessed with an orderly transition from President Mandela to President Mbeki, and we have much to celebrate in the efforts of most of our leaders, both in the public and private sector, to be transformative in their own portfolios or areas of work.

We now need to consolidate our democracy by restoring the link between ordinary citizens and those representing them in public office. The proportional representation system should be tempered with some form of direct representation of constituencies that can hold their leaders accountable. If we do not address this, the lack of voice among the poorest people is going to extract a huge cost from the rest of society. Khutsong, Soweto, Mamelodi and other areas where destructive protests have broken out are simply the beginning of social instability that comes from a sense of betrayal. We are seeing the re-enactment of the street fights and destruction of property of the 1970s and 1980s.

Transformative leadership is needed to remind those communities that what they are destroying are their assets that they own by virtue of their citizenship. The kind of anti-government tactics that were directed at an illegitimate government cannot be allowed in a democracy. Children's education is again being sacrificed to settle political scores between adults in violation of the rights of those children as set out in our Bill of Rights.

Effective multiparty democracy as an essential pillar of our governance system is critical. We have not done a good job of signalling to ordinary South Africans that strong opposition parties are not the enemy of democracy, but the essence of it. I am saddened to hear educated South Africans speak about opposition party leaders as either racists or misguided black people who should be in the tent of the ruling party. Of particular concern is the increasing tendency by public commentators in the media to label black people who criticise the government or other public officials as agents of evil anti-transformation forces.

Black people, like anyone else, are entitled to express their views on matters they disagree with. That is the responsibility of citizens who are stewards of a vibrant democracy. It is equally the responsibility of commentators in the media to defend the right to free expression of all citizens, whether one agrees with them or not.

The conflation of liberation-movement politics with democratic practice poses serious risks to our democracy, as it has done for the rest of Africa. Liberation leaders do not necessarily make good transformative leaders. The strengths needed to sustain a struggle for freedom might become liabilities in sustaining a democracy. For example, liberation struggles demand unquestioning loyalty to the cause and the closing of ranks behind the leadership regardless of personal misgivings.

Democracy, in contrast, is about being open to questioning to ensure that the best policy options emerge. Implementation of public policies must be open to review and correction as mistakes are discovered. Doubt and questioning are important attributes of open societies that cherish good governance. The militaristic culture of liberation movements is not the best breeding ground for leaders of open societies. Each epoch in history needs its own leaders as well as its own institutions to promote appropriate cultural shifts to meet new demands. Breaking the chains of the habits of liberation-struggle politics is essential to consolidating our democracy.

The continuing Tripartite Alliance between the ruling ANC and its partners the SACP and Cosatu contributes to the conflation in the minds of many South Africans of liberation-movement politics with democratic practice. Until the ANC is transformed from a 'broad church' into a fully-fledged political party, held accountable by its members and the wider voting public, the consolidation of South Africa's democracy will remain incomplete. The net effect of the persistence of this dysfunctional alliance is to perpetuate the romanticism of the ANC as a liberator – and thus untouchable. As in much of Africa, the unspoken taboo of not criticising one's liberators curtails public criticism. For as long as this romanticism lasts South African voters will deny themselves an effective political voice. Regular elections without real political alternatives do not constitute true democracy.

The 'hegemony' of any one political party is anathema to democratic culture. What incentive can a political party have to listen to citizens if it is assured of their votes regardless of its performance? The Zanu-PF example in Zimbabwe is a classic current case. Even Zimbabweans who disagree with President Mugabe are trapped by the lack of a viable opposition party.

We need to learn the lessons of our continent and nurture opposition political discourse while we still have the luxury of a committed ruling party. No country – developed or developing – is immune to abuse of power by political leaders. As citizens of a democracy we have the responsibility of stewardship. We must ensure that alternative political voices have the space to emerge. It is in the interests of the ANC to have strong competitors to safeguard our democracy.

The need for competing political voices raises another issue undermining public debate in our society. There is an increasing tendency to demonise liberalism as a political orientation. There is a dismissive view about the role of liberals in our political history, although many fine South Africans made significant contributions to the anti-apartheid struggle from the platform of liberalism. Its limitations as a political force in racist South Africa should not justify its demonisation in our post-apartheid society. There is much irony in the ease with which former Afrikaner elites are embraced, in contrast to fellow liberation-movement comrades from other parties. Afrikaner Broederbond members fare better with the new political elites than liberals. This may signal the comfort between the two elites in terms of shared political cultures. That should worry democrats.

The *Oxford English Dictionary* defines 'liberal' as that frame of mind that is respectful and accepting of behaviour and opinions that are different from one's own. Liberal politics promote and protect individual rights and freedoms. There is no clash between this understanding of liberalism and our constitution that entrenches and protects individual rights. Liberalism in South Africa acquired a bad name during the 1960s and 1970s owing to claims by some of those passively supporting apartheid that theirs was a liberal cause. The effectiveness of those who did stand up to apartheid was undermined by the banning of the Liberal Party in the 1960s. Some alienated themselves from activists because of their failure to understand the call for black leadership in the struggle as articulated by the Black Consciousness Movement (BCM), which they interpreted as caving in to racism. Liberal principles should not be confused with inaction by those calling themselves liberals.

Anti-liberalism today has elements that remind me of US Republican Party rhetoric. That anti-liberalism rhetoric labels anyone with an open mind on issues like abortion rights or who favours social welfare programmes for poor people as a 'liberal' and therefore a risky candidate for public office. As citizens of a new democracy we should guard against closing our minds to the views of others. The tendency to silence those we disagree with by labelling and demonising them is profoundly undemocratic.

Proportional representation has not helped in educating the electorate about the value of different voices on public issues. Constituency-based politics have a better chance of creating a platform for competing voices than our current system. The hybrid model of citizen representation proposed by the Van Zyl Slabbert Commission should be revisited. We need to draw the best from both proportional and constituency representation. The exemplary constituency work that Helen Suzman of the opposition Progressive Party undertook in the apartheid-era parliament as a lone voice for nearly three decades is a model young MPs should be learning from.

Authoritarianism has also promoted the notion that leaders speak and voters listen. What the president, the minister or the public official says is rarely challenged. People disagree in silence until their anger breaks out in a torrent of raging fires. Citizenship as stewardship demands much more from those living in a democracy.

The ANC 2007 Polokwane Conference represents a welcome break from the disconnection between leaders and grassroots members. For the first time since 1994, ANC members broke with their president's wishes. They signalled their displeasure with the style of leadership and refused to let the president hold the leadership for a third term. Whatever views one might have about the leaders elected in Polokwane, it is clear that the people found their voice and spoke. The question is how the new leaders will conduct themselves to continue the journey of transformation.

The need for transformative leadership is all the more urgent given the increasing loss of confidence in the government and public institutions beyond the ANC's membership. The Institute for Justice and Reconciliation 2007 survey[218] shows an across-the-board loss of confidence by South Africans in leadership in both government and other key public institutions. The greatest concerns are about transparency and accountability, where only 39% of those surveyed had confidence in the government compared to 67% in 2006. Among institutions, the national government suffered the greatest loss of confidence, from 73% to 63%. Not a single measure of confidence showed any improvement. It will take a visionary, inspirational leader to re-establish trust in our national institutions and system of government.

Educating for democracy is essential to help us towards a shared understanding of our founding documents. It would be instructive to see how many public servants have read and understood the basic tenets of our constitution and know how to apply them in their daily responsibilities.

Non-racism

The foundations of a non-racial society are strong in our society. We have been bold in tackling the ghost of racism in the formal sphere of public life. There are admirable examples of non-racialism in our public life and the private sector. The envisaged enrichment that comes from the diversity of our people is flowering in many important places. Many of the post-apartheid generation, young people who have grown up without having to deal with 'it is reserved for whites', have seamless relationships that span all boundaries.

Our challenges lie in persistent tensions among South Africans in domains where racial categories retain value as currency in social, economic and political transactions. The dilemma lies in redressing the imbalances of the past without deepening the imprints of our divided society.

From the perspective of our need for transformative leadership, BEE should be linked to reciprocal contributions by those who have been enabled to access opportunities that enhance their material position. There is value in the greater visibility of black people in decision-making positions in both the public and private sectors. Leadership is no longer the sole preserve of white males. But visibility of wealthy black people alone, without transformative action by those in leadership positions, makes a mockery of transformation.

Institutions run by transformative leaders should look different. Their value system should be one of respect, self-discipline, integrity and commitment to serve. It becomes a fruitless exercise if transformation simply amounts to replacing one dominant group with another. Harnessing the energies and the skills of all citizens should be the central focus. We need every skilled South African to be creatively and productively engaged in growing our wealth. There is no need for a zero-sum approach to power where categories of black people scramble for positions of influence. Transformative leaders transcend divisive categories and work to mobilise all energies for the common good.

'Race' still matters because racism is still alive and well. Some white people still struggle with the notion of equality, but those willing to make the journey and to transcend their prejudices are discouraged by the mistrust that persists. Black people also need to beware of a knee-jerk reaction that any criticism by white people is fuelled by racism. Playing the race card to silence critics is not helpful. All citizens need to wean themselves from reliance on the ghosts of the past to gain short-term benefits.

Building trust takes a long time, and it takes all sides to work at it. Thirteen years is not enough to wipe away centuries of conditioning.

Most South Africans still struggle with the idea that there is only one race. The visible distinctions in terms of external appearance have conditioned us to ignore scientific evidence that there is but one race. We must find ways of de-conditioning ourselves from the deep-seated need for categories. We must de-link political patronage from racial categories as we succeed in our transformation process. We need to set ourselves a target date by when we will throw away the crutch of racial categories and become simply South Africans. It is when 'race' no longer has currency, as in fellow African countries such as Mozambique, Botswana and Zambia, that we will see ourselves as fellow citizens and not competitors.

Non-sexism

Although we have made significant progress in this area and women are increasingly able to participate in both the public and private sectors, sexism remains a big challenge. The public sector has in many ways done better than the private in terms of visible women leadership. South Africa is tenth in the world with regard to women in parliament (42%), 43% of our cabinet ministers are women, we have 40% women in local government, and women constitute 31,3% of directors of state-owned enterprises. Some of the largest stated-owned enterprises are led by women, with Transnet and the Airports Company of South Africa (ACSA) as flagships.[219]

Equally important is the impact women leaders may have in advancing transformation. One of the greatest letdowns has been the ineffectual leadership of women in public office in promoting non-sexist institutional cultures. Parliament, the custodian of our national constitution on behalf of citizens, ought to be the example of propriety, yet reports of widespread harassment of women abound.

Chapter 6 refers to the case of the ANC Chief Whip relieved of his position in 2007 after a disciplinary hearing for abuse of power and harassment of a junior woman employee. Support for the junior employee came not from the Speaker, a woman herself, but from an ordinary MP. That this happened in a Parliament with no less than 42% women tells a story of a lack of support networks and proper policies and procedures to ensure working conditions free of harassment. Women leaders who fail to be transformation agents are undermining the cause of gender equality.

It is disappointing that in the face of so much gender-based violence in our society women's organisations are not demanding action. Where is the practical impact of the brave slogan *Wathint' abafazi wathint' imbokodo?* – you touch women, you dislodge a boulder? Where is the ANC's Women's League on this issue? What about the Inkatha Freedom Party Women's League and other women's formations? What about men's groups who care about the image of men?

Women leaders delay transformation when they fail to enlarge the circle of successful women, thus undermining the definition of leadership as male. Successful change agents must ensure that sanctions against harassment and abuse of women are strong enough to deter would-be perpetrators. It can be done.

One success I was involved in was at the World Bank, setting up a framework for gender equality in the selection, promotion and treatment of staff. Women with the same qualifications and experience had lagged behind their male colleagues as a matter of custom. How could the World Bank preach gender equality in development policy to its members when it did not practise it on the home front? Anti-harassment policies also became part of the framework of ethical behaviour demanded of staff members. The success of such policies depends on consistent leadership enforcing a zero-tolerance approach from the top. Economists understand incentives and sanctions, and many of my colleagues at the World Bank were economists.

Sexism is a thorny issue because it plays itself out at the intersection of the personal, the political and the professional. Both men and women need to make transformative leaps in attitude and conduct to celebrate our biological differences while affirming our equality as partners.

South African citizens have an opportunity to use the 2009 national elections to spell out their demands for inspirational transformative leadership to complete the maturation process into the democracy we envisage in our constitution. Mandela led us into the 'promised land';

Mbeki has taken steps to make it more prosperous. Much remains to be done to ensure that its fruits are shared by all. We require transformative leadership to tackle the dilemmas outlined in this book and lay the roaming ghosts of racism, sexism and authoritarianism to rest. Such leadership exists in our midst. We have the opportunity to elect such leadership. But do we have the courage to do so?

Our long road to transformation has only begun. In this book, I have explored some of the dilemmas we face at each level of the process. One of the meanings of the word dilemma is 'a state of indecision between two alternatives'.[220] One alternative is for us to remain prisoners of our history; the other is to become agents of its making. Transformative leadership is needed to help us acknowledge our dilemmas openly, and inspire us to transcend them. The question each one of us must ask every day is whether we are giving the best we can to enable our society to transcend the present and become its envisaged self.

NOTES

1 I am indebted to Bishop David Russell for the term 'civic-mindedness', on which I expand in Part III.

2 'Black' is used in this book as a generic term for all those who were classified as 'non-white' under the apartheid system and, as a result, were disadvantaged and oppressed.

3 Frantz Fanon, *Black Skin, White Masks*, trans. Charles Lam Markmann. (St. Albans, Herts: Paladin, 1970).

4 Steve Biko, *I Write What I Like*. (Johannesburg: Picador Africa, 2004), p 74.

5 Jonathan Sacks, *To Heal a Fractured World: The Ethics of Responsibility*. (New York: Schocken Books, 2005), pp 17-28.

6 To paraphrase the famous statement by Kwame Nkrumah, quoted in Anthony Daniels, 'The corrupt continent,' N.d., <http://www.telegraph.co.uk/arts/main.jhtml?xml=/arts/2004/04/18/bogue18.xml> (1 August 2007).

7 Kiswahili for 'freedom'.

8 I had the privilege of being a team member of the Old Mutual/Nedcor scenario exercise as set out in Bob Tucker and Bruce Scott (eds.), *South Africa: Prospects for Successful Transition*. (Cape Town: Juta, 1992). See also Guillermo O'Donnell and Philippe Schmitter, *Transitions from Authoritarian rule: Tentative Conclusions about Uncertain Democracies*. (Baltimore: John Hopkins University Press, 1986).

9 World Bank, *Development Committee Reports (1990-2000)*. (Washington, DC: World Bank, 1990) and *World Bank Annual Reports (1991-2000)*. (Washington, DC: World Bank, 2000).

10 Bob Tucker and Bruce Scott, *South Africa: Prospects for Successful Transition*. (Cape Town: Juta, 1992), pp 50-56.

11 The Mont Fleur Scenarios were facilitated by sympathetic economists to help ANC leaders anticipate the complexities of economic-policy choices.

12 Francis Wilson and Mamphela Ramphele, *Uprooting Poverty: The South African Challenge*. (Cape Town: David Philip, 1989), p 4.

13 Nelson Mandela, *Long Walk to Freedom: The Autobiography of Nelson Mandela*. (London: Little, Brown, 1994), p 513.

14 Rosamund Stone Zander and Benjamin Zander, *The Art of Possibility: Transforming Professional and Personal Life.* (Boston: Harvard Business School Press, 2000), p 26.

15 Andrew Feinstein, *After the Party: A Personal and Political Journey Inside the ANC.* (Johannesburg: Jonathan Ball, 2007), p 77.

16 Walter Sisulu's passing in May 2003 days before his 91st birthday was an occasion both of mourning and of celebrating a life of exemplary service. The biography of Sisulu and his wife Albertina by their daughter-in-law, Elinor, captures the intimacies of a husband-and-wife partnership that served South Africa well. See Elinor Sisulu, *Walter and Albertina Sisulu: In our Lifetime.* (Cape Town: David Philip, 2002).

17 Harry Gwala, the then leader of the ANC/SACP in KwaZulu-Natal, was a strong opponent of any *rapprochement* between the ANC and Buthelezi in the negotiation process.

18 SAIRR, *Monthly Totals of Political Fatalities in South Africa.* (Johannesburg: SAIRR, 2007), p 600.

19 An average of 260 political fatalities per month occurred in the first three years of this period. In the ten months leading up to the election this increased to an average of 460 deaths per month. A total of 600 political fatalities occurred in the month (July 1993) in which the date for the election was announced.

Sapa, 'Most political deaths occurred in run-up to 1994 election: HRC.' 26 May 2007, <http://www.doj.gov.za/trc/media/1997/9705/s970527e.htm> (15 November 2007).

20 Neville Alexander, *An Ordinary Country: Issues in the Transition from Apartheid to Democracy in South Africa.* (New York: Berghahn Books, 2003), p 48.

21 Desmond Tutu, *No Future Without Forgiveness.* (London: Rider Press, 1999), p 87.

22 Kader Asmal made this point to me in a discussion on the framing of the 1996 TRC Act. My insistence on including socio-economic rights in the TRC brief was seen as unrealistic.

23 Dave Steward, 'A common map of the past is needed before we can walk freely into the future.' *Sunday Independent*, 17 December 2006.

24 Gail Gerhart and Thomas Karis, *From Protest to Challenge: A Documentary History of African Politics in South Africa 1882-1964.* Vol 4. (Stanford, CA: Hoover Institution Press, 1972), pp 147-149.

25 Hermann Giliomee and Bernard Mbenga (eds.), *New History of South Africa*, (Cape Town: Tafelberg, 2007), p 334.

26 Richardson testimony at the TRC, and Desmond Tutu, *No Future Without Forgiveness*, p 103.

27 This Football Club, created by Winnie Mandela in the heady 1980s, acted as a platform for the political mobilisation of youths. It gained an unflattering reputation in the end.

28 Desmond Tutu, *No Future Without Forgiveness*, p 135.

29 *Ibid*, pp 201-202.

30 Sapa, 'Vlakplaas policeman, four others to be arrested for Mxenge murder.' 11 July 1996, <http://www.doj.gov.za/trc/media/1996/9607/s960711a.htm> (29 August 2007).

31 The Mxenges were respected activist lawyers who defended many political prisoners and detainees in the 1970s and 1980s. Both were brutally murdered.

32 Pumla Gobodo-Madikizela, *A Human Being Died That Night: A Story of Forgiveness*. (Cape Town: David Philip, 2003).

33 *Ibid*, p 17.

34 F.W. de Klerk, *The Last Trek: A New Beginning*. (London: Pan Books, 1999).

35 *Ibid*, p 398

36 These are equivalents of 1999 US dollar exchange rates.

37 Joseph Nevins, 'Truth, lies, and accountability: In search of justice in East Timor.' *Boston Review* (January/February 2007).

38 Basil Davidson, *The Black Man's Burden: Africa and the Curse of the Nation-State*. (New York: Three Rivers Press, 1992), pp 134-149.

39 *Ibid*, p 138.

40 *Ibid*, pp 290-291.

41 Ibbo Mandaza, 'Reconciliation and social justice in Southern Africa' in Malegapuru William Makgoba (ed.), *African Renaissance*. (Johannesburg: Mafube Publishing, 1999), pp 77-90.

42 Basil Davidson, *The Black Man's Burden.*

43 Frantz Fanon, *Black Skin, White Masks*. (St. Albans, Herts: Paladin, 1970).

44 Colin Eglin, *Crossing the Borders of Power*. (Johannesburg: Jonathan Ball, 2007).

45 'Black' is used here to denote all those classified under apartheid as not white: Africans, Indians and Coloured people.

46 *Employment Equity Act, 55 of 1998*, section 15 (1).

47 Allyson Lawless, *Numbers and Needs: Addressing Imbalances in the Civil Engineering Profession*. (Midrand: SAICE, 2005), p 5.

48 Statistics South Africa. 'Provincial Profile 2004 Western Cape.' N.d., <http://www.statssa.gov.za/publications/Report-00-91-01/Report-00-91-012004.pdf> (29 August 2007).

49 Basil Davidson, *The Black Man's Burden*, p 11.

50 *Ibid*, p 85.

51 Bruce Berman, 'Ethnicity, patronage and the African state: The politics of uncivil nationalism.' *African Affairs* 97(1998): pp 305-341.

52 The Washington Consensus of the 1990s was based on the assumption that if macroeconomic variables such as proportion of government expenditure, debt and inflation were stabilised, the economy would grow and benefit all.

53 Peter Unwin, 'Prejudice, crisis and genocide in Rwanda.' *African Studies Review* 40 (1997): pp 91-115.

54 Gérard Prunier, *Darfur: The Ambiguous Genocide*. (London: Hurst & Co., 2005).

55 Juma Okuku, *Ethnicity, State Power and the Democratisation Process in Uganda*. (Uppsala: Nordic Africa Institute, 2002).

56 Thandabantu Nhlapo, 'The African family and women's rights: friends or foes?' *Acta Juridica* 135 (1991): pp 135-146.

57 Joe Tefo, 'Monarchy and democracy: Toward a cultural renaissance.' *Journal on African Philosophy* 1,1 (2002): 1-17.

58 Mavivi Myakayaka-Manzini, 'Women empowered – Women in Parliament in South Africa,' in Azza Karam (ed.), *Women in Parliament: Beyond Numbers*. (Stockholm: International IDEA, 1998).

59 Fred Khumalo, *Sunday Times*, 12 August 2007.

60 Lisa Vetten, 'Gender, race and power dynamics in the face of social change: Deconstructing violence against women in South Africa.' In: Yoon Jung Park, Joanne Fedler, and Zubeda Dangor, *Reclaiming Women's Spaces: New Perspectives on Violence Against Women and Sheltering in South Africa*. (Lenasia: NISAA, 2000), pp 47-75.

61 The South African National Editors' Forum (Sanef), *Glass Ceiling Two: An Audit of Women and Men in South African newsrooms*. (Rosebank: Sanef, 2007). This second phase of the study put numbers to what was reported in the first phase, released on Women's Day (9 August) 2006. The 2007 study, which covered 4 364 employees (an estimated half of all journalists), found that women constituted 45% of staff in newsrooms (compared to 33% in a 1995 study). Progress was being made towards gender balance in staff profiles. But black women, who constitute 46% of the population, only accounted for 18% of newsroom staff. Black men, 45% of the population, constituted 28% of newsroom staff. White men, 4% of the population, were over-represented at 28% of newsroom staff, reflecting their historical dominance.

Disparities between men and women were also prevalent in the pay structures. At R184 387 per annum the annual average salary of women in newsrooms was 21% less than that of men in newsrooms, who earned R233 737. Pay disparities partly reflect the position of women within the management hierarchy of the media. Women occupied less than 30% of top management posts and constituted one out of three senior managers in newsrooms. Not surprisingly, women were over-represented at junior management level at 48%, and were almost 70% of all semi-skilled workers. While black men had constituted 16% of top and senior managers in newsrooms in 1999, their representation increased to 23,5% in 2006. In contrast, black women made less progress, with their representation at senior management levels a mere 6% in 2006.

Women dominated the lowest-paying administrative categories while men made up 86% of the better-paid technical category. Male journalists dominated in all the 'hard' beats – politics, economics, investigative reporting, crime and sport. These beats enhance promotion chances. Women journalists tend to be relegated to the 'soft' beats, covering entertainment, education and general reporting.

62 Thapelo Sakoana, 'South Africa: KZN women fill seats of power.' N.d., <http://www. allafrica.com/stories/200708100021.html> (30 August 2007).

63 Myakayaka-Manzini, 'Women empowered: Women in Parliament in South Africa,' in Azza Karam (ed.), *Women in Parliament: Beyond Numbers*. (Stockholm: International IDEA, 1998).

64 Business Women's Association of South Africa, 2007 Annual Report.

65 Shanaaz Matthews, Naeemah Abrahams, Lorna Martin, Lisa Vetten, Lisa van der Merwe and Rachel Jewkes, *Every Six Hours a Woman is Killed by her Intimate Partner: A National Study of Female Homicide in South Africa*. (Tygerberg: MRC, 2004).

66 Ilse Terblanche, 'The Mind of a Family Murderer'. N.d. <http://www.health24. com/mind/Other/1284-1303,15821.asp> (30 January 2008).

67 *Ibid.*

68 SAPS, 'Rape in RSA for the period April to March 2001/2002 to 2006/2007.' N.d., <http://www.saps.gov.za/statistics/reports/crimestats/2007_pdf/category/ rape.pdf> (24 November 2007).

69 Richard Knight, *South Africa 2006 Population and HIV*, 2006, Nov., 2006. <http:// www.richardknight.com/files/SouthAfrica2006-PopulationandHIV-AIDS.pdf> (16 November 2007)

70 *Business Day*, 10 September 2007.

71 Hillary Clinton, *It Takes a Village to Raise a Child*. (New York: Simon & Schuster, 1996).

72 A Sesotho word for a discussion forum in a village setting to share information and settle disputes.

73 In 2002 alone 3 789 incidents of child abuse were reported. The Western Cape is the province with the highest incidence, while the Northern Cape shows the largest increase between 1994 and 2002, by a frightening 188%. The North West and Mpumalanga are also showing large increases of 100% and 168% respectively. From April 2001 to March 2007, 28 604 cases of neglect and ill-treatment of children were reported to the SAPS. See SAPS, 'Neglect and ill-treatment of children in the RSA for the period April to March 2001/2002 to 2006/2007,' N.d., <http:// www.saps.gov.za/statistics/reports/crimestats/2007/_pdf/category/neglect_ children.pdf> (24 November 2007).

74 See http://www.childwelfaresa.org.za.

75 Jolyon Nuttall, *The First Five Years: The Story of the Independent Development Trust*. (Cape Town: IDT, 1997).

76 Amartya Sen, *Development as Freedom*. (Oxford: Oxford University Press, 2001).

77 David Robertson (ed.), *The Routledge Dictionary of Politics*. (London: Routledge, 2002), pp. 64-65 and Vernon Bogdanor (ed.), *The Blackwell Encyclopaedia of Political Science*. (Oxford: Blackwell, 1993), pp 94-95.

78 The Stewardship Project. 'The stewardship.' N.d., <http://the-stewardship.org/stewardship.htm> (16 May 2007).

79 Jeremy Gordin and Eleanor Momberg, 'Security guards die like dogs. So who cares', *Sunday Independent,* 3 June 2007.

80 At the time, an urban Grade C security guard earned about R2 400 a month (R101 a 12-hour shift) and a rural Grade E security guard about R1 080 a month. Sapa, 'Guards want higher wages, benefits.' 23 March 2006, http://www.business.iafrica.com/news/985388.htm (16 May 2007).

81 Jeremy Gordin and Eleanor Momberg, 'Security guards die like dogs. So who cares,' *Sunday Independent,* 3 June 2007, 1.

82 Ivor Chipkin, *Do South Africans Exist?* (Johannesburg: Wits University Press, 2007), p 151.

83 *Ibid*, p 213.

84 Basil Davidson, *The Black Man's Burden: Africa and the Curse of the Nation-State.* (New York: Three Rivers Press,1992), p 246.

85 Between April 2001 and March 2007, 83 188 car hijackings were reported to the SAPS. SAPS, *Carjacking (subcategory of aggravated robbery) in the RSA for the period April to March 2001/2002 to 2006/2007,* N.d., <http://www.saps.gov.za/statistics/reports/crimestats/2007_pdf/category/carjacking.pdf> (24 November 2007).

86 Christine Qunta, 'When blacks are made to turn on their own race,' *The Star,* 25 July 2007.

87 *Daedalus*, Fall 2007.

88 As quoted by William Galston, 'An old debate renewed: the politics of the public interest,' *Daedalus*, Fall 2007, p 10.

89 Personal communication in face-to-face encounters in 1993/4.

90 Václav Havel, *The Art of the Impossible: Politics as Morality in Practice.* (New York: Knopf, 1997).

91 *Daedalus*, Fall 2007, p 10.

92 *Ibid*, p 24.

93 As quoted by R.K. Pachauri, Chairman of the International Panel on Climate Change (IPCC) and Director-General of Teri, Speech to Rockefeller Foundation Board, 29 November 2007.

94 Johann Wilhelm Grosskopf, *The Poor White Problem in South Africa: Report of the Carnegie Commission.* (Stellenbosch: Pro Ecclesia, 1932).

95 Shaun Johnson, *The Native Commissioner.* (Johannesburg: Penguin Books, 2006).

96 Francis Wilson and Mamphela Ramphele, *Uprooting Poverty: The South African Challenge: Report for the Second Carnegie Inquiry into Poverty and Development in Southern Africa.* (Cape Town: David Philip, 1989).

97 Marita Golden, 'Carnegie Corporation in South Africa: A difficult past leads to a commitment to change.' *Carnegie Results* 4 (2004): pp 1-8.

98 Hermann Giliomee, 'Manipulating the Past.' In Rainer Erkens and John Kane-Berman (eds.), *Political Correctness in South Africa.* (Braamfontein: SAIRR, 2000).

99 Sipho Sibanda, *Land Reform and Poverty Alleviation in South Africa.* (Pretoria: HSRC, 2001).

100 The black sector of the population was classified into Coloured, Indian and Bantu groups, and the Bantu group into further ethnic groups: Zulu, Xhosa, North Sotho, South Sotho, Ndebele, Venda, Tsonga, Tswana.

101 These were: University of the North (previously Turfloop), University of Durban Westville, University of Zululand, University of the Western Cape, and the Universities of Transkei, Venda, Bophuthatswana, Vista and The Medical University of South Africa (Medunsa) as a dedicated medical school for Africans. Fort Hare University was reinvented as part of the scheme, which undermined its long, proud history.

102 This study was commissioned by the ANC government-in-waiting and conducted by the South African Labour and Development Research Unit at UCT under Francis Wilson in the early 1990s.

103 - 3 million more people have access to potable water
   - 486 new health clinics have been built providing free care to pregnant women and children under five
   - 3,8 million more people have been connected to the national electricity grid
   - 1,4 million hectares of land have been redistributed
   - 1,8 million housing subsidies have been awarded and 1,5 million more new houses constructed
   - primary school nutrition programme has been extended to 5 million children in 15 000 schools.

104 Ivor Chipkin, *Do South Africans Exist?* (Johannesburg: Wits University Press, 2007), pp 152-153.

105 *The Development Indicators Mid-Term Review, 2007* is the first such report produced by the Presidency to take stock of the performance of the government in meeting its own policy objectives.

106 According to Medical Research Council (MRC) figures, infant mortality has increased significantly from 58 per 1 000 live births in 2001 to 59 per 1 000 live births in 2004. Figures for child mortality for those between 1-5 years are even more alarming at 96 per 1 000 in 2001 rising to 106 per 1 000 in 2004. Trends in maternal

mortality are very worrying, given the impact of death of the mother on families. Maternal mortality rates have risen from a high of 115 per 100 000 births in 2001 to 166 per 100 000 in 2003. Recent reports from poor provinces such as Limpopo and the Eastern Cape show a worsening trend in maternal mortality rates. See MRC Annual Reports 2002-2006.

107 The HIV/Aids prevalence rate, according to ante-natal surveys, increased from 7,6 % in 1994 to over 30% in 2005. In the general population prevalence rates have grown from less than 9% in 2001 to over 11% in 2006. The number of new infections between 2001 and 2005 was at 370 000 and 590 000, according to actuarial estimates. Tracking immune system weaknesses is the rise of TB from a notification level of 90 000 per year in 2001 to a frightening above 300 000 per year level in 2006. It is estimated that more than 60% of those presenting with TB are also HIV positive. The emergence of drug-resistant TB, including extreme and multi-drug varieties, has added to the challenge. See the South African Government's *The Development Indicators Mid-Term Review, 2007* and UNICEF. *South Africa: Epidemiological Fact Sheet on HIV/AIDS and Sexually Transmitted Infections*, (Pretoria: UNICEF, 2006).

108 Sakhela Buhlungu, John Daniel, Roger Southall, Jessica Lutchman (eds.), *State of the Nation: South Africa 2005-2006.* (Cape Town: HSRC, 2006), p 14.

109 For example Director-General of National Intelligence, Billy Masethla (2006); Deputy Minister of Health, Nozizwe Madlala-Routledge and Vusi Pikoli, Director of Public Prosecutions (2007).

110 Adam Wolfson, 'From James Madison to Abraham Lincoln,' *Daedulus*, Fall 2007, p 24.

111 Duxita Mistry, Anthony Minnaar, Jean Redpath and Jabu Dhlamini, *Research Report: The Use of Force by Members of the South African Police Service: Case Studies from Seven Policing Areas in Gauteng.* (Florida: Institute for Human Rights and Criminal Justice Studies, Technikon SA, 2001), pp i-ii.

112 The Mo Ibrahim Foundation was established in 2006 to promote good governance in Africa. The founder, Mo Ibrahim, made his money through Celtel, a cellphone company he founded. He has invested significant resources in establishing measurable indicators of good governance and rewarding excellence in African leadership through the Ibrahim Prize to former heads of state.

113 Andrew Feinstein, *After the Party: A Personal and Political Journey Inside the ANC.* (Johannesburg: Jonathan Ball, 2007), p 208.

114 Angela Quintal, 'Social grant fraudsters feel the heat,' *The Independent on Saturday*, 9 April 2005. By early 2008, 21 588 government employees had been found to be on the system irregularly and had been removed. Disciplinary action ranged from warnings to dismissals. 6 693 public servants had been arrested and taken to

court, with a conviction rate of more than 80%, while 123 610 beneficiaries had been cancelled. The investigation saved the government approximately R7,7 billion. South African Government, *Fraudsters referred to their employers for disciplinary action*, 29 January 2008, <http://www.info.gov.za/speeches/2008/08012916151001.htm> (5 February 2008).

115 Apartheid was the ultimate example of 'state capture'. A 2006 report by civil-society groups led by the Institute of Security Studies, *Apartheid Grand Corruption*, details corruption between 1976 and 1994.

116 Albert Luthuli, *Let My People Go*. (Cape Town: Tafelberg & Mafube, 2006), p 186.

117 Carl Dahlman, Jourma Routti and Ylä-Anttila Pekka, *Finland as a Knowledge Economy*. (Washington, DC: World Bank, 2006) pp 33-37.

118 Hansard reference for Verwoerd's statement quoted in David Johnson, 'Building citizenship in fragmented societies: the challenges of democratizing and integrating schools in post-apartheid South Africa.' *International Journal of Educational Development* 27(3) 2007: 307.

119 Sarah Howie, *Third International Mathematics and Science Study-Repeat (TIMSS-R): What has changed in pupils' performance in mathematics 1995-1998?* (Pretoria: HSRC, 1998).

120 77% of South African teachers had a three-year qualification (REQV 13). The current quality framework (norms and standards for educators 2000) raised the minimum qualification from a three-year post-school level qualification to a four-year degree (REQV 14). Initiatives by the Department of Education have reduced levels of unqualified and under-qualified teachers by as much as 36% since 1994. By 2001 the proportion of unqualified and under-qualified teachers fell to 18% with a further fall to 8,3% by 2004. Department of Education, *Teachers for the Future, 2005: Meeting Teacher Shortages to Achieve Education for All*. (Pretoria: Department of Education, 2005), pp 46-7.

121 Department of Education, *National Strategy for Mathematics, Science and Technology Education in General and Further Education and Training*. (Pretoria: Department of Education, 2001), p 12.

122 Nazma Dreyer, 'School education is "dumbed-down" – principal,' *Cape Times*, 5 December 2003.

123 *Umalusi* is isiXhosa for 'shepherd'.

124 Matseleng Allais, *Business Day*, 13 September 2007.

125 Nick Taylor, 'Schools, Skills and Citizenship,' in *2006 Transformation Audit: Money and Morality*. (Cape Town: Institute for Justice and Reconciliation, 2006).

126 Sakhela Buhlungu, John Daniel, Roger Southall and Jessica Lutchman (eds.), *State of the Nation: South Africa 2005-2006*. (Cape Town: HSRC, 2006), pp 397-400.

127 Firoz Patel and Luis Crouch, *Investment Choices in Education: The South African Experience*. Conference paper, p 15.

128 Personal comunication from John Gilmour, Director, 2007.

129 Be kind. Be honest. Be healthy. Be punctual. Look good. Work hard. Never give up. Admit mistakes. Learn from mistakes. Confront issues. Be open to change. Work together. Share as much as possible.

130 John Gilmour, 'End of 2005 report.' N.d., <http://www.leapschool.org.za/archive/dec-05> (28 November 2007).

131 Personal communication, John Gilmour.

132 Z.K. Matthews, 'Native Education in South Africa in last 25 years', *S.A. Outlook*, 76: pp 138-141, 1946, as quoted by Michael Kahn for the Historic Schools Project Concept note.

133 Department of Labour, *Skills Development Levies Act, 1999*. (Pretoria: Department of Labour, 2004), p 3.

134 Sasseta, 'Learnership implementation process – 10 steps.' <http://www.sasseta.org.za/docs/Whats-new/learnerships/annexures1/LEARNERSHIP%20IMPLE-MENTATION%20PROCESS%2010%20steps.pdf>

135 Lavinia Mahlangu, 'Learnerships, apprenticeships – both important for skills development.' (BuaNews Online, 13 February 2007). <http://www.buanews.gov.za/view.php?ID=07021313451004&coll=buanew07>

136 *Joint Initiative on Priority Skills Report March – December 2006*. <http://www.info.gov.za/otherdocs/2007/jipsarep.pdf>

137 'Siemens restarts apprenticeship training programme'. *SA Instrumentation & Control*, May 2007. <http://instrumentation.co.za/news.aspx?pklNewsId=24705&pklCategoryID=65>

138 Department of Labour, *State of Skills in South Africa, 2005*. (Pretoria: Department of Labour, 2005), p. 31.

139 Thabo Mohlala, 'Setas to be cut down to size.' *Mail & Guardian Online*, 12 January 2008. <http://www.mg.co.za/articlePage.aspx?articleid=329432&area=/insight/insight__national/>

140 *Ibid*.

141 Kader Asmal, 'Speech at the unveiling of the inauguration plaque at Central Johannesburg Further Education and Training College, 2 June 2003.' <http://www.info.gov.za/speeches/2003/03060310461001.htm>

142 Lavinia Mahlangu, *Ibid*.

143 Ronel Blom, 'Parity of esteem: hope or despair?' Paper prepared for the Annual SADC Conference Assessment in Education, University of Johannesburg, 25-30 June 2006. <http://www.saqa.org.za/docs/events/rblom-sadcassess06.pdf>

144 *Weekend Argus*, 15 September 2007.

145 Jonathan Jansen, 'Why I support the teachers' strike', *Sunday Independent*, 8 July 2007.

146 Department of Education, *Education Statistics in South Africa at a Glance in 2005*. (Pretoria: Department of Education, 2006) p 29.

147 UCT pioneered an Alternative Admission Research Project (AARP) in the late 1980s to assess students' potential to succeed at the higher-education level. The core test is based on assessing the ability to learn and think logically.

148 See, for example, Stuart Saunders, *Vice-Chancellor on a Tightrope: A Personal Account of Climactic Years in South Africa*. (Cape Town: David Philip, 2000).

149 See Basil Davidson, *The Black Man's Burden*.

150 Amartya Sen, *Identity and Violence*. (New York: W.W. Norton, 2006), p 17.

151 Ian Scott, *Department of Education 2000-2004 Cohort Study*.

152 Stuart Saunders, *Vice-Chancellor on a Tightrope*.

153 The 'gravy train' was a metaphor used in the early part of the new democracy to refer to the benefits of high salaries and allowances that came with joining the public service. The reality is that in 1995 the salary of a vice-chancellor at UCT was R600 000 – hardly a fortune to fight for.

154 Pfizer, *Clinical trials*, N.d.,<www.pfizer.com/research/clinical-trials.jsp> (28 November 2007).

155 NSFAS, '2006 Annual Report.' N.d., <https://www.nsfas.org.za/web/view/general/reports/annual_rep2006> (28 November 2007).

156 Department of Education, *Education Statistics in South Africa at a Glance in 2005*. (Pretoria: Department of Education, 2006).

157 Allyson Lawless, *Numbers and Needs: Addressing Imbalances in the Civil Engineering Profession*. (Midrand: SAICE, 2005).

158 The Deputy Presidency, SABC, interview on Morning Live, 16 July 2007.

159 Mamphela Ramphele, *A Bed Called Home*. (Cape Town: David Philip, 1991).

160 This reference was to religious leaders, including the Archbishop of Cape Town, Njongonkulu Ndungane, who participated in protest action to demand treatment for those living with HIV/Aids.

161 Nicoli Nattrass, *The Moral Economy of AIDS in South Africa*. (Cambridge: Cambridge University Press, 2004.)

162 Jane Galvão, 'AIDS no Brasil: A agenda de construção de uma epidemia.' *Editora 34* (2000) p 182.

163 UNICEF, *South Africa: Epidemiological Fact Sheets on HIV/Aids and Sexually Transmitted Infections*. (Pretoria: UNICEF, 2006) pp 2, 5.

164 This calculation assumes that an average jumbo jet carries 400 passengers when fully loaded.

165 Clive Bell, Shantayanan Devarajan and Hans Gersbach, *The Long-run Economic*

Costs of AIDS: Theory and an Application to South Africa. (Washington, DC: World Bank, 2003).

166   Rob Dorrington, Leigh Johnson, Debbie Bradshaw and Timothy-John Daniel, 'The demographic impact of HIV/Aids in South Africa: National and provincial indicators 2006.' N.d., <http://www.mrc.ac.za/bod/DemographicImpactHIVIndicators. pdf> (28 November 2007).

167   South African Government, *Development Indicators Mid-term Review, 2007.* (Pretoria: South African Government, 2007) pp 5, 12, 18-19, 25, 28-31.

168   Eileen Meier, 'Child rape in South Africa.' N.d., <http://www.medscape.com/ viewarticle/444213)> (28 November 2007).

169   Personal communication from Dr. Brian Brink, Anglo American Executive Director of Health, 2007.

170   Khehla Shubane and Colin Reddy. *BEE 2007: Empowerment and its Critics.* (Johannesburg: BusinessMap Foundation, 2007).

171   2006/07 Report of the Commission on Employment Equity.

172   Christy van der Merwe, 'South African tooling industry not struggling to survive.' 23 February 2007, <http://www.engineeringnews.co.za/article.php?a_id=101471> (28 November 2007).

173   Paul Vecchiatto, 'Government doesn't care about software.' 10 May 2007, <http:// www.itweb.co.za/sections/software/2007/0705101044.asp> (28 November 2007).

174   The Employment Equity Report is based on data from over 6 000 returns from mainly private institutions of which over 4 000 were analysed in detail.

175   Justice Sandra Day O'Connor as quoted in William Bowen, Martin Kurzweil and Eugene Tobin, *Equity and Excellence in American Higher Education.* (Charlottesville: University of Virginia Press, 2005), p 148.

176   David Benatar is Professor of Philosophy at UCT. In his inaugural lecture in early 2007 he critiqued affirmative action.

177   Neville Alexander, *An Ordinary Country: Issues in the Transition from Apartheid to Democracy in South Africa.* (New York: Berghahn Books, 2003).

178   AngloZimele Annual Reports.

179   UCT conducted a cohort study of the generation of young black upwardly mobile professionals with considerable purchasing power. The study, 'Black Diamond', conducted by UCT's Unilever Institute of Strategic Marketing, is the most comprehensive of its kind. Unilever Institute of Strategic Marketing, *New Study Explodes Myths about SA's Black Middle Class*, 27 February 2006/7.

180   'Booming economy not to blame.' *Mail & Guardian*, 1-7 February 2008.

181   An 'equity kicker' is a provision in funding deals that enables the provider of finance to acquire a portion of the equity of the enterprise being financed as a condition for funding. Equity kickers have the effect of reducing the economic

value that ultimately accrues to the entrepreneur, and provide financiers with additional benefits from funding those without adequate capital.

182 76,2% of the total land surface of South Africa is privately held; the rest is held by the state (24,4%) or in trust on behalf of the state (3,4%). 73,2% of land use is for natural pasture, 12% for arable productive agriculture, 12% for nature conservation and 1% for urban and residential purposes. Department of Agriculture and Land Affairs, *Report and Recommendations by the Panel of Experts on the Development of Policy Regarding Land Ownership by Foreigners in South Africa* (Pretoria: Department of Agriculture and Land Affairs, 2007), pp 17-18.

183 Sapa, 'Land Bank board members sacked.' 15 November 2007, <http://www.iol.co.za/index.php?set_id=1&click_id=3045&art_id=nw20071115190524341C111841> (28 November 2007) and Thabo Mabaso, 'Land Bank report reveals shocking results,' *Cape Times*, 8 November 2007.

184 Pradeep Mitra and Marcelo Selowisky, *Transition, The First Ten Years – Analysis and Lessons for Eastern Europe and the Former Soviet Union*. (Washington, DC: World Bank, 2002), pp 107-110.

185 This speech is likely to have been inspired by a similar one made in 1905 by Pixley ka Seme at Columbia University as part of an oratory contest. Seme's topic 'The Regeneration of Africa' resonates with Mbeki's African Renaissance, as quoted in M.W. Makgoba (ed.), *African Renaissance*, Mafube & Tafelberg, 1999, Cape Town, p 31.

186 Thabo Mbeki, 'Statement on Behalf of the African National Congress, on the Occasion of the Adoption by the Constitutional Assembly of The Republic of South Africa Constitutional Bill 1996'. (Cape Town: Office of the Deputy President, 8 May 1996). <http://www.anc.org.za/ancdocs/history/mbeki/1996/sp960508.html>

187 *Ibid.*

188 Thabo Mbeki, 'The African Renaissance Statement of Deputy President Thabo Mbeki, SABC, Gallagher Estate, 13 August 1998.' <http://www.dfa.gov.za/docs/speeches/1998/mbek0813.htm>

189 *The Economist*, 13 May 2000, vol. 355.

190 The English poet John Donne wrote in 1624: 'No man is an island, entire of itself; every man is a piece of the continent, a part of the main ... any man's death diminishes me, because I am involved in mankind. And therefore never send to know for whom the bell tolls. It tolls for thee.' In John Hadfield, *A Book of Beauty*. (London: Hulton Press, 1952), p 147.

191 Department of Foreign Affairs, 'An overview of Nepad.' <http://www.dfa.gov.za/au.nepad/nepad_overview.htm>

192 Institute for Security Studies, 'ISS Profile: African Peer Review Mechanism.'

<http://www.iss.co.za/index.php?link_id=3893&slink_id=3945&link_type=12&slink_type=12&tmpl_id=3>

193 'Peer review highlights SA strengths, weaknesses.' (7 December 2007.) http://www.sagoodnews.co.za/politics/peer_review_highlights_sa_strengths_weaknesses.html

194 World Economic Forum, *The Africa Competitiveness Report 2007*. (Geneva: World Economic Forum, 2007).

195 Commission for Africa, *Our Common Interest: The Commission for Africa: An Argument* (London: Penguin, 2005), p 46.

196 The largest proportion of legal entrants are migrant mine workers, at 140 000. Another 80 000 are legally employed in other sectors, and refugees are around 100 000. Undocumented migrants constitute the majority of migrants.

197 Basil Davidson, *The Black Man's Burden*, pp 290-291.

198 Anonymous, 'Brain drain in Africa: Facts and figures.' N.d., <http://web.ncf.ca/cp129/factsandfigures.pdf> (28 November 2007).

199 Thirty-eight countries in sub-Saharan Africa (SSA) have less than the 20 medical doctors per 100 000 of the population recommended by the World Health Organisation (WHO). Thirteen African countries have less than 5 doctors per 100 000 people. In addition, 17 SSA countries have less than the WHO minimum standard of 100 nurses per 100 000 population. For example, Malawi has 17 per 100 000 people compared to 1000 per 100 000 in developed countries.

200 Commission for Africa, *Our Common Interest: The Commission for Africa −An Argument* (London: Penguin, 2005), pp 262-265.

201 The number of member countries are given in brackets:
* Arab Maghreb Union (AMU) (5)
* Economic and Monetary Community of Central Africa (CEMAC) (6)
* Common Market for Eastern and Southern Africa (COMESA) (20)
* Economic Community of Central States (ECCAS) (11)
* Economic Community of West African States (ECOWAS) (16)
* Southern African Development Community (SADC) (14)
* West African Economic and Monetary Union (WAEMU) (8)

202 Commission for Africa, *Our Common Interest*, pp 261-265.

203 *Ibid*, p 263.

204 A 2003 Organisation for Economic Cooperation and Development study estimates that sub-Saharan Africa (SSA) could gain almost 1% of GDP from tackling these non-tariff reforms. For example, it is estimated that every day spent in customs adds 0,8% to the cost of goods. The Economic Commission of Africa's study found that average customs delays for Africa as a whole were 11,4 days and for SSA 12,1 days, comparing unfavourably with Latin America at 7,2 days, Asia at 5,5 days and Western Europe at 3,9 days. *Ibid*, p 266.

205 World Economic Forum, *The Africa Competitiveness Report 2007*. (Geneva: World Economic Forum, 2007), pp 70-82.

206 Kym Anderson, Bernard Hoekman and Anna Strutt, 'Agriculture and the WTO: Next Steps.' *Review of International Economics*, 9 (2), 2001.

207 African field officers of the Rockefeller Foundation initiated this project.

208 In 2007, MPs earned R572 873, cabinet ministers R804 487 – R884 994, and provincial MPs R410 315 – R451 352. Ethel Hazelhurst, 'Public servant pay uproar pits MP's against president.' 11 April 2007, <www.busrep.co.za/index.php?fSectionId=566&fArticleId=3773712> (28 November 2007) and Angela Quintal, 'MP's hoping for salary increases.' *Cape Times*, 15 February 2007.

209 Carl Dahlman, Jourma Routti and Ylä-Anttila Pekka, *Finland as a Knowledge Economy: Elements of Success and Lessons Learnt*. (Washington, DC: World Bank, 2006) pp 33-37.

210 World Bank WDR 2006 and World Bank Institute Finland, *Knowledge Society Report*, 2005.

211 Guillermo O'Donnell & Philippe C.Schmitter, *Transitions from Authoritarian Rule: Tentative Conclusions about Uncertain Democracies*. (Baltimore: John Hopkins University Press, 1986).

212 National treasury, *Budget at a Glance*, N.d., <http://www.treasury.gov.za/documents/national%20budget/2007/default.aspx> (28 November 2007).

213 Health Systems Trust Annual Review, 2006.

214 The Anti-Corruption Commission chaired by the Minister of Public Service and Administration commissioned a report entitled *Apartheid Grand Corruption, 2006*. In its detailed study, defrauding of poor white people by public servants did not feature.

215 Department of Social Development, 'General information on the national investment into the abuse of the social grant system.' N.d. <http://www.sui.org.za/index.asp?include=about/dsd.html> (28 November 2007).

216 Gumisai Mutuime, 'Women break into African politics: Quota systems allow more women to gain elected office.' *Africa Recovery* 18 (2004).

217 Francis Wilson and Mamphela Ramphele, *Uprooting Poverty: The South African Challenge*. (Cape Town: David Philip, 1989), p 5.

218 Institute for Justice and Reconciliation, *Leadership and Legitimacy, 2007*, an annual publication of the Institute for Justice and Reconciliation, pp 10-11.

219 219 Thapelo Sakoana, 'South Africa: KZN women fill seats of power.' N.d., <http://www.allafrica.com/stories/200708100021.html> (30 August 2007).

220 Sara Tulloch (ed.), *The Reader's Digest Oxford Complete Wordfinder*. (London: The Reader's Digest Association Limited, 1993), p 406.

SELECT BIBLIOGRAPHY

Alexander, Neville. *An Ordinary Country: Issues in the Transition from Apartheid to Democracy in South Africa*. New York: Berghahn Books, 2003.

Bell, Clive, Devarajan, Shantayanan and Gersbach, Hans. *The Long-run Economic Costs of AIDS: Theory and an Application to South Africa*. Washington, DC: World Bank, 2003.

Biko, Steve. *I Write What I Like*. Johannesburg: Picador Africa, 2004.

Bogdanor, Vernon (ed.). *The Blackwell Encyclopaedia of Political Science*. Oxford: Blackwell Press, 1993.

Bowen, William, Kurzweil, Martin and Tobin, Eugene. *Equity and Excellence in American Higher Education*. Charlottesville: University of Virginia Press, 2005.

Buhlungu, Sakhela, Daniel, John, Southall, Roger and Lutchman, Jessica (eds). *State of the Nation: South Africa 2005-2006*. Cape Town: HSRC, 2006.

Cameron, Edwin. *Witness to AIDS*. Cape Town: Tafelberg, 2005.

Chipkin, Ivor. *Do South Africans Exist?* Johannesburg: Wits University Press, 2007.

Clinton, Hillary. *It Takes a Village to Raise a Child*. New York: Simon & Schuster, 1996.

Commission for Africa. *Our Common Interest: The Commission for Africa: An Argument*. London: Penguin, 2005.

Dahlman, Carl, Routti, Jourma and Pekka, Ylä-Anttila. *Finland as a Knowledge Economy: Elements of Success and Lessons Learnt*. Washington, DC: World Bank, 2006.

Davidson, Basil. *The Black Man's Burden: Africa and the Curse of the Nation-State*. New York: Three Rivers Press, 1992.

De Klerk, F.W. *The Last Trek: A New Beginning*. London: Pan Books, 1999.

Eglin, Colin. *Crossing the Borders of Power*. Johannesburg: Jonathan Ball, 2007.

Fanon, Frantz. *Black Skin, White Masks*, trans. Charles Lam Markmann. St. Albans, Herts: Paladin, 1970.

Feinstein, Andrew. *After the Party: A Personal and Political Journey Inside the ANC*. Johannesburg: Jonathan Ball, 2007.

Galston, William. 'An Old Debate Renewed: The Politics of the Public Interest', *Daedalus*, Fall, 2007.

Gerhart, Gail and Karis, Thomas. *From Protest to Challenge: A Documentary History of African Politics in South Africa 1882-1964*, Vol. 4. Stanford, CA: Hoover Institution Press, 1972.

Giliomee, Hermann. 'Manipulating the Past', in Erkens, Rainer and Kane-Berman, John (eds). *Political Correctness in South Africa*. Braamfontein: SAIRR, 2000.

Giliomee, Hermann and Mbenga, Bernard (eds). *New History of South Africa*. Cape Town: Tafelberg, 2007.

Gobodo-Madikizela, Pumla. *A Human Being Died that Night: A Story of Forgiveness*. Cape Town: David Philip, 2003.

Golden, Marita. 'Carnegie Corporation in South Africa: A Difficult Past Leads to a Commitment to Change', *Carnegie Results*, 4, 2004.

Hadfield, John (ed.). *A Book of Beauty*. London: Hulton Press, 1952.

Havel, Václav. *The Art of the Impossible: Politics as Morality in Practice*. New York: Knopf, 1997.

Howie, Sarah. *Third International Mathematics and Science Study-Repeat (TIMSS-R): What Has Changed in Pupils' Performance in Mathematics 1995-1998?* Pretoria: HSRC, 1994.

Institute for Justice and Reconciliation. *2007 Transformation Audit: Leadership and Legitimacy*. Cape Town: IJR, 2007.

Jacobs, Sean and Calland, Richard (eds). *Thabo Mbeki's World: The Politics and Ideology of the South African President*. Pietermaritzburg: University of Natal Press, 2002.

Johnson, David. 'Building Citizenship in Fragmented Societies: The Challenges of Democratizing and Integrating Schools in Post-apartheid South Africa', *International Journal of Educational Development*, 27 (3), 2007.

Lawless, Allyson. *Numbers and Needs: Addressing Imbalances in the Civil Engineering Profession*. Midrand: SAICE, 2005.

Lehohla, Pali. *South African Statistics, 2006*. Pretoria: Statistics South Africa, 2006.

Luthuli, Albert. *Let My People Go*. Cape Town: Tafelberg and Mafube, 2006.

Makgoba, Malegapuru William (ed.). *African Renaissance: The New Struggle*. Johannesburg: Mafube, 1999.

Mandela, Nelson. *Long Walk to Freedom: The Autobiography of Nelson Mandela*. London: Little, Brown, 1994.

Matthews, Shanaaz, Abrahams, Naeemah, Martin, Lorna, Vetten, Lisa, Van der Merwe, Lisa and Jewkes, Rachel. *Every Six Hours a Woman is Killed by her Intimate Partner: A National Study of Female Homicide in South Africa*. Tygerberg: MRC, 2004.

Matthews, Z.K. 'Native Education in South Africa in Last 25 Years', *S.A. Outlook*, 76, 1946.

Mistry, Duxita, Minnaar, Anthony, Redpath, Jean and Dhlamini, Jabu. *Research Report: The Use of Force by Members of the South African Police Service: Case Studies from*

Seven Policing Areas in Gauteng. Florida: Institute for Human Rights and Criminal Justice Studies, Technikon SA, 2001.

Mitra, Pradeep and Selowsky, Marcelo. *Transition, the First Ten Years: Analysis and Lessons for Eastern Europe and the Former Soviet Union*. Washington, DC: World Bank, 2002.

Mutuime, Gumisai. 'Women Break into African Politics: Quota Systems Allow More Women to Gain Elected Office', *Africa Recovery*, 18, 2004.

Myakayaka-Manzini, Mavivi. 'Women Empowered – Women in Parliament in South Africa', in Karam, Azza (ed.), *Women in Parliament: Beyond Numbers*. Stockholm: International IDEA, 1998.

Nattrass, Nicoli and Seekings, Jeremy. *Class, Race, and Inequality in South Africa*. New Haven: Yale University Press, 2005.

Nattrass, Nicoli. *The Moral Economy of AIDS in South Africa*. Cambridge: Cambridge University Press, 2004.

Nhlapo, Thandabantu. 'The African Family and Women's Rights: Friends or Foes?' *Acta Juridica*, 135, 1991.

Nuttall, Jolyon. *The First Five Years: The Story of the Independent Development Trust*. Cape Town: Independent Development Trust, 1997.

O' Donnell, Guillermo and Schmitter, Philippe. *Transitions from Authoritarian Rule: Tentative Conclusions about Uncertain Democracies*. Baltimore: Johns Hopkins University Press, 1986.

Okuku, Juma. *Ethnicity, State Power and the Democratisation Process in Uganda*. Uppsala: Nordic Africa Institute, 2002.

Ramphele, Mamphela. *A Bed Called Home*. Cape Town: David Philip, 1991.

Rehle, Thomas, Shisana, Olive, Pillay, Victoria, Zuma, Khangelani, Purren, Adrian and Parker, Warren. 'National HIV Incidence Measure – New Insights into the South African Epidemic', *South African Medical Journal*, 97 (3), 2007.

Robertson, David (ed.). *The Routledge Dictionary of Politics*. London: Routledge, 2002

Sacks, Jonathan. *To Heal a Fractured World: The Ethics of Responsibility*. New York: Schocken Books, 2005.

Saunders, Stuart. *Vice-Chancellor on a Tightrope: A Personal Account of Climactic Years in South Africa*. Cape Town: David Philip, 2000.

Sen, Amartya. *Development as Freedom*. Oxford: Oxford University Press, 2001.

Sen, Amartya. *Identity and Violence*. New York: W.W. Norton, 2006.

Shubane, Khehla and Reddy, Colin. *BEE 2007: Empowerment and its Critics*. Johannesburg: BusinessMap Foundation, 2007.

Sibanda, Sipho *Land Reform and Poverty Alleviation in South Africa*. Pretoria: HSRC, 2001.

Sisulu, Elinor. *Walter and Albertina Sisulu: In our Lifetime*. Cape Town: David Philip, 2002.

South African National Editors' Forum. *Glass Ceiling Two: An Audit of Women and Men in South African Newsrooms.* Rosebank: Sanef, 2007.

Taylor, Nick. 'Schools, Skills and Citizenship', in *2006 Transformation Audit: Money and Morality.* Cape Town: Institute for Justice and Reconciliation, 2006.

Tefo, Joe. 'Monarchy and Democracy: Toward a Cultural Renaissance', *Journal on African Philosophy*, 1, 2002.

Tucker, Bob and Scott, Bruce (eds.). *South Africa: Prospects for Successful Transition.* Cape Town: Juta, 1992.

Tulloch, Sara (ed.). *The Reader's Digest Oxford Complete Wordfinder.* London: The Reader's Digest Association Limited, 1993.

Tutu, Desmond. *No Future Without Forgiveness.* London: Rider Press, 1999.

Unwin, Peter. 'Prejudice, Crisis and Genocide in Rwanda', *African Studies Review*, 40, 1997.

Vetten, Lisa. 'Gender, Race and Power Dynamics in the Face of Social Change: Deconstructing Violence Against Women in South Africa', in Park, Yoon Jung, Fedler, Joanne and Dangor, Zubeda, *Reclaiming Women's Spaces: New Perspectives on Violence Against Women and Sheltering in South Africa.* Lenasia: NISAA, 2000.

Wilson, Francis and Ramphele, Mamphela. *Uprooting Poverty: The South African Challenge: Report for the Second Carnegie Inquiry into Poverty and Development in Southern Africa.* Cape Town: David Philip, 1989.

Wolfson, Adam. 'From James Madison to Abraham Lincoln', *Daedalus*, Fall, 2007.

World Economic Forum. *The Africa Competitiveness Report 2007.* Geneva: WEF, 2007.

Zander, Rosamund Stone and Zander, Benjamin. *The Art of Possibility: Transforming Professional and Personal Life.* Boston: Harvard Business School Press, 2000.

INDEX

child abuse 107, 110, 114, 238–239
corporal punishment 115
impact on social relationships 132–134
'necklace' murders 48–49, 112, 132, 133
Vlakplaas 59
Vlok, Adriaan 60, 64
Vorster, John 33

Waemu (West African Economic and
Monetary Union) 285
Walus, Janusz 38
Washington Consensus 292
white South Africans
denial of apartheid benefits 76, 77–78
effects of TRC 50–51
impact of affirmative action 86, 250
impact of racism 16–17
women
see also gender equality
abuse within universities 211–213

constant challenge of sexism 309–310
discrimination against 99–102
entry into BEE 264–265
harmful cultural practices 75
role in ANC Youth League 115
role in economy 286
violence against 101, 103–108, 287
vulnerability to HIV/Aids 239
white women and employment equity
252–254, 265
World Bank 22, 282, 287, 292–294, 310
World Bank Africa Regional Strategy 277

xenophobia 162, 289

Zambia 91, 229, 276, 279, 309
Zille, Helen 89, 222
Zimbabwe 31, 133, 144, 184–185, 275,
276, 278–279, 280–281, 289, 305
Zuma, Jacob 95

MAMPHELA RAMPHELE is a medical doctor with a Ph.D. in Social Anthropology and 23 honorary degrees from local and international institutions.

She first rose to prominence in the 1970s as an activist and founder member, with Steve Biko, of the Black Consciousness Movement. They started Black Community Programmes in the Eastern Cape, and she founded the Zanempilo Community Health Centre in Zinyoka, a village outside King William's Town. Her project was cut short when she was detained in 1976 under section 10 of the Terrorism Act. From 1977 to 1984 she was banished to Lenyenye near Tzaneen, where she established the Ithuseng Community Health Programme.

She served at various institutions including the South African Labour and Development Research Unit at the University of Cape Town, the Equal Opportunities Research Project and Idasa. Her academic career culminated in her appointment as Vice-Chancellor of the University of Cape Town, where she steered the university during the crucial transformative years between 1996 and 2000. She was appointed Managing Director at the World Bank in Washington DC in 2000, and was co-chair of the Global Commission on International Migration from 2004 to 2005.

In 2004 she returned to South Africa where she currently chairs Circle Capital Ventures. She serves on the boards of major corporations and non-governmental organisations.

Ramphele has written a number of books, including *My Life*, her autobiography, *Steering by the Stars: Being young in South Africa* and *Uprooting Poverty: The South African Challenge*, for which she received the Noma Award for Publishing in Africa. Among many other awards she has received the NRF Lifetime Achiever Award, the Global Health Sciences Award, the Kilby Award and the Outstanding International Leadership and Commitment Award for Health, Education and Social Development. She contributes actively to the national debate, with frequent newspaper columns and opinion pieces.